LaTeX Beginner's Guide

Second Edition

Create visually appealing texts, articles, and books
for business and science using LaTeX

Stefan Kottwitz

BIRMINGHAM—MUMBAI

LaTeX Beginner's Guide
Second Edition

Copyright © 2021 Packt Publishing

Group Product Manager: Rohit Rajkumar
Publishing Product Manager: Ashitosh Gupta
Senior Editor: Hayden Edwards
Content Development Editor: Rashi Dubey
Technical Editor: Simran Haresh Udasi
Copy Editor: Safis Editing
Project Coordinator: Manthan Patel
Proofreader: Safis Editing
Indexer: Manju Arasan
Production Designer: Roshan Kawale

First published: March 2011
Second edition: August 2021

Production reference: 1030921

Published by Packt Publishing Ltd.
Livery Place
35 Livery Street
Birmingham
B3 2PB, UK.

ISBN 978-1-80107-865-8
www.packt.com

To the members of TUG and DANTE for supporting TeX and LaTeX development, infrastructure, and education. To all the helpers on internet forums for their tireless support for LaTeX beginners.

– Stefan Kottwitz

Contributors

About the author

Stefan Kottwitz studied mathematics in Jena and Hamburg. He works as a network and IT security engineer both for Lufthansa Industry Solutions and for Eurowings Aviation.

For many years, he has been providing LaTeX support on online forums. He maintains the web forums LaTeX.org and goLaTeX.de and the Q&A sites TeXwelt.de and TeXnique. fr. He runs the TeX graphics gallery sites TeXample.net, TikZ.net, and PGFplots.net, the TeXlive.net online compiler, the TeXdoc.org service, and the CTAN.net software mirror. He is a moderator of the TeX Stack Exchange site and matheplanet.com. He publishes ideas and news from the TeX world on his blogs LaTeX.net and TeX.co.

Before this book, he authored the first edition of *LaTeX Beginner's Guide* in 2011, and *LaTeX Cookbook* in 2015, both published by Packt.

About the reviewers

LianTze Lim has reveled in the joys and beauty of LaTeX typesetting for nearly two decades. She is currently Community TeXpert at Overleaf and has been helping Overleaf users with LaTeX-related questions since 2014.

Joseph Wright is the author of the popular siunitx package for units, leads maintenance of the beamer class, and is a member of the LaTeX project. He is also one of the moderators on the popular TeX – LaTeX Stack Exchange Q&A site.

Table of Contents

Preface

1

Getting Started with LaTeX

Technical requirements	2
What is LaTeX?	2
Benefits of LaTeX	3
Virtues of open source	3
Separation of form and content	4
Portability	4
Protection for your work	4
How to get started with LaTeX	5
Approaches to working with LaTeX	5

Installing and using LaTeX	5
Installing TeX Live using the net installer wizard	8
Installing TeX Live offline	11
Installing TeX Live on other operating systems	12

Updating TeX Live and installing new packages	12
Creating our first document	14
Checking out advanced LaTeX editors	15

Working with LaTeX online using Overleaf	16
What Overleaf requires and delivers	16
Benefits of Overleaf	17
Caveats of working online	18
Creating our first document online	18
Exploring Overleaf	20
Grammar and language feedback with Writefull	23
Reviewing and commenting	24

Accessing documentation	25
Summary	25

2

Formatting Text and Creating Macros

Technical requirements	28
Working with logical formatting	28
Creating a document with a title and heading	29

Exploring the document structure	31
Understanding LaTeX commands	31
Understanding LaTeX environments	32

Understanding how LaTeX reads our input   33
Printing out special symbols   34

Modifying the text fonts   35
Adjusting the font shape   36
Choosing the font family   37
Confining the effect of commands by braces   40
Exploring font sizes   41

Creating our own commands   42
Using macros for simple text   42
Proper spacing after commands   43
Creating more universal commands and using arguments   44

Using boxes to limit the width of paragraphs   46
Creating a narrow text box   47
Producing common paragraph boxes   48

Exploring further features of paragraph boxes   49
Using mini pages   49

Breaking lines and paragraphs   51
Improving hyphenation   51
Preventing hyphenation   52
Improving the justification   53
Breaking lines manually   53
Exploring line breaking options   55
Preventing line breaks   55

Turning off full justification   56
Creating ragged-right text   56
Creating ragged-left text   57
Centering text   57
Using environments for justification   58

Displaying quotes   60
Quoting longer text   61

Summary   64

3

Designing Pages

Technical requirements   66
Creating a book with chapters   66
Defining the margins   69
Using class options   72
Designing headers and footers   75
Understanding page styles   78
Customizing headers and footers   79
Using decorative lines in headers or footers   80
Changing LaTeX's header marks   80

Using footnotes   81
Modifying the footnote line   82
Using packages to expand footnote styles   83

Breaking pages   84
Enlarging a page   88
Changing the line spacing   91
Creating a table of contents   93
Summary   97

4
Creating Lists

Technical requirements	99	Getting compact lists	107
Building lists	100	Choosing bullets and numbering format	110
Creating a bulleted list	100	Suspending and continuing lists	113
Building an enumerated list	103		
Producing a definition list	105	Summary	115
Customizing lists	106		

5
Including Images

Technical requirements	117	Understanding placement options	125
Including an image	118	Forcing the output of figures	125
Choosing an optimal file type	120	Limiting floating	126
Scaling an image	121	Avoiding floating at all	126
Including whole pages	121	Arranging several images	127
Putting images behind the text	122	Letting text flow around images	128
Managing floating images	122	Summary	130

6
Creating Tables

Technical requirements	131	Spanning entries over multiple columns	144
Using tab stops to write in columns	132	Inserting code column-wise	145
		Spanning entries over multiple rows	146
Typesetting tables	136		
Drawing lines in tables	138	Adding captions to tables	147
Understanding formatting arguments	138	Placing captions above	150
Increasing the row height	140	Customizing captions	151
Beautifying tables	141		
Adjusting lengths	143	Using packages for further customizations	151
		Auto-fitting columns to the table width	151

Generating multi-page tables   152
Coloring tables   153
Using landscape orientation   153

Aligning columns at the decimal point   153
Handling narrow columns   154

Summary   **154**

7
Using Cross-References

Technical requirements   **156**
Setting labels and references   **156**
Assigning a label   159
Referring to a label   160
Referring to a page   160

Using advanced referencing   **161**
Producing intelligent page references   161
Fine-tuning page references   163

Referring to page ranges   164
Using automatic reference names   164
Combining intelligent references
with automatic naming   167

**Referring to labels
in other documents**   **167**
**Turning references into
hyperlinks**   **168**
Summary   169

8
Listing Contents and References

Technical requirements   **172**
**Customizing the table of
contents**   **172**
Adjusting the depth of the TOC   174
Shortening entries   175
Adding entries manually   176
Creating and customizing
lists of figures   177
Creating a list of tables   178
Using packages for customization   178

Generating an index   **179**
Defining index entries and subentries   181
Specifying page ranges   182
Using symbols and macros in the index   182
Referring to other index entries   183

Fine-tuning page numbers   183
Designing the index layout   184

Creating a bibliography   **185**
Using the standard bibliography
environment   186
Using bibliography databases with
BibTeX   187
Looking at the BibTeX entry fields   189
Referring to Internet resources   190
Understanding BibTeX entry types   191
Choosing the bibliography style   192
Listing references without citing   194

Changing the headings   **194**
Summary   **195**

9

Writing Math Formulas

Technical requirements	197	Binary relation symbols	213
Writing basic formulas	198	Inequality relation symbols	214
Embedding math expressions within text	200	Subset and superset symbols	214
		Arrows	214
Displaying formulas	201	Harpoons	215
Numbering equations	202	Symbols derived from letters	215
Adding subscripts and superscripts	202	Miscellaneous symbols	215
Using operators	203	Writing units	217
Taking roots	204	Variable sized operators	217
Writing fractions	205	Variable sized delimiters	218
Writing Greek letters	205		
Writing script letters	206	**Building math structures**	**219**
Producing an ellipsis	207	Creating arrays	219
Changing the font, style, and size	207	Typesetting matrices	219
Customizing displayed formulas	209	Writing binomial coefficients	220
		Underlining and overlining	221
Typesetting multi-line formulas	**209**	Setting accents	222
Numbering rows in multi-line formulas	212	Putting a symbol above or below another one	222
Inserting text into formulas	212	Writing theorems and definitions	223
		Further tools for writing mathematics	224
Exploring the wealth of math symbols	**212**		
Binary operation symbols	213	**Summary**	**226**

10

Using Fonts

Technical requirements	228	Serif fonts	233
Using comprehensive font bundles	228	Sans-serif fonts	236
		Typewriter fonts	239
Latin Modern – a replacement for the standard font	231	Calligraphic fonts	240
Kp-Fonts – another extensive set of fonts	231	**Using arbitrary fonts**	**242**
		Selecting the main font	242
Using specific font families	**232**	Selecting multiple font families	243
		Summary	**245**

11

Developing Large Documents

Technical requirements	248	Creating front and back matter	254
Splitting the input	248	Designing a title page	256
Including small pieces of code	251	Working with templates	258
Including bigger parts of a document	251	Summary	267
Compiling parts of a document	252		

12

Enhancing Your Documents Further

Technical requirements	270	Creating bookmarks manually	277
Using hyperlinks and bookmarks	270	Using math formulas and special symbols in bookmarks	277
Adding hyperlinks	270	Designing headings	279
Customizing hyperlinks	272	Coloring our documents	283
Creating hyperlinks manually	276	Summary	284

13

Troubleshooting

Technical requirements	285	General syntax errors	293
Understanding and fixing errors	286	Handling warnings	294
Handling the preamble and document body	289	Justifying text	295
Using commands and environments	290	Referencing	296
Writing math formulas	291	Choosing fonts	297
Working with files	291	Placing figures and tables	297
Creating tables and arrays	292	Customizing the document class	298
Working with lists	293	Avoiding obsolete classes and packages	298
Working with floating figures and tables	293	General troubleshooting	300
		Summary	303

14

Using Online Resources

Web forms, Q&A sites,
and discussion boards   306
LaTeX.org   306
TeX and LaTeX on Stack Exchange   307
Forums in other languages   308
Usenet groups   308

Lists of frequently asked
questions   309
Mailing lists   310
TeX user group sites   311
The TeX Users Group   311
DANTE   311
The LaTeX project   312

UK TUG – TeX in the United Kingdom   312
Other local user groups   312

Websites for LaTeX software
and editors   312
LaTeX distributions   312
LaTeX editors   313
CTAN – the Comprehensive TeX
Archive Network   314

Graphics galleries   315
LaTeX blogs   315
Twitter messages   316
Summary   316

Other Books You May Enjoy

Index

Preface

LaTeX is a high-quality open source typesetting software that produces professional prints and PDF files. However, as LaTeX is a powerful and complex tool, getting started can be intimidating, and specific aspects such as layout modifications can seem rather complicated. Using Microsoft Word or other word-processing software may seem more straightforward, but once you've become acquainted, LaTeX's capabilities far outweigh any initial difficulties. This book guides you through these challenges and makes beginning with LaTeX easy. If you are writing mathematical, scientific, or technical papers, this is the perfect book for you.

LaTeX Beginner's Guide Second Edition offers you a practical introduction to LaTeX. Beginning with the installation and basic usage, you will learn to typeset documents containing tables, figures, formulas, and common book elements such as bibliographies, glossaries, and indexes. Lots of step-by-step examples start with fine-tuning text, formulas, and page layout, and proceed with managing complex documents and using modern PDF features. It's easy to start with LaTeX when you have LaTeX Beginner's Guide Second Edition at hand.

This practical book will guide you through the essential steps of LaTeX, from installing LaTeX, formatting, and justification, to page design. Right from the beginning, you will learn to use macros and styles to maintain a consistent document structure while saving typing work. This book will help you learn to create professional-looking tables, along with including figures and writing complex mathematical formulas. You will see how to generate bibliographies and indexes with ease. Finally, you will learn how to manage complex documents and how to benefit from modern PDF features. Detailed information about online resources such as software archives, web forums, and online compilers complement this introductory guide.

Who this book is for

If you are about to write mathematical or scientific papers, seminar handouts, or even plan to write a thesis, then this book offers you a fast-paced and practical introduction. Those studying in school and university as mathematicians or physicists will benefit greatly, as well as engineers and humanities students. Anybody with high expectations who plans to write a paper or a book will be delighted by this high-quality, stable software.

What this book covers

Chapter 1, Getting Started with LaTeX, introduces LaTeX and explains its benefits. It guides you through the download and installation of a comprehensive LaTeX distribution and shows you how to create your first LaTeX document. It also introduces the use of the online LaTeX software Overleaf. Furthermore, you will get familiar with accessing package documentation.

Chapter 2, Formatting Text and Creating Macros, explains how to vary font, shape, and text styles. It deals with centering and justification of paragraphs and how we can improve line breaks and hyphenation. It introduces logical formatting and describes how to define macros and how to use environments and packages.

Chapter 3, Designing Pages, shows how you can adjust the margins and change the line spacing. It demonstrates portrait, landscape, and two-column layouts. In this chapter, we will create dynamic headers and footers and learn how to control page breaking and how to use footnotes. Along the way, you will also learn about redefining existing commands and using class options.

Chapter 4, Creating Lists, deals with arranging text in bulleted, numbered, and definition lists. You will learn how to choose bullets and numbering styles and how to design the overall layout of lists.

Chapter 5, Including Images, shows you how to include external pictures with captions in your documents. You will learn how to benefit from LaTeX's automated figures placement and how to fine-tune it.

Chapter 6, Creating Tables, shows you how to create professional-looking tables and goes deep into formatting details.

Chapter 7, Using Cross-References, introduces intelligent referencing to sections, footnotes, tables, figures, and numbered environments in general.

Chapter 8, Listing Contents and References, deals with creating and customizing a table of contents and lists of figures and tables. Furthermore, it explains how to cite books, create bibliographies, and generate an index.

Chapter 9, Writing Math Formulas, explains mathematical typesetting in depth. It starts with basic formulas and continues with centered and numbered equations. It shows how to align multi-line equations. In detail, it shows how to typeset math symbols such as roots, arrows, Greek letters, and operators. Moreover, you will learn to build complex math structures such as fractions, stacked expressions, and matrices.

Chapter 10, Using Fonts, takes us into the world of fonts and demonstrates various fonts, including Roman, sans-serif, and typewriter fonts, in different shapes.

Chapter 11, Developing Large Documents, helps in managing large documents by splitting them into several files. After reading this chapter, you will be able to create complex projects building upon sub-files. Furthermore, we deal with front matter and back matter with different page numbering and separate title pages. We will work through this by creating an example book. By doing this, you will get familiar with using document templates, and finally you can write your own thesis, book, or report.

Chapter 12, Enhancing Your Documents Further, brings color into your documents. It shows you how to modify headings of chapters and all kinds of sections. We will learn how to create feature-rich PDF documents with bookmarks, hyperlinks, and metadata.

Chapter 13, Troubleshooting, provides us with tools for problem-solving. We will learn about different kinds of LaTeX errors and warnings and how to deal with them. After reading this chapter, you will understand LaTeX's messages and know how to use them to fix errors.

Chapter 14, Using Online Resources, guides you through the vast amount of LaTeX information on the internet. We will visit an online LaTeX forum and a LaTeX Q&A site. This chapter points the way to the huge LaTeX software archives, TeX user groups' homepages, mailing lists, Usenet groups, and LaTeX graphics galleries. It tells you where you can download LaTeX-capable editors and where you can meet LaTeX friends on blogs and Twitter.

To get the most out of this book

You need access to a computer with LaTeX on it. An online connection would be helpful regarding installation and updates. We can install LaTeX on most operating systems, so you can use Windows, Linux, macOS, or Unix.

This book uses the freely available TeX Live distribution, which runs on all mentioned platforms. You just need an internet connection or the TeX Live DVD to install it. In the book, we work with the cross-platform editor TeXworks, but you could use any editor you like.

Without installing LaTeX, you can work with the code examples at `https://latexguide.org`*, which comes with an online compiler.*

If you are using the digital version of this book, we advise you to type the code yourself or access the code from the book's GitHub repository (a link is available in the next section). Doing so will help you avoid any potential errors related to the copying and pasting of code.

Download the example code files

You can download the example code files for this book from GitHub at `https://github.com/PacktPublishing/LaTeX-Beginner-s-Guide-Second-Edition`. If there's an update to the code, it will be updated in the GitHub repository.

The book's website at `https://latexguide.org` offers code downloads as well. You may also visit `https://latex-cookbook.net`, which provides further complete code examples with an online compiler.

We also have other code bundles from our rich catalog of books and videos available at `https://github.com/PacktPublishing/`. Check them out!

Conventions used

There are a number of text conventions used throughout this book.

`Code in text`: Indicates code words in text, database table names, folder names, filenames, file extensions, pathnames, dummy URLs, user input, and Twitter handles. Here is an example: "Load the `fontenc` package and choose T1 font encoding."

A block of code is set as follows:

```
\[
  \int_a^b \! f(x) \, dx = \lim_{\Delta x \rightarrow 0}
  \sum_{i=1}^{n} f(x_i) \,\Delta x_i
\]
```

When we wish to draw your attention to a particular part of a code block, the relevant lines or items are set in bold:

```
\documentclass{book}
\usepackage{cleveref}
\crefname{enumi}{position}{positions}
\begin{document}
\chapter{Statistics}
\label{stats}
\section{Most used packages by LaTeX.org users}
\label{packages}
```

Bold: Indicates a new term, an important word, or words that you see onscreen. For instance, words in menus or dialog boxes appear in **bold**. Here is an example: "Click the **Typeset** button to compile the document."

> **Tips or important notes**
> Appear like this.

Get in touch

Feedback from our readers is always welcome.

General feedback: If you have questions about any aspect of this book, email us at customercare@packtpub.com and mention the book title in the subject of your message.

LaTeX questions: If you have any question about LaTeX, you can visit the author's forum at https://latex.org

Errata: Although we have taken every care to ensure the accuracy of our content, mistakes do happen. If you have found a mistake in this book, we would be grateful if you would report this to us. Please visit www.packtpub.com/support/errata and fill in the form.

Piracy: If you come across any illegal copies of our works in any form on the internet, we would be grateful if you would provide us with the location address or website name. Please contact us at copyright@packt.com with a link to the material.

If you are interested in becoming an author: If there is a topic that you have expertise in and you are interested in either writing or contributing to a book, please visit authors.packtpub.com.

1
Getting Started with LaTeX

You are familiar with **word processing** software: you type something, and the software prints it as it is on screen. In contrast, LaTeX, as **typesetting** software, receives instructions and text from you, and then creates the output. It produces high-quality output based on sophisticated algorithms for justification, text alignment, whitespace balancing, figure placement, and more, such as predefined formatting styles for headings and general page layout, which you can customize.

Are you ready to leave those "what you see is what you get" word processors behind and to enter the world of accurate, reliable, and high-quality typesetting? Yes? Then let's go together!

It's great that you decided to learn LaTeX. This book will guide you along the way to help you get the most out of it. Let's speak briefly about LaTeX's benefits and the challenges, and then we shall prepare our tools.

In this chapter, we will get to know LaTeX, as well as how to install and use it. Specifically, our topics will be as follows:

- What is LaTeX?

- Installing and using LaTeX

- Working with LaTeX online using Overleaf

- Accessing documentation

At the end of this chapter, you will have working LaTeX software, and you will know how to edit and typeset a document and how to obtain further documentation.

So, let's get started.

Technical requirements

We will focus on the Windows operating system here, but you can also install LaTeX on Mac OS X, Linux, and other systems.

A complete installation takes about 8 GB of disk space.

If you have an internet connection, you don't have to install LaTeX. You can use online LaTeX software, such as Overleaf. We will look at Overleaf at the end of this chapter.

All code examples of this book are available on GitHub at `https://github.com/PacktPublishing/LaTeX-Beginner-s-Guide`.

On the book's website, `https://latexguide.org`, you can read, edit, and compile every code example in this book online without installing anything. An internet browser with JavaScript enabled is all you need for this, and a PC, laptop, tablet, or smartphone.

What is LaTeX?

LaTeX is free, open source software for typesetting documents. In other words, it's a document preparation system. LaTeX is not a word processor, but it's a document markup language.

It was initially written by Leslie Lamport and is based on the TeX typesetting engine by Donald Knuth. People often refer to it as just TeX, meaning LaTeX. It has a long history; you can read about it at `https://tug.org/whatis.html`.

For now, let's continue by looking at how we can make the most of LaTeX.

Benefits of LaTeX

LaTeX is especially well suited for scientific and technical documents. LaTeX's superior typesetting of mathematical formulas is legendary. Suppose you are a student or a scientist. In that case, LaTeX is by far the best choice, and even if you don't need its scientific capabilities, there are other uses—it produces very high-quality output and is incredibly stable. It handles complex documents easily, no matter how large they are.

Some more remarkable strengths of LaTeX are its cross-referencing capabilities, the ability for automatic numbering, and the generation of lists of contents, figures and tables, indexes, glossaries, and bibliographies. It is multilingual with language-specific features, and it can use PostScript and PDF features.

Apart from being perfect for scientists, LaTeX is incredibly flexible—there are templates for letters, presentations, bills, philosophy books, law texts, music scores, and even chess game notation. Hundreds of LaTeX users have written thousands of templates, styles, and valuable tools for every possible purpose. It is collected and categorized online on archiving servers.

You could benefit from its impressive high quality by starting with its default styles and relying on its intelligent formatting, but you are free to customize and modify everything. People of the TeX community have already written a lot of extensions addressing nearly every formatting need.

Virtues of open source

The code of LaTeX is entirely **open source**, free, and readable for everyone. This enables you to study and change everything, from the core of LaTeX to the latest extension packages. But what does this mean for you as a beginner? There's a huge LaTeX community with a lot of friendly, helpful people. Even if you cannot benefit from the open source code directly, they can read the source and assist you. Just join a LaTeX web forum and ask your questions there. Helpers will, if necessary, dig into LaTeX sources and, in all probability, find a solution for you, sometimes by recommending a suitable package, often providing a redefinition of a default command.

Today, we're already profiting from about 30 years of development by the LaTeX community. The open source philosophy made it possible, as every user is invited to study and improve the software and develop it further. *Chapter 14, Using Online Resources*, will point the way to the community.

Separation of form and content

A fundamental principle of LaTeX is that the author should not be distracted too much by formatting issues. Usually, the author focuses on the content and formats logically. For example, instead of writing a chapter title in big, bold letters, you just tell LaTeX that it's a chapter heading. You can let LaTeX design the heading or decide in the document's settings what the headings will look like—just once for the whole document. LaTeX extensively uses style files called **classes** and **packages**, making it easy to design and modify the entire document's appearance and all of its details.

Portability

LaTeX is available for nearly every operating system, such as Windows, Linux, Mac OS X, and many more. Its file format is plain text, readable and editable on all operating systems, which means LaTeX will produce the same output on each system. There are several LaTeX software packages, which we call **TeX distributions**. We will focus on the **TeX Live** distribution since this one is available for Windows, Linux, and Mac OS X. On the Mac, the native TeX Live version is called **MacTeX**.

LaTeX doesn't have a graphical user interface; that's one of the reasons why it's so portable. You can choose any text editor. There are many editors, even specialized in LaTeX, for every operating system. Some editors are available for several systems; for instance, **TeXworks** runs on Windows, Linux, and Mac OS X, which is one of the reasons why we will use it in our book. Another significant reason is that it's probably best suited for beginners.

LaTeX generates PDF output, which is printable and readable on most computers and looks identical regardless of the operating system. Besides PDF, it supports DVI, PostScript, and HTML output, preparing the ground for distribution both in print and online, such as on personal computers, electronic book readers, and smartphones. To sum up, LaTeX is portable in three ways: your source, implementation, and output.

Protection for your work

LaTeX documents are stored in human-readable text format, not in some obscure proprietary word processing format, that may be altered in a different version of the same software.

Try to open a 20-year-old document written with a commercial word processor. What might your modern software show? Even if you can read the file, its visual appearance would undoubtedly be different than before. LaTeX promises that the document will always be readable and will result in the same output. Even though it's further developed, it will remain backward compatible.

Word processor documents could be infected with viruses, and malicious macros could destroy the data. Did you ever hear of a virus "hiding" in a text file? LaTeX documents are not threatened by viruses.

How to get started with LaTeX

The learning curve could be steep, but this book will help you master it.

Though writing LaTeX looks like programming, don't be afraid. Soon you will know the frequently used commands, while text editors with auto-completion and keyword highlighting will support you. They might even provide menus and dialogs with commands for you.

Do you still think it will take a long time until you can learn to achieve creditable results? Don't worry; this book will give you a quick start. You will learn by practicing with a lot of examples. Many more examples can be read and downloaded from the internet. In *Chapter 14, Using Online Resources*, we will explore online resources. There are LaTeX help forums where you get answers to your questions. Specifically, `https://latex.org` has a forum dedicated to the readers of this book. Visit us there!

Approaches to working with LaTeX

There are two ways to approach working with LaTeX:

- The traditional way is to install LaTeX on your own computer. It's pretty straightforward, and we will walk through installing on Windows in the *Installing and using LaTeX* section.

- Another way is to use LaTeX online *in the cloud*. No installation is needed; all you need is an internet-connected computer, tablet, or phone. We will explore this option in the *Working with LaTeX online using Overleaf* section at the end of this chapter.

Now, we will continue with the setup of LaTeX on our computer. If you like, you could skip it for the moment and jump to the *Working with LaTeX online using Overleaf* section, and then decide which approach you would like to take.

Installing and using LaTeX

Let's start with the installation of the LaTeX distribution, **TeX Live**. This distribution is available for Windows, Linux, Mac OS X (**MacTeX**), and other Unix-like operating systems. TeX Live is well maintained, and it is actively developed.

> **Alternative LaTeX distribution**
>
> Another excellent and user-friendly LaTeX distribution for Windows
> is **MiKTeX**. It's easy to install, like any other Windows application.
> You can download it from `https://miktex.org`. Visit
> `https://latexguide.org/distributions` for a detailed,
> up-to-date comparison.

You can install TeX Live for a single user (that's you) or as a shared installation for all
users on a computer. The latter is called **admin mode**. It requires running the installation
as an administrator: either log in with an administrator account or right-click on the
install program and choose **Run as administrator**.

It is recommended to install in **single-user mode**.

First, we will visit the TeX Live homepage and take a survey of the installation possibilities.
To do this, open the TeX Live homepage using `https://tug.org/texlive/`:

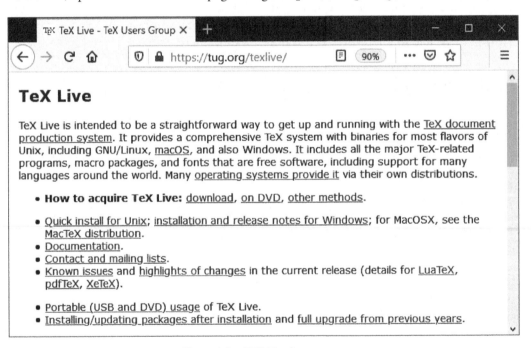

Figure 1.1 – TeX Live home page

Feel free to explore the home page in depth to study the information offered there, though, in this book, we will cover two types of installation:

- Installing TeX Living using the net installer wizard; this will be online and requires an internet connection.

- Installing TeX offline; this starts with a considerable download, but then we can do it offline.

Before we start the installation, let's have a look at LaTeX packaging conventions with different granularity:

- A **package**, also called a **style** file, is a single LaTeX file with some macros to add specific features or provide a particular look and document style. It has the filename extension `.sty`.

- A **bundle** is a set of packages with a similar purpose. It may also contain class files that have the filename extension `.cls`.

- A **collection** is a larger set of packages for a field of interest. That can be, for example, an extensive set of math and natural science packages, music packages, or graphics-related packages.

- A **scheme** is a LaTeX installation of a specific size. That can be **minimal** (the smallest to be able to work), **basic** (commonly needed stuff), or **full** (everything available).

We can now install and update LaTeX with this understanding. The easiest option is to install everything fully, that is, the **full scheme**. That way, you will not miss any packages.

Let's check out two installation methods on a Windows PC. The first one will be installing over the internet, which requires a good internet connection. If you don't have a good internet connection, go to the next section, *Installing TeX Live offline*.

Installing TeX Live using the net installer wizard

We will download the TeX Live net installer and install the complete TeX Live distribution on our computer. To do this, follow these steps:

1. Click on **download** as seen in *Figure 1.1*, or go to `https://tug.org/texlive/acquire-netinstall.html`:

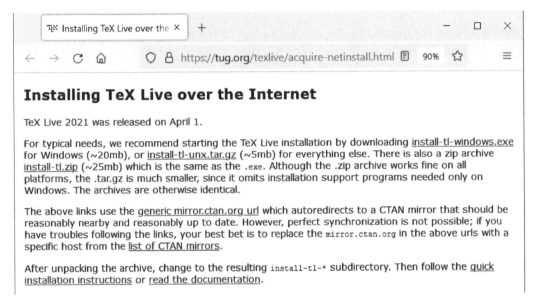

Figure 1.2 – Installation instructions

2. Download the executable installer program, `install-tl-windows.exe`, and run the program.

3. Confirm the installation mode (as a **Single-user** or as the **Administrator**), click **Next**, and then **Install**.

4. The net installer will automatically detect your operating system language. You can change the language of the **Graphical User Interface** (**GUI**) by clicking on **GUI language** in the menu of the window that opens, as we can see in *Figure 1.3*:

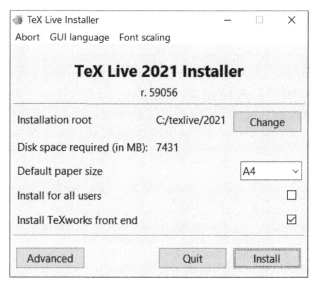

Figure 1.3 – TeX Live Installer

5. You can change the installation root, that is, the location of all TeX Live installed files on your hard drive. That complete default installation is fine, though you can click on **Advanced** to determine what shall happen more specifically, as you can see here:

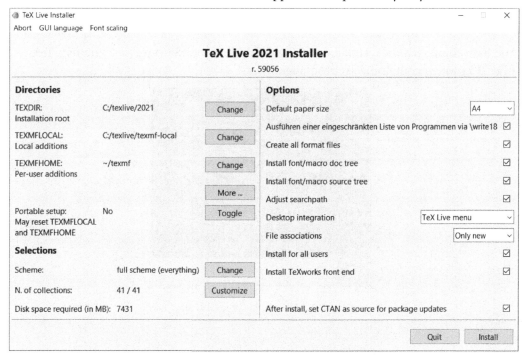

Figure 1.4 – TeX Live Installer advanced options

6. You can change the **Scheme** (options include **Full**, **Medium**, and **Small**) and customize the number of software collections, such as installed formats, fonts, styles, graphics packages, editor, language support, and many more. As the recommended options are already the most significant parts of the installation, unchecking some collections won't save much space. The full scheme is recommended.

7. Click on **Install** to proceed. Now, there's no interaction needed for a long time, and you can lean back while all the thousands of TeX packages are downloaded and installed:

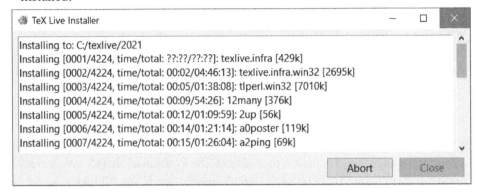

Figure 1.5 – Installation progress

8. Finally, you will get a welcome message. Finish by clicking on **Close**.

You have completed the installation of TeX Live. Now your Start menu contains a **TeX Live 2021** folder containing six programs:

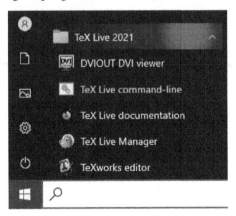

Figure 1.6 – TeX Live in the Windows Start menu

Let's briefly look at each of the programs:

- **DVIOUT DVI viewer**—a viewer program for the classic LaTeX output format DVI (today, most people choose PDF output, so you probably won't need this).

- **TeX Live command-line**—use this if you would like to run other TeX live programs at the command line.

- **TeX Live documentation**—opens the TeX Live manual in your web browser.

- **TeX Live Manager**—this is your tool for package management (for example, for installing and updating LaTeX packages).

- **TeXworks editor**—this is an editor that was developed to create LaTeX documents comfortably. We will make extensive use of TeXworks in this book.

- **Uninstall TeX Live**—use this before you install a new TeX Live version from scratch, or if you would like to install MiKTeX instead.

Now we will go through the offline installation of TeX Live.

Installing TeX Live offline

Every year, the TeX user group creates a TeX software collection DVD and sends it to their members. You can get a DVD from a TUG member or purchase it from the TUG web store, where it's listed for $16 in 2021. But we can download the DVD's content for free.

We will now download an ISO image of TeX Live with a size of about 4 GB. After extraction, we can burn it on a DVD and run the installation from there. To do this, follow these steps:

1. Visit the download area at `https://tug.org/texlive/acquire-iso.html`.

2. Download the `texlive.iso` file. If possible, use a download manager, especially if your internet connection is not stable.

3. Either burn the ISO file on a DVD using burning software that supports the ISO format, or extract it to your hard disk drive. For example, the free program **7-zip** can extract ISO files.

4. Among the extracted files or on your DVD, you will find the installer batch files `install-tl` and `install-tl-advanced`. Choose one, start it, and go through the installation similar to the online installation. More information is available on `https://tug.org/texlive/quickinstall.html`.

Installing TeX offline was just like the first installation. Still, this time you've got all the data, and you won't need an internet connection during the installation or for another installation. This download approach is especially recommended if it's foreseeable that you will install TeX Live on another computer later, or if you would like to give it to friends or colleagues.

As TeX runs on other operating systems as well, let's take a brief look at other systems.

Installing TeX Live on other operating systems

TeX also runs on a lot of systems other than Windows. Here's a quick glance:

- **Mac OS X**: You can download a customized version of TeX Live at `https://tug.org/mactex/`. Download the huge `.pkg` file and double-click on it to install. It will print very straightforward instructions.

- **Ubuntu Linux**: Use the **Software Center** to install TeX Live packages, or run `sudo apt-get install texlive-full` to get everything.

- **Debian Linux**: Use **Synaptic** to install TeX Live packages, or run `apt-get install texlive-full` (via `sudo` or as root user) to get everything.

- **Red Hat, CentOS, and Fedora Linux**: Use the **Red Hat package manager**, or `yum` via Command Prompt, such as `yum install texlive-scheme-full`, or DNF: `sudo dnf install texlive-scheme-full`.

- Others: Visit `https://tug.org/texlive/quickinstall.html` and follow the instructions.

If you want to stay on the edge, you could download and install the most current version of TeX Live from its home page instead of the version from the operating system's repositories, as mentioned in the last point.

If we need to update or add packages, the following section shows you how.

Updating TeX Live and installing new packages

The LaTeX developers update it continuously, both for new features and for bug fixes. From time to time, you can update your system.

To do this, go to the **Start** menu, then the **TeX Live** folder, and start the **TeX Live Manager** (also referred to as `tlmgr` for short, and also called **TeX Live Shell**). This application is both for updating and installing additional packages. Take a look at this screenshot so we can talk about how to use the TeX Live Manager:

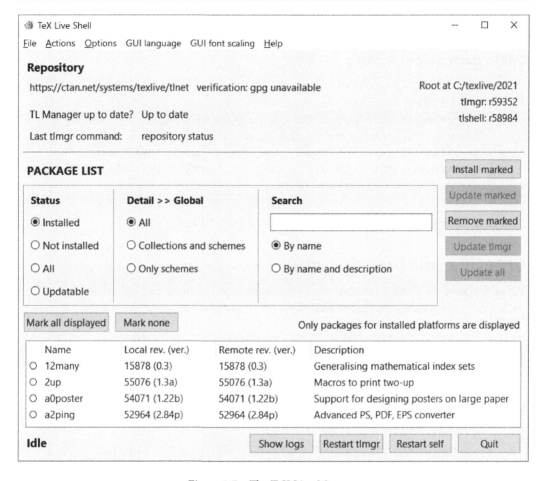

Figure 1.7 – The TeX Live Manager

The first section in the TeX Live Manager shows the **Repository**. A repository is a server with a TeX Live software archive. If the default repository is unavailable or is too slow in your area, you can click on **Options** to choose another repository from a list.

Click on **File | Load repository** to synchronize LaTeX with the latest software status.

In the **PACKAGE LIST** section, you can search packages by name or filter the view to see all available packages or only those installed, not installed, or updatable. In the middle of *Figure 1.7*, you can see an option to change the granularity to see all the packages or only collections or schemes.

The lowest section shows the packages when a filter is selected, with a short description and the version. You can choose packages here. Then you can click on **Install marked** if you would like to install the selected packages or click on **Remove marked** to uninstall them.

An easy way is just to click on **Update all**. If the **Update tlmgr** button is enabled and clickable, then there's a TeX Live Manager update available, and you can click the **Update tlmgr** button to update.

Yearly updates

The update procedure is only for the same TeX Live version. Every year, there's a new TeX Live version with the year as the version number. It would be best to uninstall the current TeX Live for a yearly upgrade and then install the new version from scratch. On `https://tug.org/texlive/`, you can see the upgrade plan with estimated dates.

Now that we've prepared the ground, let's start to write LaTeX!

Creating our first document

We've installed TeX and an editor; now, let's jump in at the deep end by writing our first LaTeX document using the TeXworks editor.

For Mac users

Please use the *Cmd* key when you see the *Ctrl* key here.

Our first goal is to create a document that prints out just one sentence. We want to use it to understand the basic structure of a LaTeX document. To do this, follow these steps:

1. Launch the TeXworks editor by clicking on the desktop icon or by opening it in the **Start** menu. In *Figure 1.8*, you can see the editor with the menu, buttons, and toolbar.

2. Click on the **New** button (or type *Ctrl + N*) or choose **File | New** in the menu.

3. Enter the following lines:

```
\documentclass{article}
\begin{document}
This is our first document.
\end{document}
```

4. Click on the **Save** button (or type *Ctrl + S*) to save the document. Choose a location where you want to store your LaTeX documents, ideally in its own folder.

5. Make sure that in the drop-down field in the TeXworks toolbar, **pdfLaTeX** is selected (this should be the default anyway):

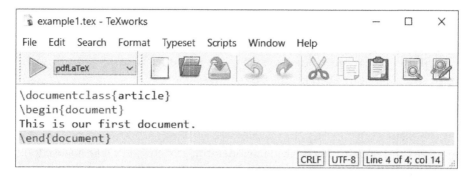

Figure 1.8 – The TeXworks editor

6.   Click the **Typeset** button or press *Ctrl + T*.

7.   The output window will automatically open. Have a look at it:

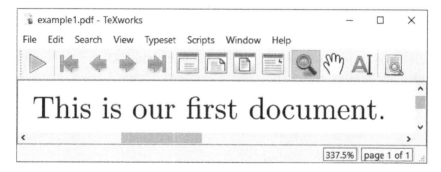

Figure 1.9 – The PDF output in the TeXworks editor

Those were the first few minutes of the life of a LaTeX document. You may edit it, typeset and check the output, and edit again. Don't forget to save your document frequently.

As mentioned earlier, in contrast to the classic word processor software, you cannot see the effect of changes immediately—but the result is just one click away.

Checking out advanced LaTeX editors

Do you have experience in working with complex programs? Do you like using a feature-rich and powerful editor? Then have a look at these LaTeX editors. Visit their websites to find screenshots and to read about their features:

- **Texmaker**—a cross-platform editor running on Windows, Linux, Mac OS X, and Unix systems: `https://xm1math.net/texmaker/`

- **TeXstudio**—another cross-platform editor for Windows, Linux, Mac OS X, and Unix systems: `https://texstudio.org/`

- **Kile**— a user-friendly editor for operating systems with KDE, such as Linux: `https://kile.sourceforge.io/`
- **TeXShop**—an easy-to-use and very popular editor for Mac OS X: `https://pages.uoregon.edu/koch/texshop/`

These editors are free, open source software. You can find more at `https://latexguide.org/editors`.

Online editors run on any internet-capable operating system. Let's take a close look at an online editor and compiler in the following section.

Working with LaTeX online using Overleaf

Installing LaTeX on your computer is recommended, but it can take up about 8 GB on your hard drive and two hours to install it.

How about simply using LaTeX in your internet browser? Here comes **Overleaf**. It's a pure online LaTeX service that mathematicians enthusiastic about TeX started in 2011. You can access it through this link: `https://www.overleaf.com`.

In this section about Overleaf, we will do the following:

- Check the Overleaf requirements
- Look at the benefits of Overleaf
- Evaluate possible caveats
- Use the Overleaf editor
- Try out Writefull

Let's go online now.

What Overleaf requires and delivers

To use Overleaf, you need the following:

- Any internet browser, such as Firefox, Chrome, Opera, or Edge.
- You don't need any other local software such as a LaTeX compiler, editor, or PDF viewer.

It is free for basic usage, and that covers *a lot*. It provides a complete TeX Live with unlimited projects and a feature-rich editor, real-time-sync collaboration with another user, and hundreds of templates to start with. You can easily write your thesis or book with Overleaf with free usage.

An advanced personal or professional subscription costs money and provides additional features, such as the following:

- Unlimited collaborators per project
- Document history (going back and forth between document versions)
- Advanced bibliography management (with Mendeley)
- Dropbox sync integration
- GitHub integration
- Priority personal support

The advanced features go beyond regular LaTeX. You can check if you are eligible; many universities and institutions partner with Overleaf to provide their members the full service.

Benefits of Overleaf

Let's look at what you can gain when using Overleaf, compared to using classic editors locally on your computer. With Overleaf, you can do the following:

- Use it on any device, such as a PC, laptop, tablet, or smartphone.
- Use it on a locked-in work computer where you cannot install anything yourself.
- Access your own files on any device (be it a private or work or library computer) once you log in with your password.
- If you invite somebody to work with you, both of you can instantly edit and see each other's changes, making collaboration easy.
- Have an automatic real-time view of the PDF result while you type.
- Access a version history for LaTeX projects to track changes.
- Annotate LaTeX source code with comments and answers to them.
- Work with a new LaTeX software without doing an upgrade.

However, there are some challenges to Overleaf. Let's think about that now.

Caveats of working online

To be clear, there can be some caveats:

- You always need the internet available.

- As your documents are stored online, you have to rely on data security and privacy by Overleaf. See `https://www.overleaf.com/legal`.

- You depend on Overleaf's features; their TeX version could be a bit behind the official TeX Live until they update theirs.

- The speed depends on their servers and your network connection, not just on your own computer's performance.

Let's take a closer look at how Overleaf works.

Creating our first document online

We want to create our own space on Overleaf in two steps. Then we will start our first LaTeX project:

1. Register for the service. Either click on **Register** on the Overleaf home page or go to `https://www.overleaf.com/register`. Enter your email address and choose a password.

2. Log in to Overleaf. Either click on **Login** on the front page or go to `https://www.overleaf.com/login`:

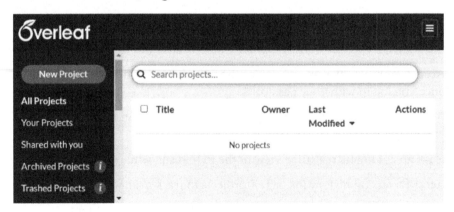

Figure 1.10 – Creating a new project

> **Why do we need to register?**
>
> To be reachable via an email address is basically to comply with data protection law. If you forget your password, you can ask Overleaf to send a password reset link to your email address. In general, by using your email address, you can prove your identity and ownership of your data if you ever need to.

3. Click the **New Project** button. A drop-down list will appear, where you can choose to have a blank project or one based on a template, such as a book, presentation, CV, or thesis template. For now, we just choose **Blank Project**.

4. Overleaf asks you for a name; choose one. That's it! This is what you have now:

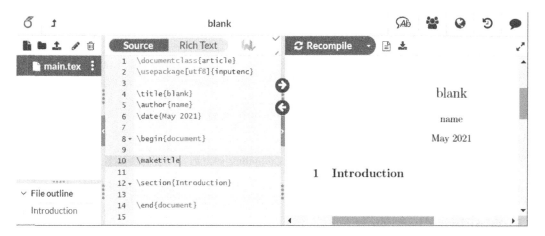

Figure 1.11 – A new project

It's not entirely blank as it contains a small code frame, so you got a quick start, and you can begin filling in your text.

Whenever you click the **Recompile** button or press *Ctrl + Enter*, the preview on the right side will be refreshed. You can enable automatic typesetting if you open the **Recompile** menu and choose **Auto Compile** in the drop-down menu, which is switched on in *Figure 1.12*. The document refreshes frequently and automatically while you are typing:

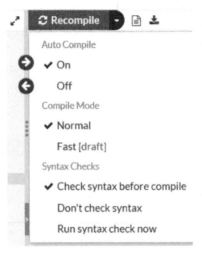

Figure 1.12 – Compiling settings

Since Overleaf is so different from classic LaTeX editors, let's have a closer look at it.

Exploring Overleaf

To quickly see a more complex document in action and to understand what you can expect from Overleaf, let's open the *Masters/Doctoral Thesis* template from `https://www.latextemplates.com/template/masters-doctoral-thesis`. Once you are there, simply click the **Open in Overleaf** button. Then Overleaf creates a project for you:

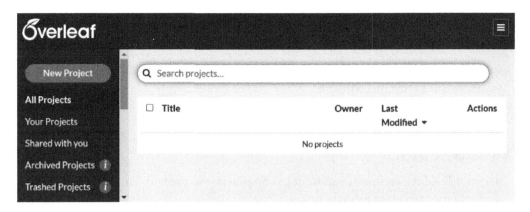

Figure 1.13 – A thesis template in the Overleaf editor

In *Figure 1.13*, on the very left, you can see your folder structure and files. Next to it, there is the LaTeX source code. On the right, you can see the output in a PDF preview.

In its most basic form, you write your code on the left, click the **Recompile** button, and see the result on the right, as we previously did in our example.

While you are working, Overleaf keeps track of the history. You can label versions to check them later. Clicking on the **History** button at the top shows you the versions:

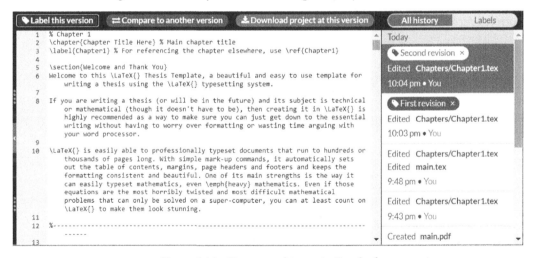

Figure 1.14 – Document history in Overleaf

Click a version on the right to switch to it.

Without looking at too many screenshots, this is what you can do if you click on the **Menu** button in the top-left corner:

- Let Overleaf count the words in your document, excluding code syntax such as commands and environments

- Synchronize with Dropbox or GitHub

- Choose the compiler (pdfLaTeX, classic LaTeX, XeLaTeX, LuaLaTeX, for advanced users)

- Set a TeX Live version if you want to compile an old file with an old TeX Live version or switch to a newer one

- Select a main `.tex` document if your project consists of several documents

- Choose a visual style editor theme for the code markup and background, changing colors between light, pastel, dark, and others

- Choose the editor font (such as Consolas or Lucida) and the font size

- (De)activate spell checking, auto-completion, auto-closing of brackets, and code-checking

The integrated spell checker of Overleaf marks issues with a wavy line. Just right-click on it to get replacement suggestions, as shown in the following screenshot:

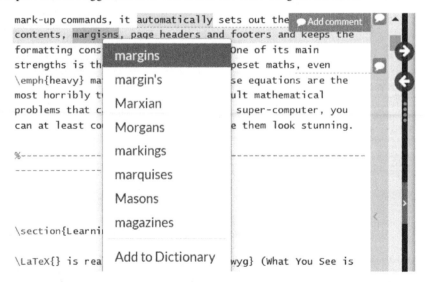

Figure 1.15 – Spellchecking in Overleaf

Apropos spellchecking, there's more.

Grammar and language feedback with Writefull

The **Writefull** Overleaf extension checks grammar and provides phrasing suggestions for your text. It's designed for scientific writing, and it's trained on millions of research journal articles. It can correct typos, grammar mistakes, vocabulary issues, punctuation, and more.

Let's see it in action on our previous thesis template example:

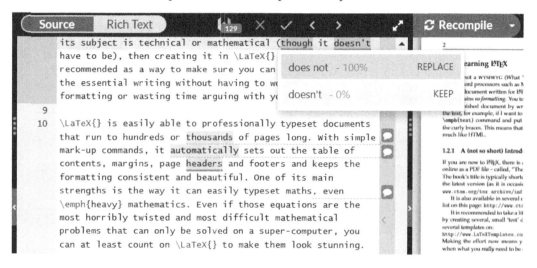

Figure 1.16 – Grammar checking with Writefull

While the spellchecker doesn't complain, the trained AI of the Writefull extension shows 129 potential issues and gives suggestions to the words underlined in red:

- *Though* may be replaced by *although*.

- *Doesn't* may be replaced by *does not*, in formal writing.

After **headers** (in the previous image), there should be an Oxford comma, that is, a comma before the word "and" at the end of a list.

You can take it easy as I do in this book, not so formal, but your thesis or research articles and any scientific writing may benefit from these suggestions.

The Writefull extension was available for the Chrome browser at first. It was announced that other web browsers, such as Firefox, will be supported in the future. It's free in a basic version, and there is a premium version that you can read about on their website.

Reviewing and commenting

You probably noticed the text highlighted in yellow and the speech bubble symbols in the previous screenshot. When you click the **Review** button, the review bar expands and the comments will be shown:

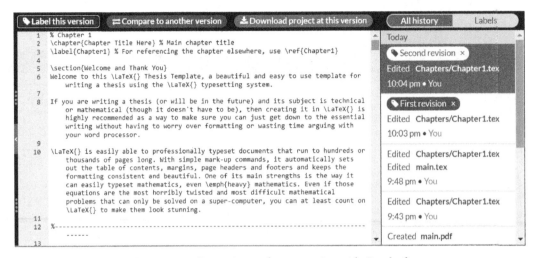

Figure 1.17 – Reviewing and commenting with Overleaf

You can mark text snippets, click on **Add comment**, write what you think, and also reply to other people's comments. That helps both in your own writing and in collaborating with colleagues or an editor.

This and the previously mentioned features should provide a good insight into current cloud LaTeX services.

Using Overleaf with our book examples

The complete set of the *LaTeX Beginner's Guide* code examples can be opened in Overleaf simultaneously, with a single click. Visit `https://latexguide.org/code` to get the entire package and have your own project with all book examples included, ready to edit and compile.

The following section will provide you with a way to access additional supporting documentation and references while working with this book.

Accessing documentation

There are many hundreds of LaTeX classes and packages available. No book could ever explain all its features on its own. But most of those packages offer good documentation that you can easily open and read. If you work your way through this book and supplement it with the documentation of the packages mentioned, you're on the right track to becoming a LaTeX power user.

In the following chapters, you will learn about many LaTeX packages that provide additional capabilities. To be prepared, you should just know how to access package documentation.

You can open a package manual directly on your computer after you have installed LaTeX:

- On Windows computer: In the **Start** menu, choose the **TeX Live** folder, and click TeX Live command-line. Alternatively, just run the Windows **cmd** app.

- On a Mac or any Linux computer: Start a **Terminal** app.

Then, just type `texdoc packagename` and press *Enter*. For example, typing `texdoc geometry` opens a PDF document that is the manual for the `geometry` package.

If you did not install LaTeX, you could obtain the documentation online. In your browser, open `https://texdoc.org/pkg/packagename`. That is just a template URL, so if you want the geometry package, you should type `https://texdoc.org/pkg/geometry`. That's an easy method for Overleaf users.

> **Remember throughout this book**
>
> We will often refer to a package manual or package documentation in this book later on. Remember that you can open documentation with the `texdoc` command or on `https://texdoc.org`, as described previously.

Finally, there's a lot of LaTeX-related documentation available online, including tutorials and references. We will talk more about it in *Chapter 14, Using Online Resources*.

Summary

We learned in this chapter about the benefits of LaTeX; soon, it will be our turn to use the virtues of LaTeX to achieve the best possible results. Furthermore, we covered installing, editing, and using LaTeX, both locally on your computer and online in the cloud.

Now that we've got a functional and tested LaTeX system, we're ready to write our own LaTeX documents. In the next chapter, we will talk about formatting text in detail.

2
Formatting Text and Creating Macros

In the last chapter, we installed LaTeX and used the TeXworks editor, as well as Overleaf, to write our first document. Now, we will look at the structure of text and focus on the text details and its formatting.

In this chapter, we will talk about the following:

- Working with logical formatting
- Understanding how LaTeX reads our input
- Modifying the text fonts
- Creating our own commands
- Using boxes to limit the width of paragraphs
- Breaking lines and paragraphs
- Turning off full justification
- Displaying quotes

By working with examples and trying out new features, we shall learn some basic concepts of LaTeX. By the end of this chapter, you will be familiar with commands and environments. You will even be able to define your own commands.

Now that you've started working intensively, you may encounter error messages when there's a problem with the document code. In such a case, you can look to *Chapter 13, Troubleshooting*, for possible solutions.

Technical requirements

You either need a LaTeX installation on your computer or you can use Overleaf. You can also edit and compile all the examples online on the book's web page: `https://latexguide.org/chapter-02`.

The code is also available on GitHub: `https://github.com/PacktPublishing /LaTeX-Beginner-s-Guide-2nd-Edition-/tree/main/Chapter_02_-_ Formatting_Text_and_Creating_Macros`.

In this chapter, we will use the following LaTeX packages: `hyphenat`, `microtype`, `parskip`, `url`, and `xspace`. If you don't work online, make sure you have them installed, or you have a full LaTeX installation as suggested.

Working with logical formatting

Within a LaTeX document, we should not apply **physical formatting**, for example, making words bold or italic or in a different size. Instead, we should use **logical formatting**, such as declaring a title and the author and giving a section header. The actual formatting, such as printing the title in big letters and making a section heading bold, is done by LaTeX.

> **Physical formatting in this book**
>
> In some examples later in this chapter, we will use physical formatting commands, such as making words bold or italic. However, that's for practicing font commands. The goal of this chapter is to define our own logical commands with the help of font commands.

In a good LaTeX document, physical formatting is only used within the definition of logical formatting commands. If we need some format style, such as for keywords, we will define a suitable logical command in the document preamble. In the document body text, we should only use the logical formatting commands. This gives us consistent formatting throughout the text, and whenever we change our mind on formatting details, we can modify the logical commands in the preamble. We will go through this in the next sections.

First, to understand the typical document structure, let's start with a short, illustrative example.

Creating a document with a title and heading

We will create a short example with some basic formatting. It shall include a title, the author's name, the date, a heading, and some regular text:

1. Type the following code into your editor to start a small document:

   ```
   \documentclass[a4paper,11pt]{article}
   ```

2. Specify the title, author, and date:

   ```
   \title{Example 2}
   \author{My name}
   \date{May 5, 2021}
   ```

3. Begin the document:

   ```
   \begin{document}
   ```

4. Let LaTeX print the full title, which will include the author and date:

   ```
   \maketitle
   ```

5. Make a section heading and add some text:

   ```
   \section{What's this?}
   This is our second document. It contains a title and a
   section with text.
   \end{document}
   ```

6. Save the document by clicking the **Save** button (or press *Ctrl + S*). Give it a name, such as example2.tex.

7. Compile the document by clicking the **Typeset** button (or press *Ctrl + T*); this translates your code into a PDF file.

8. View the output:

Example 2

My name

May 5, 2021

1   What's this?

This is our second document. It contains a title and a section with text.

Figure 2.1 – Text with a heading

The TeXworks editor immediately shows the PDF preview after you press the **Typeset** button. At the same time, a PDF file is also created. In this case, it's called `example2.pdf` and it's in the same folder as your original code file, `example2.tex`.

In the first chapter, we talked about logical formatting; let's look at this example from that point of view. We told LaTeX the following:

- Our document is of the `article` type. It will be printed on A4 paper using a size of 11 points for the base font.
- The title of the document is **Example 2**.
- It shows the author's name.
- The document was written on **May 5, 2021**.

Concerning the content of the document, we stated the following:

- It begins with a title.
- The first section includes the heading **What's this?**
- Following the heading is the text **This is our second document. It contains a title and a section with text.**.

Note we did not choose the font size of the title or heading, and neither did we make something bold or centered. Such formatting is done by LaTeX but nevertheless, you're free to tell LaTeX how it actually should look.

> **Auto-saving**
>
> Once we have saved a document, we do not need to press the **Save** button again. TeXworks automatically saves the document when we click the **Typeset** button.

Exploring the document structure

Let's look at the details of the example we just created. A LaTeX document doesn't stand alone—commonly, the document is based on a versatile template. Such a fundamental template is called a **class**. It provides customizable features, usually built for a certain purpose. There are classes for books, journal articles, letters, presentations, posters, and many more; hundreds of reliable classes can be found in internet archives, but also on your computer after you've installed TeX Live. In our example, we have chosen the `article` class, a standard LaTeX class suitable for smaller documents.

The first line starts with `\documentclass`. This word begins with a backslash; such a word is called a **command** or a **macro**. We already used commands to specify the class and to state document properties in our first example in this chapter: `\title`, `\author`, and `\date`. These commands store the properties; they don't print something.

This first part of the document is called the **preamble** of the document. This is where we choose the class, specify properties, and in general make document-wide definitions.

`\begin{document}` marks the end of the preamble and the beginning of the actual document. `\end{document}` marks the end of the document. Everything that follows would be ignored by LaTeX. Generally, such a piece of code that's framed by a `\begin` and `\end` command pair is called an **environment**.

In the actual document, we've used the `\maketitle` command, which prints the title, author, and date in a nicely formatted manner. With the `\section` command, we produced a heading, bigger and bolder than normal text. Then, we let some text follow. What we wrote after the preamble, in the document environment, will be printed out. However, the preamble itself will never produce any output.

Now that you've seen what commands look like, let's look at command syntax in detail.

Understanding LaTeX commands

LaTeX commands begin with a backslash, followed by big or small letters, and are usually named in a descriptive way. There are exceptions: you will see some commands consisting of a backslash and just one special character.

Commands can have **parameters**, that is, options that determine in which way the command does its work. The values that we hand over as parameters are called **arguments**. They are given in curly braces or square brackets, as we will explain now.

So, calling a command can look like this:

```
\command
```

Or, it can look like this:

```
\command{argument}
```

Or, it can look like this:

```
\command[optional argument]{argument}
```

There could be several arguments, each of them in braces or brackets. Arguments in curly braces are mandatory. If a command is defined to require an argument, one has to be given. For example, calling \documentclass would be futile if we haven't stated a class name.

Arguments in square brackets are optional; they may be given but it's not a must. If no optional argument is provided, the command will use a default one. For instance, in the first example in *Chapter 1, Getting Started with LaTeX*, we wrote \documentclass{article}. This document was typeset with a base font size of 10 points because this is the class's default base font size. In the second document, we wrote \documentclass[a4paper,11pt]{article}; here, we replaced the default values with the given values, so now the document will be adjusted for A4 paper using a base font size of 11 points.

Commands, macros, and declarations

Most LaTeX commands, including those we define ourselves, consist of other commands. That's why LaTeX commands are also called **macros**, and the terms *macro* and *command* are used interchangeably. A command or macro that doesn't print something but just changes current settings, such as the font shape or text alignment, is also called a **declaration**.

Now, let's look at the syntax of environments.

Understanding LaTeX environments

LaTeX environments start with \begin and end with \end. Both commands require the name of the environment as their argument.

Simple environments look like this:

```
\begin{name}
   ...
\end{name}
```

Such environments can be used for each declaration called \name.

Like commands, environments may have arguments. Exactly like in the case of commands, mandatory arguments are written in curly braces and optional arguments in square brackets. So, you will encounter an environment like this:

```
\begin{name}{argument}
   ...
\end{name}
```

You will also encounter environments like this:

```
\begin{name}[optional argument]{argument}
   ...
\end{name}
```

Environments are like declarations with a built-in scope. With \begin, the environment introduces a change in layout, font, or other properties. There must be an \end command, where this change will be canceled. The effect of the environment name is delimited to the piece of code between \begin{name} and \end{name}.

Furthermore, the effect of all local declarations used inside an environment will end together with the surrounding environment.

Now that we know the syntax of LaTeX commands and environments, let's see how LaTeX treats what we type.

Understanding how LaTeX reads our input

Before we continue writing, let's look at how LaTeX understands what we type:

- Besides simple alphabet characters, we can directly type (or copy and paste) accented characters, such as ä, ü, and ö, as well as further characters from other languages, such as Greek or Russian.

- A space in the input code will appear as a space in the output document. Several consecutive spaces are treated as one space.

- An end of a line in the source code is treated as a space.

- An empty line in the source code is treated as a paragraph break.

There are some characters with special meanings:

- A backslash, \, starts a LaTeX command or a LaTeX macro.

- Curly braces and square brackets are used for command arguments.

- A dollar sign, $, starts and ends math mode, which we will explore in *Chapter 9, Writing Math Formulas*.

- A percent sign, %, tells LaTeX to ignore the rest of the line.

Let's expand upon that last point: the percent sign introduces a **comment**. Everything following a percent sign until the end of the line will be ignored by LaTeX and won't be printed out. This enables you to insert notes into your document. It's often used in LaTeX templates to inform the user of what the template does or requires the user to do at a certain point. Note that the end of the line, normally behaving as a space, will also be ignored after a percent sign.

Easing experimenting by trial and error

If you want to disable a command temporarily, it may be favorable to insert a percent sign instead of deleting the command. That way, you're able to undo this change easily by removing the percent sign.

If that is how the percent sign works, what should we do if we want to write 100% in our text? And what about the other special symbols? Let's figure out how to solve that issue in the next section.

Printing out special symbols

Common text mostly contains uppercase and lowercase letters, digits, and punctuation characters that you can simply type into your editor. However, some characters are reserved for LaTeX commands and cannot be used directly. We already encountered such characters, including the percent sign and curly braces. To fix this issue, there are LaTeX commands to print such symbols.

We will write a very short example printing out an amount of dollars and a percent number, along with some other symbols:

1. Create a new document and enter the following lines:

```
\documentclass{article}
```

```
\begin{document}
Statement \#1:
50\% of \$100 equals \$50.

More special symbols are \&, \_, \{ and \}.
\end{document}
```

2. Click the **Typeset** button to compile the document.

3. Check out the output:

> Statement #1: 50% of $100 equals $50.
> More special symbols are &, _, { and }.

Figure 2.2 – Special symbols

By putting a backslash before a special symbol, we turned it into a LaTeX command. The only purpose of this commend is to print out that symbol.

Printing the backslash

You may be wondering how to print a backslash. The command for printing a backslash is `\textbackslash`. If you would like to know what `\\` might be used for, it is used as a shortcut for a line break. That may seem a bit odd, but line breaks occur frequently whereas backslashes are rarely needed in the output, therefore this shortcut has been chosen.

There's a wealth of symbols that we can use for math formulas, chess notation, zodiac signs, music scores, and more. We don't need to deal with those symbols for now, but we shall return to that subject in *Chapter 9, Writing Math Formulas*, when we will need symbols to typeset math formulas.

Now that we know how to enter pure text, let's find out how we can format it.

Modifying the text fonts

LaTeX already does some formatting automatically; for example, we've seen that section headings are bigger than normal text and bold-faced. Now we will learn how to modify the appearance of the text ourselves.

Adjusting the font shape

In this example, we will emphasize an important word in our text, and we will see how to make words appear in bold, italic, or slanted. We shall also figure out how to highlight words in a specific part of the text that's already emphasized.

Let's take a look:

1. Create a new document containing the following code:

```
\documentclass{article}
\begin{document}
Text can be \emph{emphasized}.

Besides from \textit{italics}, words can be
\textbf{bold}, \textsl{slanted}, or typeset
in \textsc {Small Caps}.

Such commands can be \textit{\textbf{nested}}.

\emph{See how \emph{emphasizing} looks when nested.}
\end{document}
```

2. Click **Typeset** and have a look at the output:

Text can be *emphasized*.
Besides from *italics*, words can be **bold**, *slanted*, or typeset in SMALL CAPS.
Such commands can be ***nested***.
See how emphasizing *looks when nested.*

Figure 2.3 – Emphasizing phrases

At first, we used the \emph command, giving one word as an argument to this command. This argument will be typeset in italic because this is the default way LaTeX emphasizes text.

Text-formatting commands usually look like \text**{argument}, where ** stands for a two-letter abbreviation such as bf for bold face, it for italic, and sl for slanted. The argument will then be formatted accordingly, as we've seen in our example. After the command, the subsequent text will continue being typeset as it was before the command—precisely after the closing curly brace, marking the end of the argument.

We nested the \textit and \textbf commands, which allowed us to achieve a combination of those styles, and the text appears in both italic and bold.

Most font commands will show the same effect if they are applied twice, such as \textbf{\textbf{words}}. Here, the words won't become bolder.

But \emph behaves differently. We've seen that \emph changes text to italic, but if we use \emph on a piece of text that is already in italic, it will change from italic to upright font. Imagine an important theorem completely typeset in italic and you would like to highlight a word inside this theorem; that word should not be in italic but formatted as upright font again.

Change the font shape sensibly

Combining font shapes, such as marking bold and italic at the same time, might be considered a questionable style choice. Change the font shape wisely—and consistently.

Choosing the font family

The default LaTeX font is a **serif** font (also called a **Roman** font). That means small lines or strokes, called **serifs**, are attached to letters. If such serifs are absent, we call the font a **sans-serif** font.

Compare the two lines in *Figure 2.4*. Look closely at the first letter, **T**, which clearly shows the difference between serif and sans-serif fonts:

This is serif

This is sans-serif

Figure 2.4 – Serif versus sans-serif font

These different types of fonts are called **font families** or **typefaces**.

Another typeface is **monospaced**; here, all letters have the same width. Monospaced fonts are also called **typewriter** fonts.

Let's switch font families in a small example document. We will start with bold text, but bold text with serif looks very heavy. So, we will use sans-serif bold text instead. The following text will contain an internet address, and we will choose a typewriter font to emphasize it.

Follow these instructions:

1. Create a LaTeX document with the following code:

```
\documentclass{article}
\begin{document}
\textsf{\textbf{Get help on the Internet}}

\texttt{https://latex.org} is a support forum for \LaTeX.
\end{document}
```

2. Click on **Typeset** and look at the result:

> **Get help on the Internet**
> https://latex.org is a support forum for LaTeX.

Figure 2.5 – Text with a URL

Here, we encountered further font commands—by using \textsf, we've chosen the sans-serif font in the heading line, and we used the \texttt command to get the typewriter font for the internet address. Those commands can be used just like the font commands we've learned about before.

Serifs, those small decorative details at the end of a letter's strokes, improve readability by leading the reader's eyes along the line; therefore, they are widely used in printed books and newspapers.

Headings are often done without serifs. Sans-serif fonts are also a good choice for screen text because of their better readability on lower-resolution screens or on mobile phone displays with small font sizes. Sans-serif fonts are often preferred for text in e-books and on internet pages.

Monospaced or typewriter fonts are preferred for writing the source code of computer programs, both in print and in text editors. As in our previous example, this book generally uses a typewriter font to distinguish source code and web addresses from normal text.

The commands we've seen applied formatting to the text in the argument in curly braces. LaTeX also provides commands without arguments, which work like switches.

Using the following instructions, we will modify the previous example using font family switching commands:

1. Edit the previous example to get the following code:

```
\documentclass{article}
\begin{document}
\sffamily\bfseries Get help on the Internet

\normalfont\ttfamily https://latex.org\normalfont\ is
a support forum for \LaTeX.
\end{document}
```

2. Click on **Typeset** to compile.

3. Compare the output to the previous example; it's the same.

By using the \sffamily command, we switched to the sans-serif typeface. The \bfseries command switched the text to bold. We used the \normalfont command to return to the default LaTeX font, and then we used the \ttfamily command to switch to a typewriter font. After the internet address, we used \normalfont again to switch to the default font.

Such switching commands don't produce any output themselves, but they will affect the text that follows it, so they are **declarations**.

Let's summarize the font commands and their corresponding declarations together with their meanings:

Command	Declaration	Meaning
\textrm{...}	\rmfamily	roman family
\textsf{...}	\sffamily	sans-serif family
\texttt{...}	\ttfamily	typewriter family
\textbf{...}	\bfseries	**bold-face**
\textmd{...}	\mdseries	medium
\textit{...}	\itshape	*italic shape*
\textsl{...}	\slshape	*slanted shape*
\textsc{...}	\scshape	SMALL CAPS SHAPE
\textup{...}	\upshape	upright shape
\textnormal{...}	\normalfont	default font

Figure 2.6 – Font commands

> **Note on emphasizing**
>
> The corresponding declaration to \emph is \em.

Confining the effect of commands by braces

In the previous example, we wrote \normalfont to switch the font back to the default font, but there's another way. We shall use curly braces to tell LaTeX where to apply a command and where to stop it:

1. Shorten and modify our font shape example that produced *Figure 2.3* to get this code:

```
\documentclass{article}
\begin{document}
Besides from {\itshape italics}, words can be
{\bfseries bold}, {\slshape slanted}, or typeset
in {\scshape Small Caps}.
\end{document}
```

2. Click on **Typeset** and check out the output:

Besides from *italics*, words can be **bold**, *slanted*, or typeset in SMALL CAPS.

Figure 2.7 – Using declarations to change the font weight and shape

When we change the font using a declaration, we start with an opening curly brace, and then the font declaration command follows. The effect of that command lasts until we stop it with the corresponding closing brace.

An opening curly brace tells LaTeX to begin a **group**. The following commands are valid for the subsequent text until a closing curly brace ends the group. Groups can be nested as follows:

```
Normal text, {\sffamily sans serif text {\bfseries and bold}}.
```

The area where a command is valid is called its **scope**. We have to be careful to complete each group. For every opening brace, there has to be a closing brace.

So, in short, groups are defined by curly braces and they contain and confine the effect of local commands.

Exploring font sizes

Now we will try out every font size available with LaTeX's default font size commands:

1. Create a document with the following code:

```
\documentclass{article}
\begin{document}
\tiny We \scriptsize start \footnotesize very
\smallsmall, \normalsize get \large big \Large
and \LARGE bigger, \huge huge, \Huge gigantic!
\end{document}
```

2. Click on **Typeset** and observe the output:

We start very small, get big and bigger, huge, gigantic!

Figure 2.8 – Font sizes

We used all 10 available font size declarations, starting small with \tiny and ending really big with \Huge. There are no corresponding commands taking arguments, so we would have to use curly braces to delimit their scope, as we learned before.

The actual resulting font size scales with the base font size. If your document has a base font of 12 points, then \tiny would result in text bigger than the base font of 10 points.

Use \footnotesize if you wish to get the same size LaTeX uses for footnotes or use \scriptsize if you wish to create a style with a size matching LaTeX subscripts and superscripts. Document classes provide carefully selected and well-suited font size selections, so you normally don't need to set a certain physical size. This and other advanced font tweaking commands are covered in *Chapter 3*, *Adjusting Fonts*, in the *LaTeX Cookbook, Packt Publishing*.

For practice, we used many predefined font commands in this section. The next level is to create our own logical formatting commands to use them instead of physical font commands within the document body text.

Creating our own commands

If you're frequently using the same term in your document, it would be annoying to type it again and again. What if you later decide to change that term or its formatting? To avoid searching and replacing the term in the whole document, LaTeX allows you to define your own commands in your preamble.

Remember: a command that consists of other commands is called a **macro**, and that's what we will define now. Basically, we choose a new macro name and define the sequence of text or commands to be used in that macro. Then, when we want to perform an action, we just need to use the macro's name.

We will start with simple macros that are basically abbreviations.

Using macros for simple text

Macros can save us from repeating long words or phrases and can act as placeholders. We can change the content of the macro to update the whole document with a different version of that phrase.

Here, we will define a short command that prints out the name of the **TeX Users Group** (**TUG**):

1. Type this code into a new document:

```
\documentclass{article}
\newcommand{\TUG}{\TeX\ Users Group}
\begin{document}
\section{The \TUG}
The \TUG\ is an organization for people who use
\TeX\ or \LaTeX.
\end{document}
```

2. Click on **Typeset** and look at the result:

1   The TeX Users Group

The TeX Users Group is an organization for people who use TeX or LaTeX.

Figure 2.9 – Using our first macro

\newcommand in the highlighted line defines our command. The first argument is the name we chose for the command, and the second argument is the text we want it to print out in the document.

Now, whenever we type \TUG in our document, the complete name will appear. If we later decide to change the name or its formatting, we just need to change this \newcommand line. Then, the change will be applied to the whole document.

You may use formatting commands inside your command definition. Let's say you would like to change the formatting of all occurrences of this name to be typeset in small caps; just change the definition to the following:

```
\newcommand{\TUG}{\textsc{TeX Users Group}}
```

You have also seen that we've used the \TeX command. This abbreviation command just prints out the name of the typesetting system, formatted in the same way as its logo. \LaTeX works similarly.

Note that we used a backslash after \TeX. The following space would just separate the command from the following text; it wouldn't produce a space in the output. Using the backslash followed by a space forces the output of a space that would otherwise be ignored. That also applies to the command we just created.

Now we will see how to avoid that manual spacing.

Proper spacing after commands

A backslash following a command could easily be forgotten. Can't we modify the command in order to automate that? Tasks like this, which aren't supported by LaTeX directly, could be solved by using **packages**, which are collections of styles and commands.

Here, we will load the xspace package; its only purpose is to adjust the spacing after printed output:

1. Insert this line into your preamble, that is, before \begin{document}:

    ```
    \usepackage{xspace}
    ```

2. Add the \xspace command to your macro definition:

    ```
    \newcommand{\TUG}{\TeX\ Users Group\xspace}
    ```

\usepackage{xspace} tells LaTeX to load the xspace package and to import all of its definitions. From now on, we can use all commands contained in that package.

This package provides the \xspace command, which inserts a space depending on the following character:

- If a normal letter follows, then it will print a space after the macro content.
- If a dot, a comma, an exclamation mark, or a quotation mark follows, it won't insert a space.

That automation is the defining reason for using the xspace package.

Creating more universal commands and using arguments

Imagine that your text contains a lot of keywords that you want to be printed in bold. If you use the \textbf command on all the keywords, what will happen if you later decide to use an italic shape instead, or a typewriter font? You would have to change that formatting for each keyword. There's a better way: defining your own macro and using \textbf only inside that macro definition.

Creating a macro with arguments

In this section, we will use \newcommand again, but this time we will introduce a parameter that will contain our keyword. For the example, we will use it on some terms that we've got to know in this chapter.

Let's get started:

1. Type the following code example in your editor. The highlighted line will be our own macro definition, as shown here:

```
\documentclass{article}
\newcommand{\keyword}[1]{\textbf{#1}}
\begin{document}
\keyword{Grouping} by curly braces limits the
\keyword{scope} of \keyword{declarations}.
\end{document}
```

2. Click on **Typeset** and observe the look of the keywords in the output:

Grouping by curly braces limits the **scope** of **declarations**.

Figure 2.10 – Formatting keywords

Let's look at the highlighted \newcommand line in the code. The number 1 in the square brackets marks the number of arguments that we want to use in the command. #1 will be replaced by the value of the first argument; #2 will be replaced by the value of the second argument, and so on. Now, if you want to modify the appearance of all keywords to be italic, just modify the definition of \keyword and the change will be global.

The first time we used \newcommand, in the *Creating our own commands* section, we used it with two arguments: the macro name and the macro commands. In the previous example, there were three arguments; the additional argument has been put in square brackets, which is how we mark optional arguments (those arguments may be given or may be omitted). If omitted, they would have a default value.

Previously, we've already worked with the \documentclass command, but how can we define a command with optional arguments ourselves?

Creating a macro with optional arguments

We will use \newcommand another time, but this time with an optional formatting parameter and a mandatory argument for the keyword:

1. Modify the previous example to get this code:

```
\documentclass{article}
\newcommand{\keyword}[2][\bfseries]{{#1#2}}
\begin{document}
\keyword{Grouping} by curly braces limits the
\keyword{scope} of \keyword[\itshape]{declarations}.
\end{document}
```

2. Click on **Typeset** and check out the result:

Grouping by curly braces limits the **scope** of *declarations*.

Figure 2.11 – Optional arguments

Let's look again at the highlighted \newcommand line in the code. By using [\bfseries], we introduced an optional parameter; we refer to it by #1 and its default value is \bfseries. Since we used a declaration this time, we added a pair of braces to ensure that only the keyword is affected by the declaration. Later in the document, we gave [\itshape] to \keyword, changing the default formatting to italic.

Here's the definition of \newcommand:

```
\newcommand{command}[arguments][optional]{definition}
```

These are the meanings of the parameters to \newcommand:

- command: The name of the new command, starting with a backslash followed by lowercase and/or uppercase letters, or a backslash followed by a single non-letter symbol. The name must not be already defined and is not allowed to begin with \end.

- arguments: An integer from 1 to 9, representing the number of arguments of the new command. If omitted, the command will have no arguments.

- optional: If this is present, then the first of the arguments would be optional with a default value given here. Otherwise, all arguments are mandatory.

- definition: Every occurrence of command will be replaced by definition and every occurrence of the form #n will then be replaced by the nth argument.

Use \newcommand to create styles for keywords, code snippets, web addresses, names, notes, information boxes, or differently emphasized text. How did we achieve the consistent structure of this book? Defining styles with \newcommand is the key. We should use font commands within our macro definitions, rather than in the document body text.

General good practice

As often as possible, create your own macros to achieve a logical structure. You will be rewarded with consistent formatting and changes could easily be applied to the whole document. By defining and using commands, you can ensure that the formatting remains consistent throughout your whole document.

Now that we have seen how to format words and phrases, let's look at whole paragraphs.

Using boxes to limit the width of paragraphs

We won't always write text just from left to right over the complete text width. Sometimes, we'd like a paragraph to have a smaller width, for instance, when we would like to put text and a picture side by side.

In the following sections, we will look at how to work with paragraph boxes in LaTeX.

Creating a narrow text box

For our example, we would like to explain the acronym TUG in a text column of only 3 cm width. To do this, follow these steps:

1. Create a new document containing these four lines:

```
\documentclass{article}
\begin{document}
\parbox{3cm}{TUG is an acronym. It means
\TeX\ Users Group.}
\end{document}
```

2. Click on **Typeset** and take a critical look at the output with the too-wide spacing:

TUG   is   an
acronym.   It
means   TeX   Users
Group.

Figure 2.12 – A narrow justified paragraph

We used the \parbox command in the highlighted code line to create a column. The first argument to the \parbox command sets the width to 3 cm, and the second argument to \parbox contains the text.

\parbox takes the argument text and formats the output to fit the specified width. We see that the text is fully justified; however, our example shows an obvious problem: insisting on full justification could lead to undesirable big gaps in the text. Possible solutions are as follows:

- We introduce hyphenation; the word **acronym** could easily be hyphenated.

- We improve justification in general.

- We give up on full justification; narrow text could look better when it's only left-justified.

We will check out all of these options in the *Breaking lines and paragraphs* and *Turning off full justification* sections.

But first, let's understand how \parbox works.

Producing common paragraph boxes

Usually, we just need a text box with a certain width; occasionally, we would like to have some additional alignment to the surrounding text. So, the common definition of the \parbox command is as follows:

```
\parbox[alignment]{width}{text}
```

The meanings of the parameters are as follows:

- alignment: That's the optional argument for vertical alignment. State t to align at the baseline of the top line of the box; write b to align at the baseline of its bottom line. The default behavior is to place the box such that its center is in line with the center of the current text line.

- width: That's the width of the box. It can be given in ISO units, such as 3 cm, 44 mm, or 2 in.

- text: That's the text that you want to put in that box. It should be a short piece of common text. For complicated or longer content, we can use the minipage environment, which we will use in the next section.

Here's a demonstration of the effect of the alignment parameters:

```
\documentclass{article}
\begin{document}
Text line
\quad\parbox[b]{1.8cm}{this parbox is aligned
at its bottom line}
\quad\parbox{1.5cm}{center-aligned parbox}
\quad\parbox[t]{2cm}{another parbox aligned at its top line}
\end{document}
```

The \quad command produces some space; we used it to separate the boxes a bit. Here's the output:

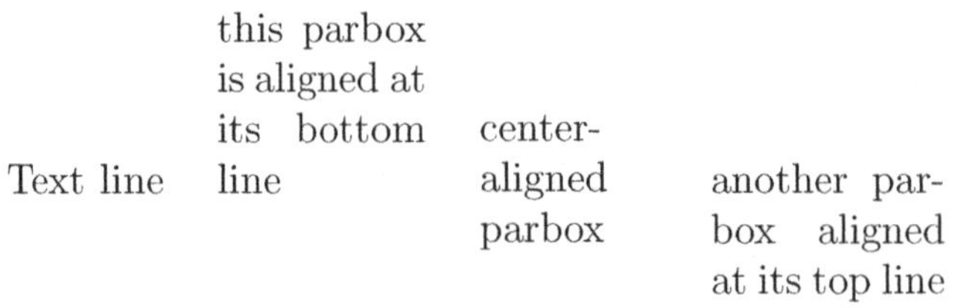

Figure 2.13 – Aligned paragraph boxes

The output in *Figure 2.13* shows how the alignment works. **Text line** is our base line, and referring to that base line, the following boxes are aligned at the bottom, the center, or the top line, respectively.

Exploring further features of paragraph boxes

\parbox is capable of doing even more. If you need advanced positioning, here's the complete \parbox definition:

```
\parbox[alignment][height][inner alignment]{width}{text}
```

The meanings of the parameters are as follows:

- height: If this optional argument isn't given, the box will have just the natural height of the text inside. Use this argument if you want to change the height of the box to make it bigger or smaller.

- inner alignment: If the height of the box is different from the natural height of the contained text, you might want to adjust the text position. You can add the following values:

  c: Vertically centers the text in the box

  t: Places text at the top of the box

  b: Places text at its bottom

  s: Stretches the text vertically (if possible)

  If you omit this argument, the alignment argument will be used here as the default value.

Take our previous demonstration example and try the effect of the optional arguments. Use the \fbox command, which helps to visualize the effect; if you write \fbox{\parbox[...]{...}{text}}, the complete parbox will be framed.

Using mini pages

Paragraph boxes are suitable for boxes with only a little text inside. In the case of a box containing a large amount of text, the closing brace could easily be forgotten or overlooked. The minipage environment would then be a better choice.

In this example, we will use the `minipage` environment instead of `\parbox` to get a sample of text with a width of just 3 cm:

1. Modify the parbox example to get the following code:

```
\documentclass{article}
\begin{document}
\begin{minipage}{3cm}
TUG is an acronym. It means \TeX\ Users Group.
\end{minipage}
\end{document}
```

2. Click on **Typeset** and look at the output:

> TUG   is   an
> acronym.   It
> means TeX Users
> Group.

Figure 2.14 – A minipage example

By using `\begin{minipage}`, we started a "page in a page." We specified that the width of 3 cm will be the mandatory argument. From this point onward, the text lines will have a width of 3 cm; they will be automatically wrapped and fully justified. We ended this restriction with `\end{minipage}`. Any text typed afterward would run over the complete body text width.

> **Preventing page breaks**
>
> There will never be a page break within a `minipage` environment, so that's a way to prevent page breaks within a text area. If that text within the `minipage` environment doesn't fit on the page, it will move to the next page.

The `minipage` environment accepts all arguments similar to `\parbox` with the same meanings.

If text is wrapped in a box or just in a normal line, it may automatically fit well. However, we may need to consider completing line breaking and justification manually. Let's see how to do this in the next sections.

Breaking lines and paragraphs

Generally, when you're writing text, you don't need to care about the line wrapping. Just by typing the text with your editor, LaTeX will make it fit to the line and it will take care of the justification. If you want to begin a new paragraph, just insert an empty line before you continue with your text for the next paragraph.

Now we will find out how to control the line wrapping. First, we will see how to improve the automatic hyphenation, and second, we will learn commands to insert breaks directly.

Improving hyphenation

If you look at longer documents, you will notice that it's outstanding how the text is fully justified by LaTeX and how the spacing between words is evenly distributed on the lines. If necessary, LaTeX will divide words and put hyphens at the end of the line in order to break the lines in a better way. LaTeX already uses very good algorithms to hyphenate words, but it may happen that it can't find an acceptable way to divide a word. The previous example pointed out this problem: breaking the word **acronym** would improve the output, but LaTeX does not know where to divide it. We shall find out how to solve that.

No matter how good the justification is, text in very narrow columns is extremely hard to justify. To achieve full justification, LaTeX inserts big gaps between the words.

In the following example, we will tell LaTeX how a word could be divided, to give LaTeX more flexibility for paragraph justification:

1. Insert the following line into the preamble of the previous example:

   ```
   \hyphenation{acro-nym}
   ```

2. Click on **Typeset** and look at the output:

   > TUG is an acro-
   > nym. It means TeX
   > Users Group.

Figure 2.15 – A paragraph with improved hyphenation

We've told LaTeX that the word **acronym** may have a division point between **acro** and **nym**. That means a hyphen might be placed after **acro** at the end of the line and **nym** moves down to the following line.

The \hyphenation command tells LaTeX where the division points of a word may be. Its argument may contain several words separated by spaces. For each word, we can indicate several points. For instance, we could extend the argument by more division points and more word variants, like this:

```
\hyphenation{ac-ro-nym ac-ro-nym-ic a-cro-nym-i-cal-ly}
```

You could also indicate division points in the body text by inserting a backslash followed by a hyphen, such as ac\-ro\-nym. But by using the \hyphenation command in the preamble, you would collect all rules there and they will be used consistently; so, use it especially in the rare cases where LaTeX's automation fails.

Preventing hyphenation

If you want to prevent the hyphenation of a certain word at all, there are two possible ways:

- Declare it in the preamble by using it in the \hyphenation argument without any division points, such as \hyphenation{indivisible}.

- Protect it inside the text using the \mbox command: The following word is \mbox{indivisible}.

Loading the hyphenat package gives us two more choices:

- \usepackage[none]{hyphenat} prevents hyphenation throughout the document.

- \usepackage[htt]{hyphenat} enables hyphenation for typewriter text; otherwise, such monospaced words won't be hyphenated by default.

These optional arguments to \usepackage are called **package options**. They configure the behavior of a package. The mentioned options may be combined, separated by commas. Even if you don't use the none option, you can disable hyphenation for short pieces of text using the \nohyphens{text} command. Try out these features if you want to benefit from them. The package documentation explains more features that you may sometimes need, such as hyphenation after special characters such as numerals and punctuation.

Improving the justification

Today's most popular TeX compiler is **pdfTeX**, which directly produces PDF output. When Hàn Thế Thành developed pdfTeX, he extended TeX with micro-typographic capabilities. When we typeset directly to a PDF, we're actually using **pdfLaTeX** and we can benefit from the new features by using the `microtype` package.

Let's improve our previous example by loading the `microtype` package:

1. Insert the following line into the preamble of the previous example:

    ```
    \usepackage{microtype}
    ```

2. Click on **Typeset** and look at the output:

> TUG is an acronym.
> It means TeX Users
> Group.

Figure 2.16 – A paragraph with better justification

We have loaded the `microtype` package without any options, relying on its default behavior. It introduces font expansion to tweak the justification and uses hanging punctuation to improve the optical appearance of the margins. This may reduce the need for hyphenation and avoids having large gaps between words for achieving full justification. You've seen its effect on a narrow column, so imagine the improvement on wide text—keep that in mind and try it out later!

Though `microtype` provides powerful features and options for the advanced typesetter, we usually won't need to do more than just load it to benefit from it. There's extensive package documentation if you want to study it in depth. `microtype` does nice tweaking but it's not a cure-all; we should still take care of proper hyphenation when necessary.

Breaking lines manually

We might choose to end a line ourselves, overriding the automation. Here, we will learn about several commands with different effects for ending a line.

We will type the beginning of a famous poem by Edgar Allan Poe. As the poet has specified where a verse has to end, we shall insert line breaks there.

So, let's write up the beginning of the poem:

1. Create a document containing these lines:

```
\documentclass{article}
\begin{document}
\noindent\emph{Annabel Lee}\\
It was many and many a year ago,\\
In a kingdom by the sea,\\
That a maiden there lived whom you may know\\
By the name of Annabel Lee
\end{document}
```

2. Click on **Typeset** and view the output:

> *Annabel Lee*
> It was many and many a year ago,
> In a kingdom by the sea,
> That a maiden there lived whom you may know
> By the name of Annabel Lee

Figure 2.17 – Manually broken lines

The very short \\ command ended a line, while the following text was moved to the next line. That's different from a paragraph break as we're still using the same paragraph. The \newline command also has the same effect.

The \noindent command suppresses the paragraph indentation. Otherwise, the first line in the paragraph would be indented by default. Indenting is actually intended for visually separating paragraphs. We suppressed indentation manually because there is no section heading. After headings, there's no indentation by default. You normally don't need the \noindent command. For generally removing paragraph indentation and replacing it with vertical inter-paragraph spacing, load the parskip package. You can see this in *Figure 2.23* and the corresponding code.

Note that although we inserted line endings, it is still a single paragraph. So, a line break doesn't cause a paragraph indentation since it's logically the same paragraph.

Exploring line breaking options

The \\ command understands optional arguments with the following syntax:

- \\[value] inserts additional vertical space after the break depending on the value, such as \\[3mm].

- *[value] is a variation of the previous argument but prevents a page break before the next line of text.

There's another command called \linebreak that tells LaTeX to end the line but to keep the full justification, therefore the space between the words would be stretched to reach the right margin. This could cause unpleasant gaps—that's why that command is rarely used.

\linebreak[number] can be used to tweak the line break. If number is 0, a line break is allowed; 1 means it's desired; 2 and 3 mark more insistent requests; 4 will enforce it. The latter is the default behavior if no number is given.

You may try out these numbers; for example, change the heading of our poem example to the following:

```
\emph{Annabel Lee}\\[3mm]
```

That inserts an additional 3 mm space between our heading and the poem fragment. Continue playing with the options to see their effects.

Preventing line breaks

The \linebreak command has a direct counterpart: \nolinebreak. This command prevents a line break at the current position.

Like its counterpart, it takes an optional argument. If you write \nolinebreak[0], you recommend not to break the line there. Using 1, 2, or even 3 makes the request stronger and \nolinebreak[4] forbids it completely. The latter option will be presumed if you don't provide an argument.

The already mentioned \mbox{text} command not only disables the hyphenation of a word but will also prevent a line break for the complete text.

LaTeX will break lines at spaces between words if meaningful. The ~ symbol stands for an interword space where no break is allowed; if you write Dr.~Watson, the title Dr. would never stand lonely at the end of a line.

By default, the text is fully justified. That means lines are stretched to the right margin if needed. This may result in undesirable gaps between words in a stretched line. Let's see how to disable it if we want to.

Turning off full justification

Though commonly your text will look fine if full justification is used, there may be occasions when it's not optimum. For instance, full justification could be displeasing if the text lines are short; in such a case, it could be sufficient to justify only to the left side. We shall see how to put this into practice, plus how to right-justify and how to get centered lines.

Creating ragged-right text

Remember the first parbox example, which was fully justified but had those big gaps between the words? In this example, we shall give up justification to the right side to avoid such gaps:

1. Create a new document containing these lines:

    ```
    \documentclass{article}
    \begin{document}
    \parbox{3cm}{\raggedright
        TUG is an acronym. It means \TeX\ Users Group.}
    \end{document}
    ```

2. Click on **Typeset** and look at the output:

    TUG is an
    acronym. It means
    TEX Users Group.

    Figure 2.18 – Left-justified text

We inserted the \raggedright declaration. From this point onward, the text will be ragged-right. In other words, the text will be moved to the left margin—"flushed-left." There won't be hyphenation.

Because we used this declaration inside a box, it's only valid there, like inside environments. After the box, the text will be fully justified again.

If we want the whole document to be ragged-right, we just need to use \raggedright in our preamble.

Creating ragged-left text

There might be occasions when we would like to achieve the opposite effect: flushing the text to the right margin. We can do this similarly by inserting the `\raggedleft` declaration. You're able to control where lines are broken by inserting \ \.

Centering text

Text can also be horizontally centered in the middle of the page. We will try centering with a few example lines.

We will manually create a nice-looking title for our document; it should contain the title, the author, and the date, all of which will be centered:

1. Write a document containing this code:

    ```
    \documentclass{article}
    \pagestyle{empty}
    \begin{document}
    {\centering
        \huge\bfseries Centered text \\
        \Large\normalfont written by me \\
        \normalsize\today


    }
    \end{document}
    ```

2. Click on **Typeset** to see the output:

Centered text
written by me
August 31, 2021

Figure 2.19 – Centered text

Because only the title should be centered, we opened a group to limit the centering. With the `\centering` declaration, the remaining text of this group will be horizontally aligned to the center. We also inserted a paragraph break with an empty line; it's recommended to do this before ending the group to apply our centering to the fully contained paragraph. By using the closing brace, we ended the group. If you complement some text after the closing brace, it will be typeset normally, not centered.

\centering is commonly used when pictures or tables are inserted, or further on title pages and sometimes for headings, but rather as part of logical command definitions.

Using environments for justification

There's a predefined center environment that centers text and prints it in a displayed paragraph at the same time.

Let's test it. We will reuse the fragment of the Edgar Allen Poe poem. This time, we shall center all verses:

1. Start a new document:

    ```
    \documentclass{article}
    ```

2. Now, let's load the url package so that we can also print a hyperlink at the end:

    ```
    \usepackage{url}
    ```

3. Begin the document with some text:

    ```
    \begin{document}
    \noindent This is the beginning of a poem
    by Edgar Allan Poe:
    ```

4. Now, write text in a center environment:

    ```
    \begin{center}
        \emph{Annabel Lee}
    \end{center}
    ```

5. Again, write text for the body of the poem:

    ```
    \begin{center}
        It was many and many a year ago,\\
        In a kingdom by the sea,\\
        That a maiden there lived whom you may know\\
        By the name of Annabel Lee
    \end{center}
    ```

6. Add some text, including a URL pointing to the poem on the internet, and finish:

```
The complete poem can be read on
\url{http://www.online-literature.com/poe/576/}.
\end{document}
```

7. Click on **Typeset** and see the output:

This is the beginning of a poem by Edgar Allan Poe:

Annabel Lee

It was many and many a year ago,
In a kingdom by the sea,
That a maiden there lived whom you may know
By the name of Annabel Lee

The complete poem can be read on `http://www.online-literature.com/poe/576/`.

Figure 2.20 – A centered poem within text

We began with \noindent again, avoiding the paragraph indentation. \begin{center} started the center environment, which begins a new paragraph, leaving some space for the preceding text. \end{center} ended this environment. We used the center environment a second time, where we inserted \\ to end the verses. After the center environment ended, some space followed, and the next paragraph began at the left margin.

There's not only an environment for centering. The corresponding environment for ragged-right text is called flushleft; that is, everything within the environment is pushed to the left and ragged at the right side, and, similarly, for ragged-left text, it's flushright.

Centering, as previously, is one way to emphasize some text. Another way is to indent it a bit and to add some vertical space before and after the text. This is a common way to display a quotation. Let's see how to do that.

Displaying quotes

Imagine your text contains a quotation from another author. It might be hard to read if it's just embedded in your text. A common way to improve the readability is setting the text off by indenting both margins. To do this, we will quote thoughts of famous physicists in our example:

1. Create a new document with some introductory text:

```
\documentclass{article}
\begin{document}
\noindent Niels Bohr said: ``An expert is a person
who has made all the mistakes that can be made in
a very narrow field.''
Albert Einstein said:
```

2. Display the quote:

```
\begin{quote}
    Anyone who has never made a mistake has never
    tried anything new.
\end{quote}
```

3. Add some more body text, and finish:

```
Errors are inevitable. So, let's be brave
trying something new.
\end{document}
```

4. Click on **Typeset** to see the result:

Niels Bohr said: "An expert is a person who has made all the mistakes that can be made in a very narrow field." Albert Einstein said:

Anyone who has never made a mistake has never tried anything new.

Errors are inevitable. So, let's be brave trying something new.

Figure 2.21 – A quote

Firstly, we quoted *inline*, that is, within the text flow in the paragraph. ` produces a left quotation mark, also called a **backtick**, and ' provides a right quotation mark. To get double quotes, we just typed two such symbols. We call this **inline quoting**.

Then, we used the quote environment to display a quotation separated from the surrounding text. We did not begin a new paragraph for it, because the quotation is already set a bit off in its own paragraph. That's called **displayed quoting**.

Quoting longer text

When writing short quotations, the quote environment looks very good. But when you would like to quote text containing several paragraphs, you might wish to have the same paragraph indentation as in your surrounding text. The quotation environment will do this for you.

Let's quote some of the benefits of TeX and LaTeX found on a web page on CTAN:

1. Start a new document and add this text:

    ```
    \documentclass{article}
    \usepackage{url}
    \begin{document}
    The authors of the CTAN team listed ten good reasons
    for using \TeX. Among them are:
    \begin{quotation}
      \TeX\ has the best output. What you end with,
      the symbols on the page, is as useable, and beautiful,
      as a non-professional can produce.

      \TeX\ knows typesetting. As those plain text samples
      show, TeX's has more sophisticated typographical
      algorithms such as those for making paragraphs
      and for hyphenating.

      \TeX\ is fast. On today's machines \TeX\ is very fast.
      It is easy on memory and disk space, too.

      \TeX\ is stable. It is in wide use, with a long
      history. It has been tested by millions of users,
      on demanding input.
      It will never eat your document. Never.
    ```

```
\end{quotation}
The original text can be found on
\url{https://www.ctan.org/what_is_tex.html}.
\end{document}
```

2. Click on **Typeset** and look at the output:

> The authors of the CTAN team listed ten good reasons for using TEX. Among them are:
>
> > TEX has the best output. What you end with, the symbols on the page, is as useable, and beautiful, as a non-professional can produce.
> >
> > TEX knows typesetting. As those plain text samples show, TeX's has more sophisticated typographical algorithms such as those for making paragraphs and for hyphenating.
> >
> > TEX is fast. On today's machines TEX is very fast. It is easy on memory and disk space, too.
> >
> > TEX is stable. It is in wide use, with a long history. It has been tested by millions of users, on demanding input. It will never eat your document. Never.
>
> The original text can be found on `https://www.ctan.org/what_is_tex.html`.

Figure 2.22 – A long section of quoted text

This time, we used the quotation environment to display some paragraphs. As in normal text, blank lines separate the paragraphs; they are left-indented at their beginning just like in all our body text.

But what if we don't like that paragraph indentation? Let's check out an alternative.

In this example, we want to avoid paragraph indentation and instead, we shall separate the paragraphs with some vertical spacing. As filler text, we will use a few sentences of the previous example about quoting, as shown here:

1. Create a small document with the following code (make sure the highlighted code is included):

```
\documentclass{article}
\usepackage{parskip}
\usepackage{url}
\begin{document}
The authors of the CTAN team listed ten good reasons
```

```
for using \TeX. Among them are:

\TeX\ has the best output. What you end with,
the symbols on the page, is as useable, and beautiful,
as a non-professional can produce\ldots

The original text can be found on
\url{https://www.ctan.org/what_is_tex.html}.
\end{document}
```

2. Click on **Typeset** and see the effect:

> The authors of the CTAN team listed ten good reasons for using TEX. Among them are:
>
> TEX has the best output. What you end with, the symbols on the page, is as useable, and beautiful, as a non-professional can produce...
>
> The original text can be found on `https://www.ctan.org/what_is_tex.html`.

Figure 2.23 – Vertical spacing between paragraphs

Here, we loaded the `parskip` package—its only purpose is to remove the paragraph indentation completely. At the same time, this package introduces a skip between paragraphs. But this package doesn't affect the definition of the `quotation` environment; you still could use the `quote` environment.

Visualizing paragraph breaks

In order to distinguish paragraphs, there are two common ways. One is to indent the beginning of each paragraph; this is the default LaTeX style. The other way is to insert vertical space between paragraphs while omitting the indentation, which is suitable for narrow columns where indenting would cost too much width.

Summary

In this chapter, we explored the basics of editing, arranging, and formatting text. Specifically, we covered modifying fonts and styles of text, using commands and declarations with mandatory and optional arguments, and defining our own commands. We also learned how to format a paragraph—including left, right, or fully justified—and we learned about quoting.

Keep in mind that even though we used formatting commands directly in the text while exploring them, it is better to use them inside command definitions in the preamble to allow easy changes for the future. As you progress through the book, you will get to know further useful commands and packages that could improve your previously written commands.

Now that we've learned about the detailed formatting of text, we're ready to enter the next chapter, which deals with the formatting and layout of whole pages, including margin sizes, headers, and footers.

3
Designing Pages

After the previous chapter, formatting text should be easy for us. So, let's turn to whole pages!

In this chapter, we will learn how to structure a document in chapters and sections, and how to modify the general appearance such as the margins, the page orientation, headers, and footers. This gives you control over the whole document design.

We will learn about the following:

- Creating a book with chapters
- Defining the margins
- Using class options
- Designing headers and footers
- Using footnotes
- Breaking pages
- Enlarging a page
- Changing the line spacing
- Creating a table of contents

By working on this, we shall gain a deeper insight into classes and packages.

We will start by writing an example document spanning over several pages. This will be our test object for our modifications.

Technical requirements

You need either a LaTeX installation on your computer, or you can use Overleaf. You can edit and compile all examples online on the book's web page: `https://latexguide.org/chapter-03`.

The code is also available on GitHub: `https://github.com/PacktPublishing/LaTeX-Beginner-s-Guide-2nd-Edition-/tree/main/Chapter_03_-_Designing_Pages`.

In this chapter, we will use the following LaTeX packages: `babel`, `blindtext`, `fancyhdr`, `geometry`, and `setspace`. If you don't work online, make sure you have them installed if you don't have a full LaTeX installation. We'll also talk about the packages `bigfoot`, `endnotes`, `footmisc`, `lipsum`, `manyfoot`, `multicol`, `safefnmark`, and `scrlayer-scrpage`, which you may optionally use.

You can find package information on CTAN at `https://ctan.org/pkg/<packagename>`, and documentation at `https://texdoc.org/pkg/<packagename>`.

Creating a book with chapters

We will start to write a book. First, we shall choose a class, and use some filler text to work out the page layout. Let's see how to do it:

1. Create a new document, and enter the following lines as our preamble:

    ```
    \documentclass[a4paper,12pt]{book}
    \usepackage[english]{babel}
    \usepackage{blindtext}
    ```

2. Proceed with writing the document body containing a chapter heading, section and subsection headings, and some filler text:

    ```
    \begin{document}
    \chapter{Exploring the page layout}
    In this chapter we will study the layout of pages.
    \section{Some filler text}
    \blindtext
    ```

```
\section{A lot more filler text}
More dummy text will follow.
\subsection{Plenty of filler text}
\blindtext[10]
\end{document}
```

3. Compile it by clicking on **Typeset**. Look at the first page:

Chapter 1

Exploring the page layout

In this chapter we will study the layout of pages.

1.1   Some filler text

Hello, here is some text without a meaning. This text should show what a printed text will look like at this place. If you read this text, you will get no information. Really? Is there no information? Is there a difference between this text and some nonsense like "Huardest gefburn"? Kjift – not at all! A blind text like this gives you information about the selected font, how the letters are written and an impression of the look. This text should contain all letters of the alphabet and it should be written in of the original language. There is no need for special content, but the length of words should match the language.

1.2   A lot more filler text

More dummy text will follow.

1.2.1   Plenty of filler text

Hello, here is some text without a meaning. This text should show what a printed text will look like at this place. If you read this text, you will get no information. Really? Is there no information? Is there a difference between this text and some nonsense like "Huardest gefburn"? Kjift – not at all! A blind text like this gives you information about the selected font, how the letters are written and an impression of the look. This text should contain all letters of the alphabet and it should be written in of the original

1

Figure 3.1 – An example page

We have chosen the document class book. As the name implies, this class is suitable for book-like documents. Books are commonly two-sided and consist of chapters. By default, and this is very common, chapters start on right-hand pages, which have odd page numbers. If it's necessary to achieve that, LaTeX inserts a blank left-hand even-numbered page so that the next chapter can start on the following right-hand page.

Furthermore, books may have front matter with one or more title pages and back matter with a bibliography, index, and so on. The book class supports all of this.

We used the option a4paper so the document would be formatted to fit on A4 paper. For the US letter paper size, we would use the letterpaper option instead.

The document class option 12pt told LaTeX to use a base font size of 12 pt.

We loaded the babel package. That package provides typographic support tools for a lot of languages, such as proper hyphenation rules for the chosen language and translations for implicit terms. For example, we used the english option with babel and got **Chapter 1** in our chapter heading. If we choose french instead of english, we will get **Chapitre 1** in our heading.

American English is the default. For British English, we would use the british option to babel. There are very small differences between the two. In British English, some words are spelled differently, and hyphenation rules are a bit different, for example.

We loaded the blindtext package, which has been developed to produce filler text. It uses babel to detect the language of the document; we stated the language english to babel, which actually means American English. Without babel, blindtext would use Latin filler text by default.

The command \blindtext prints some dummy text just to fill the space.

The command \chapter produced a large heading, which will always begin on a new page.

We've already seen the \section command. It's our second sectioning level and generates a smaller heading than \chapter. The numbering of this heading is automatically updated by LaTeX.

Lastly, we refined the sectioning with the \subsection command followed by more dummy text to fill up the page.

Lorem ipsum filler text

There's another popular package for generating dummy text. It's called lipsum and it produces the famous *Lorem Ipsum* text, which has been the typesetter's dummy text for years.

Now let's see how to change the default margin sizes.

Defining the margins

A publisher or a supervisor may request that you follow their specifications for a document. Besides font size, interline spacing, and other style issues, there may be specifications for the margins. In this case, you would need to override LaTeX's recommendations, specifying the margins precisely.

There's a package that fulfills these demands, called geometry. We shall load the geometry package and state the exact width and height of all margins:

1. Extend the preamble of the previous example in this chapter with this command:

    ```
    \usepackage[a4paper, inner=1.5cm, outer=3cm, top=2cm,
    bottom=3cm, bindingoffset=0.5cm]{geometry}
    ```

2. Click on **Typeset** to compile the code and examine the adjusted margins.

The geometry package takes care of our layout regarding the paper size, margins, and other dimensions. We chose the A4 paper size, an outer margin of 3 cm, and an inner margin of just 1.5 cm.

Inner versus outer margins

When a two-sided book lies open in front of us, the two inner margins will be perceived as one joined empty space. When we aim for equal margins—left, middle, and right—we can choose for the inner margin to be half of the size of the outer margin. That's the reason why outer margins are wider than inner margins. There could be a reason to make the inner margin just a bit wider – we might lose such space later because of binding such as gluing or stapling. But this depends on the kind of binding, and then it's done with an extra bindingoffset option.

We defined the top margin to be 2 cm, and the bottom margin to be 3 cm. Lastly, we specified a value of 0.5 cm for a binding correction.

In the early days of LaTeX, it was common to manipulate the layout dimensions directly. This approach had some disadvantages. We could easily make mistakes in calculating the lengths, for instance, the left margin plus the right margin plus the text width might not fit the paper width.

This is where the `geometry` package comes to the rescue, which provides a comfortable interface for specifying layout parameters. Further, it provides auto-completion, calculates missing values to match the paper size, and even adds missing lengths using a heuristic approach to achieve a good layout.

The `geometry` package understands options of the form `"key=value"`, separated by commas. If you load `geometry` without arguments, those arguments could alternatively be used by calling `\geometry{argument list}`.

Let's take a closer look at such `geometry` package options to control all aspects of the page layout.

Choosing the paper size

The `geometry` package provides several options to set the paper size and orientation:

- `paper=name` states the paper name, for example, `paper=a4paper`. The package supports a lot of paper sizes, such as `letterpaper`, `executivepaper`, `legalpaper`, `a0paper`, `a6paper`, `b0paper`, `b6paper`, and more.

- `paperwidth` and `paperheight` allow you to choose the paper dimensions freely, such as `paperwidth=7in` and `paperheight=10in`.

- `papersize={width,height}` sets the width and height of the paper, such as `papersize={7in,10in}`. This is an example of a double-valued argument.

- `portrait` switches the paper to portrait mode (this is the default option) while `landscape` changes the paper orientation to landscape mode.

If you already specified the paper name to the document class, `geometry` will inherit it. This works as a general rule: all document class options will be automatically given to the packages that recognize them.

Specifying the text area

The text area may be adjusted with these options:

- `textwidth` sets the width of the text area, such as `textwidth=140mm`.

- `textheight` states the height of the text area, such as `textheight=180mm`.

- `lines` provides another way to specify the text height by the number of lines, such as `lines=25`.

- `includehead` causes the header of the page to be included in the body area (this option is set to `false` by default).

- `includefoot` causes the footer of the page to be included in the body area (this option is set to `false` by default).

Setting the margins

The size of the visible margins can be specified with these options:

- `left` and `right` set the width of the left and the right margin, such as `left=2cm`. Use it for one-sided documents.

- `inner` and `outer` set the width of the inner and the outer margin, such as `inner=2cm`. Use it for two-sided documents.

- `top` and `bottom` set the height of the top and the bottom margin, such as `top=25mm`.

- `twoside` switches to two-sided mode. This means that the left and right margins will be swapped on left-hand pages, also called verso pages.

- If your book is printed and glued, stapled, or otherwise bound together, the binding may hide a part of the inner margin. You can set a value to the `bindingoffset` option to reserve width to compensate for the part of the inner margin that's hidden in the binding, so the visible inner margin looks as wide as you expect.

That's just a selection of commonly used options—there are many more. You could choose and set some options intuitively—for instance, `\usepackage[margin=3cm]{geometry}` will result in a 3 cm margin on each edge of the paper and the paper size comes from the document class option.

The auto-completion works like this:

- `paperwidth = left + width + right`, where `width=textwidth` by default

- `paperheight = top + height + bottom`, where `height=textheight` by default

If you decide to include marginal notes within the text body when calculating the layout, the width could get wider than `textwidth`. If two dimensions of the right side of each formula are given, the missing dimension will be calculated. That's why it may be enough to specify `left` and `right`, and `top` and `bottom`, respectively. Even if just one margin is specified, the other dimensions will be determined using default margin ratios:

- `top:bottom` = 2:3
- `left:right` = 1:1 for one-sided documents
- `inner:outer` = 2:3 for two-sided documents

Sounds complicated? That's just how `geometry` helps you to automatically achieve good-looking dimensions even if some values are missing.

The `geometry` package provides an extensive manual. Don't be worried by the amount of documentation; it's offered to guide you through the various features.

As we saw in *Chapter 1, Getting Started with LaTeX*, we can open the manual by typing `texdoc geometry` at the command line, that is, a terminal window, or on the internet at `https://texdoc.org/pkg/geometry`.

Now that we know how to set up the basic page geometry, we'll take a look at options to change the text layout, such as to landscape orientation and having multiple columns.

Using class options

We already know that a document class is the basis of our document. It provides commands and environments extending the LaTeX standard features. Though the class provides a default style, it's customizable with **document class options**.

We shall change the orientation of our first example to landscape. We would also like to typeset our text in two columns:

1. Add the options `landscape` and `twocolumn` to the `\documentclass` statement of our example, as follows:

    ```
    \documentclass[a4paper,12pt,landscape,twocolumn]{book}
    ```

2. Load the `geometry` package:

    ```
    \usepackage{geometry}
    ```

3. Click on **Typeset** to compile, and see how the layout has changed:

Chapter 1

Exploring the page layout

In this chapter we will study the layout of pages.

1.1 Some filler text

Hello, here is some text without a meaning. This text should show what a printed text will look like at this place. If you read this text, you will get no information. Really? Is there no information? Is there a difference between this text and some nonsense like "Huardest gefburn"? Kjift – not at all! A blind text like this gives you information about the selected font, how the letters are written and an impression of the look. This text should contain all letters of the alphabet and it should be written in of the original language. There is no need for special content, but the length of words should match the language.

1.2 A lot more filler text

More dummy text will follow.

1.2.1 Plenty of filler text

Hello, here is some text without a meaning. This text should show what a printed text will look like at this place. If you read this text, you will get no information. Really? Is there no information? Is there a difference between this text and some nonsense like "Huardest gefburn"? Kjift – not at all! A blind text like this gives you information about the selected font, how the letters are written and an impression of the look. This text should contain all letters of the alphabet and it should be written in of the original language. There is no need for special content, but the length of words should match the language. Hello, here is some text without a meaning.

1

Figure 3.2 – A landscape two-column page layout

By using the landscape option, we switched the page orientation from portrait to landscape. By using the twocolumn option, we caused the body text to be divided into two columns.

We loaded the geometry package to get the proper PDF page size in landscape mode. Without it, the PDF would remain in portrait mode.

The command \twocolumn[opening text] starts a two-column page with optional opening text over the whole width. \onecolumn begins a one-column page. If you'd like to balance the columns on the last page or if you wish to have more than two columns, use the multicols package.

The LaTeX base classes are article, book, report, slides, and letter. As the name suggests, the last one can be used to write letters, though there are further suitable classes, such as scrlttr2.

slides can be used to create presentations, but today there are more powerful and feature rich classes, such as beamer and powerdot.

Let's sum up the options of the base classes:

- `a4paper`, `a5paper`, `b5paper`, `letterpaper`, `legalpaper`, or `executivepaper`: The output will be formatted according to this paper size; for example, A4 will be formatted as 210mm x 297mm. The `letterpaper` option (8.5 in x 11 in) is the default. Loading the `geometry` package allows more sizes.

- `10pt`, `11pt`, or `12pt`: The size of normal text in the document; the default is 10 points (`10pt`). The size of headings, footnotes, indexes, and so on, will be adjusted accordingly.

- `landscape`: Switches to landscape format; the width and height of the output size will be interchanged.

- `onecolumn` or `twocolumn`: Decides whether the pages will be one-column (default) or two-column. It's not supported by the `letter` class.

- `oneside` or `twoside`: Formatting for printing on one side or both sides of a page. `oneside` is the default, except for the `book` class. `twoside` is not usable with the `slides` class and the `letter` class.

- `openright` or `openany`: The first option decides that chapters have to begin on a right-hand page (the default for the `book` class), while the second option allows chapters to start on any page (the default for the `report` class). These options are only supported by the `book` and the `report` class because the other classes don't provide chapters.

- `titlepage` or `notitlepage`: The first causes a separate title page when \maketitle is used and is the default, except for the `article` class. The default of `article` is `notitlepage`, which means that normal text may follow the title on the same page.

- `final` or `draft`: If `draft` is set, then LaTeX will mark overfull lines with a black box, which is helpful in reviewing and improving the output. Some packages support these options as well, behaving differently then, such as omitting the embedding of graphics and listings when a draft has been chosen. `final` is the default.

- `openbib`: When this option is set, a bibliography will be formatted in open style instead of compressed style.

- `fleqn`: Causes displayed formulas to be left-aligned.

- `leqno`: For numbered displayed formulas, the number will be put on the left side. The right side is the default.

Many other classes support these options as well, and even more. For an uncommon base font size, the classes `extarticle`, `extbook`, `extreport`, and `extletter` provide base font sizes from 8 points to 20 points. The **KOMA-Script** classes allow arbitrary base font sizes. They understand such a large amount of options that they additionally support a `key=value` interface as we saw with the `geometry` package.

> **KOMA-Script**
>
> KOMA-Script classes may be used like base classes: for each base class, there's a corresponding KOMA class. They extend base classes very much, providing a large set of commands and options for customizing. Visit `https://texdoc.org/pkg/koma-script` to open the manual.

As page headers have been mentioned, let's explore them now.

Designing headers and footers

When we tested the first version of our example, you might have noticed that except for the page where the chapter started, all pages showed the page number, chapter title, and section title in their header. So, in our two-sided layout, on page **2**, which is a left-hand page header, the page number is in the outer margin, here on the left side:

2   *CHAPTER 1.   EXPLORING THE PAGE LAYOUT*

language. There is no need for special content, but the length of words should match the language. Hello, here is some text without a meaning. This text should show what a printed text will look like at this place. If you read this text, you will get no information. Really? Is there no information? Is there a difference between this text and some nonsense like "Huardest gefburn"?

Figure 3.3 – The header of page 2

And this is how our right-hand page header on page **3** looks, with the page number in the outer margin, which is on the right side now:

1.2. A LOT MORE FILLER TEXT 3

> language. There is no need for special content, but the length of words should match the language. Hello, here is some text without a meaning. This text should show what a printed text will look like at this place. If you read this text, you will get no information. Really? Is there no information? Is there a difference between this text and some nonsense like "Huardest gefburn"?

Figure 3.4 – The header of page 3

In a one-sided layout, there would not be such a difference in the header layout. The headers in a one-sided layout are as in *Figure 3.4*. By default, heading text is on the left side, and the page number is on the right side.

Though these standard headers are already quite useful, we shall see how to customize them to meet our individual requirements.

The default shape of the page headings is slanted. Furthermore, they are written in capital letters. We shall use bold typeface instead and we will use a small-caps font for the chapter title. We will load the `fancyhdr` package and use its commands to achieve that:

1. Load the first example of this chapter.
2. Insert the highlighted lines to get this:

```
\documentclass[a4paper,12pt]{book}
\usepackage[english]{babel}
\usepackage{blindtext}
\usepackage{fancyhdr}
\fancyhf{}
\fancyhead[LE]{\scshape\nouppercase{\leftmark}}
\fancyhead[RO]{\nouppercase{\rightmark}}
\fancyfoot[LE,RO]{\thepage}
\pagestyle{fancy}
\begin{document}
\chapter{Exploring the page layout}
In this chapter we will study the layout of pages.
\section{Some filler text}
\blindtext
```

```
\section{A lot more filler text}
More dummy text will follow.
\subsection{Plenty of filler text}
\blindtext[10]
\end{document}
```

3. Compile the code. The footers will contain the page number on their outer side.

A right-hand page header now looks like the following:

CHAPTER 1.   EXPLORING THE PAGE LAYOUT

language. There is no need for special content, but the length of words should match the language. Hello, here is some text without a meaning. This text should show what a printed text will look like at this place. If you read this text, you will get no information. Really? Is there no information? Is there a difference between this text and some nonsense like "Huardest gefburn"?

Figure 3.5 – The new header of page 2

A left-hand header now looks like this:

1.2.   A lot more filler text

language. There is no need for special content, but the length of words should match the language. Hello, here is some text without a meaning. This text should show what a printed text will look like at this place. If you read this text, you will get no information. Really? Is there no information? Is there a difference between this text and some nonsense like "Huardest gefburn"?

Figure 3.6 – The new header of page 3

We loaded the fancyhdr package, which provides commands for customizing headers and footers. The package command names start with \fancy. Our first action was calling \fancyhf{}; this command clears the headers and footers. Furthermore, we used the following:

- \leftmark: Used by the book class to store the chapter title together with the chapter number. Capital letters are used as default.

- \rightmark: Used by the book class to store the section title together with its number. Capital letters are used as well.

- \nouppercase: This disables the (default) uppercase in its argument.

- \scshape: We switched to a small-caps font.

We used the command \fancyhead with the optional argument LE to put the chapter title into the header. LE stands for left-even and means that this chapter title will be put on the left side of the header on even-numbered pages.

Conversely, we called the command \fancyhead with RO to put the section title into the header. RO stands for right-odd and means that this section heading shall be displayed on the right side of the header on odd-numbered pages.

Afterward, we used \fancyfoot to display the page number in the footer. This time, we used LE and RO, which showed the page number on both even and odd pages, always on the outer side. Then the command \thepage prints the page number.

All those commands are used to modify a page style provided by fancyhdr; this style is called fancy. We had to tell LaTeX to use this style and we did it through \pagestyle{fancy}.

Emphasizing by writing all letters capitalized, as fancyhdr does by default, is called **all caps**. It is widely regarded as a questionable style. That's why we moved to small caps.

There are different styles of headers and footers. That combination is called a **page style**. Let's see what page styles are available.

Understanding page styles

LaTeX and its base classes provide four page styles:

- empty: Neither a header nor a footer is shown.

- plain: No header. The page number will be printed and centered in the footer.

- headings: The header contains titles of chapters, sections, and/or subsections, depending on the class and also the page number. The footer is empty.

- myheadings: The header contains user-defined text and the page number; the footer is empty.

fancyhdr adds one page style called fancy, which allows the user to customize both the header and the footer.

Two commands may be used to choose the page style:

- \pagestyle{name}: Switches to the page style name from this point onwards.
- \thispagestyle{name}: Chooses the page style name only or the current page; the following pages will have the style that's been used before.

You have seen that where a chapter starts, the page style is different from the style of other pages. Such pages will have a plain style. If you thought all pages should use the same style, look into some books: it's very common that chapter beginnings differ in style. They usually have a blank header. \thispagestyle could be used to override that.

Content and positioning in headers and footers can be modified, as we will see next.

Customizing headers and footers

Let's divide the header and footer into six pieces: left, center, and right (l, c, r) both for the header and footer. The commands to modify those areas are as follows:

- For the header: \lhead, \chead, \rhead
- For the footer: \lfoot, \cfoot, \rfoot

Each of these commands requires a mandatory argument, such as \chead{User's guide} or \cfoot{\thepage}. This argument will be put into the corresponding area of the page.

Alternatively, you could use these versatile commands:

- For the header: \fancyhead[code]{text}
- For the footer: \fancyfoot[code]{text}

Here, code may consist of one or more letters:

- L: left
- C: center
- R: right
- E: even page
- O: odd page

It doesn't matter if we choose uppercase or lowercase letters. We already used such combinations in our example.

Another customization is modifying the separation line between the text and the footer.

Using decorative lines in headers or footers

We can introduce or delete lines between the header and the body text and the body text and the footer, respectively, with these two commands:

- `\renewcommand{\headrulewidth}{width}`
- `\renewcommand{\footrulewidth}{width}`

Here, `width` may be a value such as `1pt`, `0.5mm`, and so on. The default is `0.4pt` for the header line and `0pt` for the footer line. `0pt` means that a line is not visible.

While `\newcommand` defines a new command, `\renewcommand` redefines an existing command. Incidentally, we've got to know a new concept: a lot of LaTeX commands may be redefined in this way. This can be simply changing a value like here or redefining the code for a command.

Changing LaTeX's header marks

As we already know, LaTeX classes and packages store sectioning numbers and headings in the macros `\leftmark` and `\rightmark` automatically. It will be done when we call `\chapter`, `\section`, or `\subsection`. So, we could just use `\leftmark` and `\rightmark` in the arguments of the `fancyhdr` commands.

We will sometimes want to change those entries manually, even if we rely on this automation. For instance, the starred sectioning commands such as `\chapter*` and `\section*` won't produce a header entry, as indicated earlier. In such a case, two commands will help us:

- `\markright{right head}` sets the right heading.
- `\markboth{left head}{right head}` sets both the left and right headings.

The default style `headings` is easy to use and gives good results. `myheadings` can be used together with `\markright` and `\markboth`. However, the most flexible way is given by `fancyhdr`, especially in combination with `\markright` and `\markboth`.

A very good alternative to `fancyhdr` is the package called `scrpage-scrlayer`. It belongs to KOMA-Script, but `scrpage-scrlayer` works with other classes as well. It provides similar functionality and offers even more features.

The footer is a good place to add notes. Let's see how to do that in the next section.

Using footnotes

As briefly mentioned in *Chapter 2, Formatting Text and Creating Macros*, LaTeX provides a command to typeset footnotes. Let's see it in action.

Let's go back to the very first example of this chapter. We shall insert one footnote in the body text and one in a section heading:

1. Modify the example inserting a footnote, as shown in the highlighted line:

```
\documentclass[a4paper,12pt]{book}
\usepackage[english]{babel}
\usepackage{blindtext}
\begin{document}
\chapter{Exploring the page layout}
In this chapter we will study the layout of pages.
\section{Some filler text}
\blindtext
\section{A lot more filler text}
More dummy text\footnote{serving as a placeholder}
will follow.
\subsection{Plenty of filler text}
\blindtext[10]
\end{document}
```

2. Compile the code to see how the footnote looks in print:

1.2   A lot more filler text

More dummy text[1] will follow.

1.2.1   Plenty of filler text

Hello, here is some text without a meaning. This text should show what a printed text will look like at this place. If you read this text, you will get no information. Really? Is there no information? Is there a difference between this text and some nonsense like "Huardest gefburn"? Kjift – not at all! A blind text like this gives you information about the selected font,

---

[1] serving as a placeholder

Figure 3.7 – Text with a footnote

The command `\footnote{text}` placed a superscripted number at the current position.

Furthermore, it prints its argument text at the bottom of the page, marked by the same number. As we've seen, such notes are separated from the main text by a horizontal line.

`\footnote[number]{text}` produces a footnote marked by this optional number, an integer. If we don't give the optional number, an internal counter will be stepped and used. This will be done automatically; we don't need to worry.

There are two additional commands that help us selectively put only a footnote mark or text:

- `\footnotemark[number]` produces a superscripted number in the text as a footnote mark. If the optional argument wasn't given, it's also stepping and using the internal footnote counter. No footnote text will be generated.

- `\footnotetext[number]{text}` generates footnote text without putting a footnote mark in the text, and it does not step up the internal footnote counter.

Set a footnote command right after the related text. Don't leave a space in-between, otherwise, you would get a gap between the text and the following footnote mark.

In *Figure 3.7*, we saw a line that separates the footnotes from the text. We will now see how to adjust that line.

Modifying the footnote line

The line that separates footnotes from the text is produced by the command `\footnoterule`. If we wish to omit that line or if we want to modify it, we must redefine it. We learned about `\renewcommand` earlier, so let's use it.

We will use `\renewcommand` to override the default `\footnoterule` command:

1. Take the previous example and add the following lines to the preamble:

    ```
    \renewcommand{\footnoterule}
    {\noindent\smash{\rule[3pt]{\textwidth}{0.4pt}}}
    ```

2. Click on **Typeset** to compile, and see how the line has changed:

1.2   A lot more filler text

More dummy text[1] will follow.

1.2.1   Plenty of filler text

Hello, here is some text without a meaning. This text should show what a printed text will look like at this place. If you read this text, you will get no information. Really? Is there no information? Is there a difference between this text and some nonsense like "Huardest gefburn"? Kjift – not at all! A blind text like this gives you information about the selected font,

---

[1]serving as a placeholder

Figure 3.8 – A modified footnote line

The existing \footnoterule command will be replaced by the new definition that we wrote in the second line of the first step. The command \rule[raising]{width} {height} draws a line, here 0.4 pt thick, and as wide as the text, raised a bit, by 3 pt. Through the \smash command, we let our line pretend to have a height and a depth of zero, so it's occupying no vertical space at all. This way, the page balancing will not be affected. You already know \noindent, which avoids the paragraph indentation.

If you want to omit that footnote line completely, you just need to write the following:

```
\renewcommand{\footnoterule}{}
```

Now the command is defined to do nothing, and we won't get a dividing line.

Using packages to expand footnote styles

There are different habits for setting footnotes. Some styles require footnotes numbered per page, they might have to be placed in the document as so-called endnotes, and symbols instead of numbers may be used. More demands exist and therefore several packages have been developed to comply with them. Here's a selection:

- endnotes: Places footnotes at the end of the document

- manyfoot: Allows nested footnotes

- bigfoot: Replaces and extends manyfoot and improves page break handling with footnotes

- savefnmark: Useful when you need to use footnotes several times

- footmisc: An all-round package; introduces numbering per page, is able to save space when many short footnotes are used, offers symbols instead of numbers as footnote marks, provides hanging indentation and other styles

Have a look at the respective package documentation to learn more using either the texdoc command, as explained in *Chapter 1, Getting Started with LaTeX*, or at https://texdoc.org.

As we've talked about footnotes at the end of a page, let's see how to enforce ending a page ourselves in case we don't want to let it automatically happen.

Breaking pages

As you've seen in our example, LaTeX itself took care of the page breaking. There might be occasions where we'd like to insert a page break ourselves before LaTeX does. LaTeX offers several commands to do so, with vertical balance or without.

We will now go back to the first version of our example and we shall manually insert a page break right before subsection 1.2.1:

1. Insert the highlighted line into our example, which contains the \pagebreak command:

```
\documentclass[a4paper,12pt]{book}
\usepackage[english]{babel}
\usepackage{blindtext}
\begin{document}
\chapter{Exploring the page layout}
In this chapter we will study the layout of pages.
\section{Some filler text}
\blindtext
\section{A lot more filler text}
More dummy text will follow.
\pagebreak
\subsection{Plenty of filler text}
\blindtext[10]
\end{document}
```

2. Compile the code and take a look at the result:

Chapter 1

Exploring the page layout

In this chapter we will study the layout of pages.

1.1   Some filler text

Hello, here is some text without a meaning. This text should show what a printed text will look like at this place. If you read this text, you will get no information. Really? Is there no information? Is there a difference between this text and some nonsense like "Huardest gefburn"? Kjift – not at all! A blind text like this gives you information about the selected font, how the letters are written and an impression of the look. This text should contain all letters of the alphabet and it should be written in of the original language. There is no need for special content, but the length of words should match the language.

1.2   A lot more filler text

More dummy text will follow.

1

Figure 3.9 – A stretched page

3. Replace \pagebreak with \newpage.

4. Compile again, and compare:

Chapter 1

Exploring the page layout

In this chapter we will study the layout of pages.

1.1   Some filler text

Hello, here is some text without a meaning. This text should show what a printed text will look like at this place. If you read this text, you will get no information. Really? Is there no information? Is there a difference between this text and some nonsense like "Huardest gefburn"? Kjift – not at all! A blind text like this gives you information about the selected font, how the letters are written and an impression of the look. This text should contain all letters of the alphabet and it should be written in of the original language. There is no need for special content, but the length of words should match the language.

1.2   A lot more filler text

More dummy text will follow.

1

Figure 3.10 – A non-stretched page

At first, we inserted the command \pagebreak; as its name suggests, it causes a page break. Furthermore, the text has been stretched to fill the page down to the bottom. That can be desirable for having the same text height on all pages.

Afterward, because of the obviously unpleasant whitespace between the paragraphs and the headings, we replaced \pagebreak with \newpage. This command breaks the page as well, but it doesn't stretch the text: the remaining space of the page will stay empty.

So, \pagebreak behaves like \linebreak, and \newpage works like \newline (for pages instead of lines). There's even a \nopagebreak command that's analogous to \nolinebreak and forbids page breaking. \pagebreak won't break a line, while \nopagebreak doesn't refer to the middle of a line; both commands apply at the end of the current line. Of course, they immediately have an effect when used between paragraphs.

If you use the two-column format, both \pagebreak and \newpage will begin on a new column instead of a new page.

There are two further variants: \clearpage works like \newpage, except that it will start on a new page, even in two-column mode. \cleardoublepage does the same but causes the following text to start on a right-hand page, inserting a blank page if necessary. The latter is useful for two-sided documents.

More importantly, both commands cause all figures and tables that LaTeX has in its memory to be printed out immediately.

\pagebreak and \nopagebreak can take an optional argument that requests a certain line break, as follows. The argument is an integer between 0 and 4. Here, 0 means that a page break is allowed, 1 means it's desired, 2 and 3 mark more insistent requests so LaTeX tries harder to stretch the text to reach the page bottom, and 4 will enforce a page break. \pagebreak and \nopagebreak are very similar to the command pair \linebreak and \nolinebreak, which we saw in *Chapter 2, Formatting Text and Creating Macros*.

Such manual page breaks reduce the amount of text that fits on the page. Let's now look at the opposite: getting more text on a page.

Enlarging a page

There may be occasions where we want to put a little more text onto a page, even if the text will be squeezed a bit or the text height increases. There's a command that will help us out: \enlargethispage.

We shall modify our example a bit. This time, we will try to avoid a nearly empty page by squeezing the text on the preceding page:

1. Remove the \newpage command from our example and switch to 11pt base font. This time, use less filler text in the subsection:

    ```
    \documentclass[a4paper,11pt]{book}
    \usepackage[english]{babel}
    \usepackage{blindtext}
    \usepackage[a4paper, inner=1.5cm, outer=3cm, top=2cm,
    bottom=3cm, bindingoffset=1cm]{geometry}
    \begin{document}
    \chapter{Exploring the page layout}
    In this chapter we will study the layout of pages.
    \section{Some filler text}
    \blindtext
    \section{A lot more filler text}
    More dummy text will follow.
    \subsection{Plenty of filler text}
    \blindtext[3]
    \end{document}
    ```

2. Compile, and the result will consist of two pages. This is the first page:

Chapter 1

Exploring the page layout

In this chapter we will study the layout of pages.

1.1   Some filler text

Hello, here is some text without a meaning. This text should show what a printed text will look like at this place. If you read this text, you will get no information. Really? Is there no information? Is there a difference between this text and some nonsense like "Huardest gefburn"? Kjift – not at all! A blind text like this gives you information about the selected font, how the letters are written and an impression of the look. This text should contain all letters of the alphabet and it should be written in of the original language. There is no need for special content, but the length of words should match the language.

1.2   A lot more filler text

More dummy text will follow.

1.2.1   Plenty of filler text

Hello, here is some text without a meaning. This text should show what a printed text will look like at this place. If you read this text, you will get no information. Really? Is there no information? Is there a difference between this text and some nonsense like "Huardest gefburn"? Kjift – not at all! A blind text like this gives you information about the selected font, how the letters are written and an impression of the look. This text should contain all letters of the alphabet and it should be written in of the original language. There is no need for special content, but the length of words should match the language. Hello, here is some text without a meaning. This text should show what a printed text will look like at this place. If you read this text, you will get no information. Really? Is there no information? Is there a difference between this text and some nonsense like "Huardest gefburn"? Kjift – not at all! A blind text like this gives you information about the selected font, how the letters are written and an impression of the look. This text should contain all letters of the alphabet and it should be written in of the original language. There is no need for special content, but the length of words should match the language. Hello, here is some text without a meaning. This text should show what a printed text will look like at this place. If you read this text, you will get no information. Really? Is there no information? Is there a difference between this text and some nonsense like "Huardest gefburn"? Kjift – not at all! A blind text like this gives you information about the selected font, how the letters are written and an impression of the look. This text should contain all letters of the alphabet and it should be written in

1

Figure 3.11 – A fully filled page

And this is the text on the second page:

of the original language. There is no need for special content, but the length of words should match the language.

Figure 3.12 – Remaining text on the second page

3. Insert this command right after the \subsection line:

```
\enlargethispage{\baselineskip}
```

4. Compile again and now our document fits on just one page:

Chapter 1

Exploring the page layout

In this chapter we will study the layout of pages.

1.1   Some filler text

Hello, here is some text without a meaning. This text should show what a printed text will look like at this place. If you read this text, you will get no information. Really? Is there no information? Is there a difference between this text and some nonsense like "Huardest gefburn"? Kjift – not at all! A blind text like this gives you information about the selected font, how the letters are written and an impression of the look. This text should contain all letters of the alphabet and it should be written in of the original language. There is no need for special content, but the length of words should match the language.

1.2   A lot more filler text

More dummy text will follow.

1.2.1   Plenty of filler text

Hello, here is some text without a meaning. This text should show what a printed text will look like at this place. If you read this text, you will get no information. Really? Is there no information? Is there a difference between this text and some nonsense like "Huardest gefburn"? Kjift – not at all! A blind text like this gives you information about the selected font, how the letters are written and an impression of the look. This text should contain all letters of the alphabet and it should be written in of the original language. There is no need for special content, but the length of words should match the language. Hello, here is some text without a meaning. This text should show what a printed text will look like at this place. If you read this text, you will get no information. Really? Is there no information? Is there a difference between this text and some nonsense like "Huardest gefburn"? Kjift – not at all! A blind text like this gives you information about the selected font, how the letters are written and an impression of the look. This text should contain all letters of the alphabet and it should be written in of the original language. There is no need for special content, but the length of words should match the language. Hello, here is some text without a meaning. This text should show what a printed text will look like at this place. If you read this text, you will get no information. Really? Is there no information? Is there a difference between this text and some nonsense like "Huardest gefburn"? Kjift – not at all! A blind text like this gives you information about the selected font, how the letters are written and an impression of the look. This text should contain all letters of the alphabet and it should be written in of the original language. There is no need for special content, but the length of words should match the language.

1

Figure 3.13 – All text fits on a single page

We used the command \enlargethispage to squeeze more text onto a page. This command takes the additionally requested height as its argument. The command \baselineskip returns the height of a text line that we used as the argument. So, LaTeX could put one extra line onto the page, and even the remaining line fitted in as well because LaTeX compressed some whitespace.

We could use factors: write \enlargethispage{2\baselineskip} to get two more lines on a page. It doesn't even need to be an integer value. As always, when you state a length, you could use other units such as 10pt, 0.5in, 1cm, or 5mm, and even negative values.

Only the current page will be affected by this command. There's a starred version: \enlargethispage* would additionally shrink all vertical spaces on the page to their minimum.

Though, \enlargethispage should be considered just for a possible easy fix when you quickly need to put more text on a single page. In general, we can adjust the text quantity on the page by changing the margins, as we already know, or by adjusting the line spacing within text. So, let's look at line spacing in the next section.

Changing the line spacing

Without some vertical space between the lines, the readability of our text could suffer. Adding such space would help lead the eye along the line. Though LaTeX already takes care of good readability by choosing meaningful interline spacing, publishers might require different spacing.

We shall modify the very first example of this chapter by adding half of a line height to the line spacing:

1. Extend the preamble of our example with this command:

```
\usepackage[onehalfspacing]{setspace}
```

2. Compile the code to see the change:

Chapter 1

Exploring the page layout

In this chapter we will study the layout of pages.

1.1   Some filler text

Hello, here is some text without a meaning. This text should show what a printed text will look like at this place. If you read this text, you will get no information. Really? Is there no information? Is there a difference between this text and some nonsense like "Huardest gefburn"? Kjift – not at all! A blind text like this gives you information about the selected font, how the letters are written and an impression of the look. This text should contain all letters of the alphabet and it should be written in of the original language. There is no need for special content, but the length of words should match the language.

1.2   A lot more filler text

More dummy text will follow.

1.2.1   Plenty of filler text

Hello, here is some text without a meaning. This text should show what a printed text will look like at this place. If you read this text, you will get no information. Really? Is there no information? Is there a difference between this text and some nonsense like "Huardest gefburn"? Kjift – not at all! A blind text like this gives you information about the selected font, how the letters are written and an impression of the look. This text should contain all letters of the alphabet and it should be written in of the original language. There is no need for special content, but the length of words should match the language. Hello, here is some text without a meaning. This text should show what a printed text will look like at this place. If you read this text, you will get no information. Really? Is there no information? Is there a difference between this text and some nonsense like "Huardest gefburn"? Kjift – not at all! A blind text like this gives you information about the selected font, how the letters are written and an impression of the look. This text should contain all letters of the alphabet and it should be written in of the original language. There is no need for special content, but the length of words should match the language. Hello, here is some text without a meaning.

1

Figure 3.14 – Additional interline spacing

We loaded the `setspace` package to adjust the line spacing. We provided the option `onehalfspacing`, which increases the spacing by half of a line height for the whole document.

The `setspace` package understands three options:

- `singlespacing` is the default. No additional space will be inserted. The text will be typeset with LaTeX's default interline spacing, which is about 20 percent of the line height.

- `onehalfspacing` means one-and-a-half spacing, as you can see in our example.

- `doublespacing` can be used for even more spacing; the distance between the baselines of successive text lines would be twice as high as a single line.

In typesetter's jargon, the distance between the baselines of consecutive text lines is called **leading**.

Now that we have finished designing a whole document, let's finally add a table of contents.

Creating a table of contents

A book commonly begins with a table of contents, so let's create one based on our numbered headings:

1. In our previous document, let's remove the options `landscape` and `twocolumn`.

2. Remove the `setspace` package, that is, delete this line:

   ```
   \usepackage[onehalfspacing]{setspace}
   ```

3. Add the command `\tableofcontents` right after `\begin{document}`.

   Our code shall now look like this:

   ```
   \documentclass[a4paper,12pt]{book}
   \usepackage[english]{babel}
   \usepackage{blindtext}
   \usepackage[a4paper, inner=1.5cm, outer=3cm, top=2cm,
   bottom=3cm, bindingoffset=1cm]{geometry}
   \begin{document}
   \tableofcontents
   \chapter{Exploring the page layout}
   In this chapter we will study the layout of pages.
   ```

```
\section{Some filler text}
\blindtext
\section{A lot more filler text}
More dummy text will follow.
\subsection{Plenty of filler text}
\blindtext[10]
\end{document}
```

4. Compile the code twice. Afterward, the first page of your output will contain this table:

Contents

1 Exploring the page layout   3
   1.1 Some filler text   3
   1.2 A lot more filler text   3
        1.2.1 Plenty of filler text   3

Figure 3.15 – Table of Contents

The command \tableofcontents tells LaTeX to produce and to print a table of contents. During a typesetting run, LaTeX writes the headings into an auxiliary file with the file name extension .toc. The \tableofcontents command reads that .toc file in for printing the table of contents.

The LaTeX typesetting process is linear; it runs from the start to the end of the code. The \tableofcontents command comes at the beginning, and the headings come later. That's why we had to typeset twice:

1. In the first run, \tableofcontents did not know any headings and the table of contents stayed empty. While continuing to run, LaTeX put the headings into the .toc file.

2. In the second run, \tableofcontents found and read the .toc file to print the contents.

It's good to keep that in mind for later: when you change a heading and compile the document, you can see the change in the text. But the table of contents will get this change in the next compiler run.

The table of contents entries are created by the sectioning commands. We used \chapter, \section, and \subsection, and we've got an entry for each.

A heading might be very long; it could span over two or more lines. In that case, we might wish to shorten its corresponding table of contents entry. Let's see how.

We can use the optional arguments of the section commands to produce shorter entries, different from the actual headings. Let's edit the example shown in *Figure 3.15* by inserting shorter titles in square brackets:

```
\chapter[Page layout]{Exploring the page layout}
\section[Filler text]{Some filler text}
\section[More]{A lot more filler text}
\subsection[Plenty]{Plenty of filler text}
```

Compile the example twice. You will see that the headings stay the same, but the table of contents has changed:

Contents

1   Page layout   3
   1.1   Filler text   3
   1.2   More   3
      1.2.1   Plenty   3

Figure 3.16 – Shortened table of contents entries

Besides the mandatory argument producing the heading, each sectioning command understands an optional argument. If an optional argument is given, it will be used instead of the mandatory heading for the contents table entry.

In *Chapter 8*, *Listing Content and References*, we shall take a further look at this and learn how to further customize the table of contents. Let's look again at the sectioning commands of book, report, and article. There are seven levels in those base classes:

- \part: That's for dividing the document into major units. The numbering of other sectional units is independent of \part. A part heading will use a whole page in book and report documents.

- \chapter: Gives a large heading that will start at a new page, available in the book class and in the report class.

- `\section`, `\subsection`, and `\subsubsection`: They give bold headings, and they are available in all three classes.

- `\paragraph` and `\subparagraph`: Also available in all three classes, they produce a run-in heading. That means the heading runs straight into the text; there's no line break between the heading and the following text. Also, it's a sectioning command, and should not be confused with common text paragraphs.

Except `\part`, all sectioning commands reset the counter of the section that's one level below in the hierarchy. For instance, `\chapter` resets the section counter. This way, the sections will be numbered per chapter.

To sum up, such sectioning commands are easy to use and they do a lot:

- `\part` and `\chapter` cause a page break before the heading.

- All generate a number and a presentation for it, some depending on the higher-level counters (for example, Section 1 of Chapter 2 would generate 2.1).

- Except `\part`, they reset the counter of the next-level sectional unit so that the lower-level unit will start with 1.

- They produce a table of contents entry.

- They format the heading, usually bold-faced, and the larger they are, the higher they are in the hierarchy.

- They save headings internally for using them in a page header.

All sectioning commands provide a starred form, as follows:

```
\section*{title}
```

If you use this form, the numbering will be suppressed and there won't be an entry in the table of contents or in a header. Look at the heading **Contents** in our example; this has actually been typeset by `\chapter*` inside the `\tableofcontents` macro.

Summary

In this chapter, we have worked out how to design the overall layout of a document.

Specifically, we learned about choosing page dimensions, margins, and orientation. We know how to switch to a two-column layout and how to adjust line spacing. Furthermore, we are now able to customize headers and footers, add footnotes, and add a table of contents to our document.

Furthermore, we covered some general topics, such as changing document properties by choosing document class options and package options and by redefining existing commands.

Now it's time to deal with further text structures. In the next chapter, we shall learn how to create lists to present text in an easy-to-read way.

4

Creating Lists

Arranging text in the form of a list can be very reader-friendly. You can present several key points in a clear structure that is easy to survey. Commonly, three types of lists are used:

- Bulleted lists, to emphasize several points standing out from the text
- Enumerated lists, to present points in an order
- Definition lists, to explain several points in a structured way

In this chapter, we shall learn how to create such lists. We will cover the following:

- Building lists
- Customizing lists

First, we will learn how to create these lists, and then later in the chapter, we will see how to customize them.

Technical requirements

You need to have LaTeX on your computer, or you can use Overleaf. You can also run all examples online on the book's web page: `https://latexguide.org/chapter-04`.

The code is available on GitHub: `https://github.com/PacktPublishing/ LaTeX-Beginner-s-Guide-2nd-Edition-/tree/main/Chapter_04_-_ Creating_Lists`.

In this chapter, we will use the following LaTeX packages: `enumitem`, `layouts`, and `paralist`.

Building lists

We will start with unordered lists that are structured by bullet points. Later in this section, we will deal with ordered lists that are enumerated by numbers or characters, and then we will continue with lists of explained keywords and facts.

Creating a bulleted list

We shall start with the simplest kind of list. It contains just the items without numbers. Each item is marked by a bullet. That way, we can organize a list of key points in a much more readable way compared to a long sentence within text in a paragraph.

Let's create a list of packages that we got to know in the previous chapter. Follow these steps to build a bullet list:

1. Create a new document with some introduction text:

    ```
    \documentclass{article}
    \begin{document}
    \section*{Useful packages}
    LaTeX provides several packages for designing the
    layout:
    ```

2. Now write the list, using an `itemize` environment and `\item` commands:

    ```
    \begin{itemize}
      \item geometry
      \item typearea
      \item fancyhdr
      \item scrpage-scrlayer
      \item setspace
    \end{itemize}
    ```

3. That was easy. Now we can end the document:

    ```
    \end{document}
    ```

4. Click on **Typeset** and have a look at the output:

Useful packages

LaTeX provides several packages for designing the layout:

- geometry

- typearea

- fancyhdr

- scrpage-scrlayer

- setspace

Figure 4.1 – A bulleted list

We began with a heading followed by some text. For the actual list, we used an environment called `itemize`. As we have already learned about environments in *Chapter 2, Formatting Text and Creating Macros*, `\begin{itemize}` starts it and `\end{itemize}` ends it. The `\item` command tells LaTeX that it will add a new item to the list. `\item` works only within a list. Each item can contain text of any length and even paragraph breaks. Well, that's pretty easy.

When a list gets longer, we could make it clearer by dividing it. We can create lists under a list. It's advisable to use different bullets to differentiate between the list levels easily. LaTeX does this for us automatically.

We shall refine our package list from the previous example by introducing topic categories. To do that, follow these steps:

1. Refine the aforementioned highlighted `itemize` environment of our example in the following way: make an `itemize` list for each topic, and let it be part of an `\item` point. The list code from *step 2* in our previous example shall now become this:

```
\begin{itemize}
    \item Page layout
        \begin{itemize}
            \item geometry
            \item typearea
        \end{itemize}
    \item Headers and footers
        \begin{itemize}
```

```
        \item fancyhdr
        \item scrpage-scrlayer
      \end{itemize}
  \item Line spacing
    \begin{itemize}
      \item setspace
    \end{itemize}
  \end{itemize}
```

Note that we carefully closed each environment.

2. Compile the document to see the new list:

- Page layout

    − geometry

    − typearea

- Headers and footers

    − fancyhdr

    − scrpage-scrlayer

- Line spacing

    − setspace

Figure 4.2 – A bulleted list with two levels

We used lists as part of an \item point inside a list. That way, we **nested lists**. Up to four levels are possible; otherwise, LaTeX would stop and print out an error message that says **! LaTeX Error: Too deeply nested**. As we saw, the first level is marked by a bullet, and the second by a wide dash. A third level item would start with an asterisk symbol, *. The fourth and last level would be marked by a centered dot.

Deeply nested lists are rarely used; such complicated structures might be hard to read. In such cases, it could be a good idea to revise the text structure or at least split the list.

In our own source code of this example, we indented each line within an itemize environment. So, if there's another itemize environment within a surrounding itemize environment, the \item lines are even more indented. That way, we can see which level of nested environments we are in. It's not necessary to do this, but proper indentation within environments helps in maintaining the code structure, as we can see with a glance where an environment begins and where it ends. Indenting source code lines within an environment is a very good habit in general. You can also indent code lines to indicate to yourself that it belongs to some parent line, as we did here with \item points that spanned over several lines.

> **Give your code a structure by indenting**
>
> Indenting source code with space characters or tab characters improves the readability of the code very much. It won't affect the output because LaTeX treats multiple whitespace characters in a code line as a single whitespace character.

In the next section, we will see how to list key points in a specific order and number them.

Building an enumerated list

Bulleted lists are useful if the order of the items doesn't matter. However, if the order is essential, we could organize the items by giving them numbers and creating a sorted list. That would allow the reader to follow our thoughts easily.

Let's prepare a tiny step-by-step tutorial for designing the page layout using a numbered list. Follow these steps:

1. Open a new document and enter the following code:

```
\documentclass{article}
\begin{document}
\begin{enumerate}
  \item State the paper size by an option to the
        document class
  \item Determine the margin dimensions using one
        of these packages:
    \begin{itemize}
      \item geometry
      \item typearea
    \end{itemize}
```

```
    \item Customize header and footer by one
            of these packages:
      \begin{itemize}
        \item fancyhdr
        \item scrpage-scrlayer
      \end{itemize}
    \item Adjust the line spacing for the whole document
      \begin{itemize}
        \item by using the setspace package
        \item or by the command
              \verb|\linespread{factor}|
      \end{itemize}
  \end{enumerate}
\end{document}
```

2. Click on **Typeset** to generate the instructions:

    1. State the paper size by an option to the document class

    2. Determine the margin dimensions using one of these packages:

        -   geometry
        -   typearea

    3. Customize header and footer by one of these packages:

        -   fancyhdr
        -   scrpage-scrlayer

    4. Adjust the line spacing for the whole document

        -   by using the setspace package
        -   or by the command **\linespread{factor}**

Figure 4.3 – A numbered list with bulleted lists

We used an enumerate environment in the highlighted code lines. Except for the name, we use it just like the itemize environment; each list item is introduced by the \item command. The difference is that every \item line in our enumerate environment is numbered instead of just having a bullet point in front. Again, we nested two lists, just this time, the lists are of a different kind. Mixed nesting could go further than four levels, but four is the maximum for each type of list, and six in general for mixed lists.

The default numbering scheme for the `enumerate` environment is as follows:

- **First level**: 1., 2., 3., 4., …
- **Second level**: (a), (b), (c), (d), …
- **Third level**: i., ii., iii., iv., …
- **Fourth level**: A., B., C., D., …

`\item` can have an optional argument. If you write `\item[text]`, LaTeX prints `text` instead of a number or a bullet. This way, you could use any numbering and any symbol for the bullet.

Now that we know how to create lists with bullet points and enumerated lists, let's look at a list type that we can use to present descriptions of several items.

Producing a definition list

We shall proceed to the third kind of list, namely, **definition lists**, also called **description lists**. Here, every list item consists of a term or a phrase followed by its description.

To build an example, we need some phrases to work on. As in the first example of this chapter, we will create a list of packages. This time, we will add a description of each package. Let's choose some packages from `https://ctan.org/topic/list`, which is a collection of list-related packages. This is in preparation for the next section, *Customizing lists*, where we will work with the packages we chose for the list in the following example.

We shall write a short overview to show the capabilities of each package. Follow these steps:

1. We will use a `description` environment. Create a document with the following code:

```
\documentclass{article}
\begin{document}
\begin{description}
  \item[paralist] provides compact lists and list
    versions that can be used within paragraphs,
    helps to customize labels and layout.
  \item[enumitem] gives control over labels
    and lengths in all kind of lists.
  \item[mdwlist] is useful to customize description
```

```
        lists, it even allows multi-line labels.
        It features compact lists and the capability
        to suspend and resume.
    \item[desclist] offers more flexibility in
        definition list.
    \item[multenum] produces vertical enumeration in
        multiple columns.
\end{description}
\end{document}
```

2. Click on **Typeset** to get the definition list:

paralist provides compact lists and list versions that can be used within paragraphs, helps to customize labels and layout.

enumitem gives control over labels and lenghts in all kind of lists.

mdwlist is useful to customize description lists, it even allows multi-line labels. It features compact lists and the capability to suspend and resume.

desclist offers more flexibility in definition list.

multenum produces vertical enumeration in multiple columns.

Figure 4.4 – A definition list

We used the `description` environment like the other lists, except that we used the optional argument of `\item` in square brackets. In the `description` environment, `\item` is defined such that the optional parameter will be typeset in the bold typeface.

If we compare it to a bulleted list, the bullets have been replaced with bold font keywords.

We can also change the spacing of our lists, the bullet type, and the numbering style. Let's look at this in the next section.

Customizing lists

The default appearance of lists is meaningful regarding the spacing, indentation, and symbols. Nevertheless, it may be required to use another scheme for the enumeration, for the bullets, or to modify the line spacing or their indentation. Some packages help us to save space, as well as to customize the symbols. Let's start with the spacing.

Getting compact lists

A frequently arising question is how to reduce the space in lists. LaTeX's lists are often regarded as being too spacious. We shall see how to implement that.

Let's shrink our list in this tutorial. We shall remove the whitespace around the list items and before and after the whole list as well. Follow these steps:

1. In our enumerated list example that produced *Figure 4.3*, add the `paralist` package and replace `enumerate` with `compactenum` and `itemize` with `compactitem`:

```
\documentclass{article}
\usepackage{paralist}
\begin{document}
\begin{compactenum}
  \item State the paper size by an option to
        the document class
  \item Determine the margin dimensions using one
        of these packages:
  \begin{compactitem}
    \item geometry
    \item typearea
  \end{compactitem}
  \item Customize header and footer by one
        of these packages:
  \begin{compactitem}
    \item fancyhdr
    \item scrpage-scrlayer
  \end{compactitem}
  \item Adjust the line spacing for the whole document
  \begin{compactitem}
    \item by using the setspace package
    \item or by the command \verb|\linespread{factor}|
  \end{compactitem}
\end{compactenum}
\end{document}
```

2. Compile and compare the spacing:

    1. State the paper size by an option to the document class
    2. Determine the margin dimensions using one of these packages:
        - geometry
        - typearea
    3. Customize header and footer by one of these packages:
        - fancyhdr
        - scrpage-scrlayer
    4. Adjust the line spacing for the whole document
        - by using the setspace package
        - or by the command \linespread{factor}

Figure 4.5 – A compact list

3. Now extend the highlighted list item for setspace as follows:

```
\item by using the setspace package and one
      of its options:
\begin{inparaenum}
  \item singlespacing
  \item onehalfspacing
  \item double spacing
\end{inparaenum}
```

4. Compile and look at the change in the line spacing subject:

    1. State the paper size by an option to the document class
    2. Determine the margin dimensions using one of these packages:
        - geometry
        - typearea
    3. Customize header and footer by one of these packages:
        - fancyhdr
        - scrpage-scrlayer
    4. Adjust the line spacing for the whole document
        - by using the setspace package and one of its options: (a) singlespacing (b) onehalfspacing (c) double spacing
        - or by the command \linespread{factor}

Figure 4.6 – A list within a paragraph

The `paralist` package that we used provides several new list environments designed to be typeset within paragraphs or in a very compact look. We loaded this package and replaced the standard environments with their compact counterparts, `enumerate` with `compactenum`, and `itemize` with `compactitem`. While the other syntax is the same, the new environments don't produce additional vertical whitespace before and after a list. They also don't add vertical space around list items. Lists and items are used with the same line spacing as regular text. Finally, it looks much more compact and saves space. In *step 3*, we used the new `inparaenum` environment, where the items are enumerated but stay within the same paragraph.

For each standard environment, `paralist` adds three corresponding environments.

For **bulleted lists**, it adds the following:

- `compactitem`: Compact version of the `itemize` environment without any vertical space before or after the list or its items.

- `inparaitem`: An itemized list typeset within a paragraph, rarely seen in print.

- `asparaitem`: Every list item is formatted like a separate common LaTeX paragraph but with a bullet point in front.

For **numbered lists**, it adds the following:

- `compactenum`: Compact version of the `enumerate` environment without any vertical space before or after the list or its items.

- `inparaenum`: An enumerated list typeset within a paragraph.

- `asparaenum`: Every list item is formatted like a separate common LaTeX paragraph but numbered.

For **description lists**, it adds the following:

- `compactdesc`: Compact version of the `description` environment, that is, without additional vertical space before and after the list and its items.

- `inparadesc`: A description list that's within a paragraph.

- `asparadesc`: Every list item is formatted like a separate common LaTeX paragraph, with the bold keyword, as in a `description` list, as the intro text for the paragraph.

Now that we have customized the spacing let's look at bullets and numbers.

Choosing bullets and numbering format

To follow language-specific habits or particular requirements, we might wish to enumerate lists by using Roman numbers or alphabets; parentheses or dots might also be required. Some may prefer dashes instead of bullets. The enumitem package provides sophisticated features to implement such requirements.

Let's change the numbering scheme. We shall number a list alphabetically using circled letters. Furthermore, we will replace bullets with dashes. To do that, follow these steps:

1. Instead of paralist, we are now using the enumitem package. We will turn away from the "compact" environments, so we return to the standard list notation. Still, we want to have compact lists and add the nosep parameter to lists:

```
\documentclass{article}
\usepackage{enumitem}
\setlist{nosep}
\setitemize[1]{label=---}
\setenumerate[1]{label=\textcircled{\scriptsize\Alph*},
    font=\sffamily}
\begin{document}
\begin{enumerate}
  \item State the paper size by an option to the
        document class
  \item Determine the margin dimensions using one of
        these packages:
    \begin{itemize}
    \item geometry
    \item typearea
  \end{itemize}
  \item Customize header and footer by one of these
        packages:
  \begin{itemize}
    \item fancyhdr
    \item scrpage-scrheader
  \end{itemize}
  \item Adjust the line spacing for the whole document
  \begin{itemize}
    \item by using the setspace package
```

```
    \item or by the command \verb|\linespread{factor}|
  \end{itemize}
\end{enumerate}
\end{document}
```

2. Click on **Typeset** and check the output:

   Ⓐ State the paper size by an option to the document class
   Ⓑ Determine the margin dimensions using one of these packages:
      — geometry
      — typearea
   Ⓒ Customize header and footer by one of these packages:
      — fancyhdr
      — scrpage-scrheader
   Ⓓ Adjust the line spacing for the whole document
      — by using the setspace package
      — or by the command \linespread{factor}

Figure 4.7 – A customized enumerated list

3. Right above the highlighted code line, insert the following lines:

```
\end{enumerate}
\noindent\textbf{Tweaking the line spacing:}
\begin{enumerate}[resume*]
```

4. Click on **Typeset** to see the change:

   Ⓐ State the paper size by an option to the document class
   Ⓑ Determine the margin dimensions using one of these packages:
      — geometry
      — typearea
   Ⓒ Customize header and footer by one of these packages:
      — fancyhdr
      — scrpage-scrheader
   Tweaking the line spacing:
   Ⓓ Adjust the line spacing for the whole document
      — by using the setspace package
      — or by the command \linespread{factor}

Figure 4.8 – A list that's resumed

We used the `enumitem` package commands to specify list properties. Let's take a closer look:

- `\setlist{nosep}`: `\setlist` sets properties valid for all types of lists. Here, we specified `nosep` to achieve very compact lists analogous to the compact `paralist` environment. That setting omits all extra vertical spacing.

- `\setitemize[1]{label=---}`: `\setitemize` modifies properties of bulleted lists. Here, we chose an em dash as the label to get a leading wide dash.

- `\setenumerate[1]{label=\textcircled{\scriptsize \Alph*},font=\sffamily}`: `\setenumerate` sets properties valid for numbered lists. We used it to set a label and a font for the label. The `\Alph*` command means enumeration in capital letters.

We can use those options locally as we did with `resume*`. Other examples are as follows:

- `\begin{itemize}[noitemsep]` for a compact bulleted list without any additional space between items and paragraphs

- `\begin{enumerate}[label=\Roman*.,start=3]` numbered by III., IV., and so on

- `\begin{enumerate}[label=\alph*)],nolistsep` for a very compact list numbered a), b), c), and so on

The labeling commands would achieve a numbering as follows:

- `\arabic*`: 1, 2, 3, 4, ...
- `\alph*`: a, b, c, d, ...
- `\Alph*`: A, B, C, D, ...
- `\roman*`: i, ii, iii, iv, ...
- `\Roman*`: I, II, III, IV, ...

The `*` stands for the current value of the list counter. Parentheses and punctuation may be used as required. Later in the book, you will learn to choose between thousands of symbols for labels and bullets.

There's even a short form; if you load the enumitem package with the shortlabels option, you may use a compact syntax such as \begin{enumerate}[(i)], \begin{enumerate}[(1)] where 1, a, A, i, and I stand for \arabic*, \alph*, \Alph*, \roman*, and \Roman*, respectively. This allows customization quickly and easily. However, consider using global commands to keep formatting consistent.

When we use a numbered list, we may want to stop it, write some text, and continue it. Let's see how to do that.

Suspending and continuing lists

In *step 3* of our example that produced *Figure 4.8*, we interrupted the list. We continued writing regular text until we restarted the list by using \begin{enumerate} [resume*]. The resume option tells enumitem to continue the list with the next number. The starred resume* variant does it with the same formatting as before.

LaTeX's lists have a meaningful layout. However, there might be occasions when you would like to modify this layout, such as changing the margins or the item indentation. All layout dimensions are determined by LaTeX macros, so-called lengths.

There's a package that is really great for visualizing layouts, which presents these length macros. It's called layouts. Let's use it to examine LaTeX's list dimensions. We will use this small document:

```
\documentclass[12pt]{article}
\usepackage{layouts}
\begin{document}
\listdiagram
\end{document}
```

By simply typesetting it, we will get the following diagram:

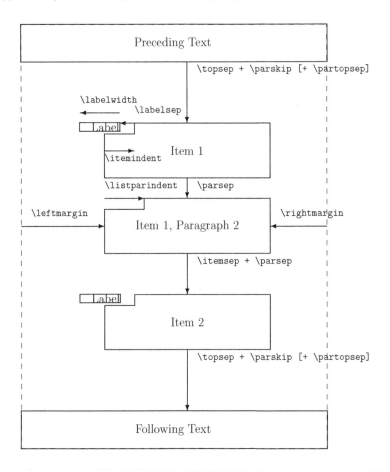

Figure 4.9 – The layout of lists

Isn't it fantastic? The `layouts` package can do even more, which you can read about in its documentation at `https://texdoc.org/pkg/layouts` or by running `texdoc layouts` at the command line. For now, we'll stay on the topic of lists.

Use the LaTeX `\setlength` command to customize those lengths, for example, `\setlength{\labelwidth}{2cm}`. Applying them to individual lists and certain nesting depths is hard. If you need to modify the list layout, the `enumitem` package comes in handy again. We can use its commands such as `\setlist` and its `key=value` interface to adjust the lengths as you can see in the previous diagram.

For example, if we would like to remove the space between list items in the description environment and to reduce the left margin, we could load the `enumitem` package and write the following:

```
\setdescription{itemsep=0cm,parsep=0cm,leftmargin=0.5cm}
```

Note we don't use the backslash for keys. Similarly, `\setitemize`, `\setenumerate`, and `\setlist` can be used for fine-tuning. Try assigning values by yourself and test the effect on our examples. If you would like to learn more, have a look at the `enumitem` documentation at `https://texdoc.org/pkg/enumitem` or by running `texdoc enumitem` at the command prompt.

Summary

In this chapter, we got to know a new way to structure our text—lists. Specifically, we learned how to create bulleted lists, numbered lists, and definition lists. Furthermore, we worked with compact and customized versions of such lists, including spacing adjustments and interrupting and resuming.

You may regard those lists as an additional possibility to structure your text. Use it to clarify your ideas.

In the next chapter, we will structure our text concerning specific alignment and work with tables.

5
Including Images

Documents do not only consist of text. You might wish to include pictures, diagrams, or drawings made with other programs. In this chapter, we will learn how to insert such images with optimal quality and good positioning.

We will now learn about the following topics:

- Including an image
- Managing floating images

By the end of this chapter, we will know how to position images within text exactly as we want.

Technical requirements

You need to have LaTeX installed, or you can use Overleaf. You can also edit and compile on the book's web page at `https://latexguide.org/chapter-05`.

The code for this chapter is available on GitHub at `https://github.com/PacktPublishing/LaTeX-Beginner-s-Guide-2nd-Edition-/tree/main/Chapter_05_-_Including_Images`.

In this chapter, we will use the following LaTeX packages: `babel`, `blindtext`, `capt-of`, `float`, `graphicx`, `pdfpages`, and `wrapfig`.

We will also briefly talk about these packages: afterpage, caption, epstopdf, eso-pic, microtype, placeins, rotating, subcaption, subfig, subfigure, and textpos.

Including an image

For including images, the standard package is called graphicx. The x in the name means it's extending the original, but outdated, graphics package.

We will create a short document, and between two paragraphs, we would like to insert a picture. We can do so with the help of the following steps:

1. Begin a new document and load babel and blindtext to print some filler text, as follows:

```
\documentclass[a5paper]{article}
\usepackage[english]{babel}
\usepackage{blindtext}
\usepackage{graphicx}
\pagestyle{empty}
\begin{document}
\section{Including a picture}
\blindtext
```

2. Open a figure environment and declare \centering, as follows:

```
\begin{figure}
   \centering
```

3. Use the \includegraphics command with the filename as the argument. We will use example-image as the filename since that's a sample image included with TeX Live. The code is illustrated in the following snippet:

```
\includegraphics[width=4cm]{example-image}
```

4. Set a caption, close the figure environment, and end the document with filler text, as illustrated in the following code snippet:

```
   \caption{Test figure}
\end{figure}
\blindtext
\end{document}
```

5. Click on **Typeset** to compile the document, and have a look at the output, which you can see in the following screenshot:

Figure 1: Test figure

1   Including a picture

Hello, here is some text without a meaning. This text should show what a printed text will look like at this place. If you read this text, you will get no information. Really? Is there no information? Is there a difference between this text and some nonsense like "Huardest gefburn"? Kjift – not at all! A blind text like this gives you information about the selected font, how the letters are written and an impression of the look. This text should contain all letters of the alphabet and it should be written in of the original language. There is no need for special content, but the length of words should match the language. Hello, here is some text without a meaning. This text should show what a printed text will look like at this place. If you read this text, you will get no information. Really? Is there no information? Is there a difference between this text and some nonsense like "Huardest gefburn"? Kjift – not at all! A blind text like this gives you information about the selected font, how the letters

Figure 5.1 – An image in a document

The most important command is \includegraphics, where we specified a filename. LaTeX loads this file if it exists; otherwise, it will show an error. LaTeX supports the following file types:

- PNG, JPG, and PDF if you directly compile to PDF (pdfLaTeX)

- EPS if you compile to DVI and convert to PS and PDF (traditional LaTeX)

To clarify, **PS** stands for **PostScript**, **EPS** stands for **Encapsulated PostScript**, and **DVI** stands for **Device Independent File Format**. The latter was the first output format to be supported by TeX and LaTeX. You definitely must know **PDF** (which stands for **Portable Document Format**) and the very popular picture formats, PNG and JPG, which are often used for screenshots and photos.

You don't need to specify a filename extension as LaTeX adds this automatically. Either put the file into the same directory as your document or specify a full or relative pathname, as follows:

```
\includegraphics{appendix/figure1}
```

In file paths, use forward slash characters (/); don't use backslash characters (\), as the latter begins a LaTeX command.

Go ahead and copy a picture of your choice into your document directory. Give \includegraphics its filename, and compile. LaTeX embeds the picture with its original size.

In the following sections, we will see how to choose an image file type and add an image of a specified size, including a whole PDF page, or place it in the background behind the text.

Choosing an optimal file type

If you have already got the final picture in JPG, PNG, or PDF format, you can use this format and include the picture in your document. Changing the image format doesn't improve quality. Before taking the picture, though, you are free to choose a file format. Let's see how to decide which file format to use.

EPS and PDF are both vector graphics formats. They are scalable, and both also look good at high resolution or if you zoom in. So, whenever possible, PDF (or EPS) should be the preferred format—for instance, when you export drawings or diagrams out of other office software. For such graphics, vector formats are common.

PNG and JPG are bitmap formats, also called raster graphics, commonly used for photos. If you zoom in, you will notice a loss of quality. PNG uses lossless compression, whereas JPG pictures may lose quality when we save them. So, if you make screenshots, use PNG, or ensure that there's no loss compression if you choose JPG. For photos, JPG is recommended to avoid getting huge PDF files.

Besides supporting vector graphics, both EPS and PDF may contain bitmap graphics. They are also called **container formats**.

There are a lot of tools to convert between graphic formats. The following three programs are beneficial, and both TeX Live and MiKTeX include them:

- dvips converts DVI files to PostScript format.
- ps2pdf converts PostScript files to PDF.

- `epstopdf` converts EPS files to PDF, the LaTeX package with the same name. `epstopdf` does it on the fly if you load it with `\usepackage`.

These are command-line tools. Some LaTeX editors use them to provide single-click compiling from `.tex` to `.dvi`, to `.ps`, and then to `.pdf`.

`epstopdf` is especially useful if you have to include PostScript pictures and wish to benefit from `pdfLaTeX` features such as font expansion and character protrusion, accessible by `microtype`.

Inkscape, ImageMagick, and GIMP are very capable free and open source programs for further working with graphics.

Scaling an image

When adding an image, you may choose a different size. For this, let's look at the definition of `\includegraphics`, as follows:

```
\includegraphics[key=value list]{file name}
```

The `graphicx` documentation lists all keys and possible values. Here are the most popular ones, and what `\includegraphics` does then:

- `width`: Resizing to this width. Example: `width=0.9\textwidth`.
- `height`: Resizing to this height. Example: `height=3cm`.
- `scale`: Scaling by this factor. Example: `scale=0.5`.
- `angle`: Turning by this angle. Example: `angle=90`.

There are also options for clipping, but you can easily do such postprocessing with any graphics software.

Instead of turning a figure by 90 degrees, you could also use the `sidewaysfigure` environment of the `rotating` package (see `https://texdoc.org/pkg/rotating`).

Including whole pages

How can we include pictures wider or higher than the text area? `\includegraphics` could do this, but LaTeX would complain about width or size and might move them to the next page.

Using the `pdfpages` package, we can include large images and even whole pages. The `pdfpages` package provides the `\includepdf` command, which can include a complete page or even a multi-page PDF document at once. Despite its name, it can also include PNG and JPG files, not just PDF files (something the documentation at https://texdoc.org/pkg/pdfpages does not mention).

An example of its basic usage could look like this:

```
\usepackage{pdfpages}
...
\includepdf[pages=-]{contract}% include entire contract.pdf
\includepdf[pages=2-4]{spec}% include pages 2-4 of spec.pdf
```

A common use is combining several PDF files into a single PDF file. We can also use `pdfpages` to resize several PDF pages and arrange them on a single sheet.

Putting images behind the text

Do you need watermarks? Background images? Textboxes positioned at arbitrary positions on the page, preferably not interfering with other text? The `eso-pic` package does this for you.

In the *LaTeX Cookbook*, you can read a step-by-step example of how to do this in the *Absolute positioning of text* section in *Chapter 2, Tuning the Text*.

The `textpos` package offers another approach. It's developed for placing boxes with text or graphics at absolute positions on a page; see https://texdoc.org/pkg/textpos.

Now, we will take a look at dynamic image positioning.

Managing floating images

When a page break occurs, regular text can be broken to continue onto the next page. However, the automatic page breaking cannot divide pictures. That's why LaTeX provides a floating environment—namely, `figure`. Such floating environments are also called **floats**. LaTeX may push their content, including captions, to a place suitable for page layout and page breaking.

We will now figure out how to deal with this.

The figure environment takes an optional argument affecting the final placement of the figure. We will test the effect in our graphics example, as shown here:

1. Go back to the previous example we had for *Figure 5.1*. This time, add the h and t options in the highlighted line (where h and t stands for *here* and *top*), as follows:

```
\begin{figure}[ht]
  \centering
  \includegraphics{example-image}
  \caption{Test figure}
\end{figure}
```

2. Compile the document, and take a look at the output. It should look like this:

1   Including a picture

Hello, here is some text without a meaning. This text should show what a printed text will look like at this place. If you read this text, you will get no information. Really? Is there no information? Is there a difference between this text and some nonsense like "Huardest gefburn"? Kjift – not at all! A blind text like this gives you information about the selected font, how the letters are written and an impression of the look. This text should contain all letters of the alphabet and it should be written in of the original language. There is no need for special content, but the length of words should match the language. Hello, here

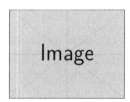

Figure 1: Test figure

is some text without a meaning. This text should show what a printed text will look like at this place. If you read this text, you will get no information. Really? Is there no information? Is there a difference between this text and some nonsense like "Huardest gefburn"? Kjift – not at all! A blind text like this gives you information about the selected font, how the letters

Figure 5.2 – An image within the text

3. Change the options in the highlighted line to !b (where b stands for *bottom)*, as follows:

```
\begin{figure}[!b]
```

4. Compile again. The figure is now forced to float to the bottom, and now we see this page:

1   Including a picture

Hello, here is some text without a meaning. This text should show what a printed text will look like at this place. If you read this text, you will get no information. Really? Is there no information? Is there a difference between this text and some nonsense like "Huardest gefburn"? Kjift – not at all! A blind text like this gives you information about the selected font, how the letters are written and an impression of the look. This text should contain all letters of the alphabet and it should be written in of the original language. There is no need for special content, but the length of words should match the language. Hello, here is some text without a meaning. This text should show what a printed text will look like at this place. If you read this text, you will get no information. Really? Is there no information? Is there a difference between this text and some nonsense like "Huardest gefburn"? Kjift – not at all! A blind text like this gives you information about the selected font, how the letters

Figure 1: Test figure

Figure 5.3 – An image at the page bottom

By adding some characters standing for placement options, we could force the figure to appear wherever we want.

> **Spanning figures over text columns**
>
> There is a starred form—namely, `figure*`—in a two-column layout that puts a figure into a single column. In one-column mode, there's no difference to the non-starred form.

Let's now take a closer look at the positioning of figures. We will see how we can set a preference as to where figures will appear, such as at the top or bottom of pages, how to force the immediate output, or at least limit the floating, and how to arrange images next to each other or within the text flow.

Understanding placement options

The optional argument of the `figure` environment tells LaTeX where it's allowed to place the figure. Four letters stand for four possible places, as outlined here:

- h stands for *here*. The figure may appear where we wrote it in the source code.

- t stands for *top*. Placing the figure at the top of a page is permitted.

- b stands for *bottom*. The figure may appear at the bottom of a page.

- p stands for *page*. The figure can appear on a separate page, where only floats may reside but no normal text.

A fifth option might come in handy, as outlined here:

- ! tells LaTeX to try harder to ignore some constraints, easing the placement.

If you don't specify any option, LaTeX can place the figure far away. New LaTeX users might be surprised by this. Specifying more options would help to put it as near as possible. The most flexible way is to use the `[!htbp]` placement, allowing the figure to go everywhere. You could still consider removing a placement specifier if you don't like it.

Forcing the output of figures

If you would like to stop LaTeX from putting the floats, there's a way to do this—the `\clearpage` command ends the current page and causes the printing out of all already defined figures. You can also use `\cleardoublepage`, which does the same but in a two-sided layout. It ensures that the next non-float page is a right-hand page. If necessary, it inserts a blank page.

Immediately ending the page might not be the best thing to do, as this could leave a lot of empty space on the current page. The `afterpage` package offers a creative solution to this. This package allows the execution of `\clearpage` to be deferred until the current page has ended, as shown here:

```
\usepackage{afterpage}
...
body text
\afterpage{\clearpage}
```

We may not need to use the `afterpage` package often, as we can just run a `\clearpage` command at the desired place, such as at the end of a section. We can automate that case. Let's look at this in the next section.

Limiting floating

Figures may float far away, perhaps even into another section. The placeins package provides a useful command to restrict the floating. If you load placeins with \usepackage{placeins} and write \FloatBarrier somewhere in your document, no figure can float past it. This macro keeps floats in their place.

A very convenient way to prevent floats from crossing section boundaries is by stating the section option, as follows:

```
\usepackage[section]{placeins}
```

This option causes an implicit \FloatBarrier at the beginning of each section. Two further options—namely, above and below—allow you to lower the restrictions, preventing floats from appearing above the start of the current section or below the beginning of the next section.

Figures don't float into the next chapter because \chapter implicitly uses \clearpage.

Avoiding floating at all

Would you like to place an image exactly where you want it? The obvious answer is: don't use a floating figure environment. We can use \includegraphics without a figure environment. For example, we could include and center an image by doing the following:

```
\begin{center}
   \includegraphics[width=4cm]{example-image}
\end{center}
```

Captions are for floating environments, though, so a \caption command won't work here. If you still want to have a caption, you may use the \captionof command. The caption package, **KOMA-Script** classes, and the tiny capt-of package provide that command, which we can use in this way:

```
\usepackage{capt-of}% or caption
...
\begin{minipage}{\linewidth}
   \centering
   \includegraphics{example-image}
   \captionof{figure}{Test figure}
\end{minipage}
```

The `minipage` environment keeps a picture and its caption together because no page break can occur in a `minipage` environment. The definition of `\captionof` is the same as `\caption`, except that there is an additional argument specifying the float type—in this case, `figure`, as illustrated in the following code snippet:

```
\captionof{figure}[short text]{long text}
```

Be aware that the numbering could go awry if you mix real floats and fixed figures. As you don't benefit from LaTeX's positioning capabilities, you have to take care that pages are still adequately filled.

The `float` package provides a convenient and consistent-looking approach to this. It introduces the H placement option, causing the float to appear right there, as illustrated in the following code snippet:

```
\usepackage{float}
...
\begin{figure}[H]
   \centering
   \includegraphics{example-image}
   \caption{Test figure}
\end{figure}
```

You may choose between these two options. If you wish to explore additional features of the `float` package, load it. Otherwise, consider using the `capt-of` one-liner. Perhaps even that is unnecessary, assuming that you're already using the `caption` package or a KOMA-Script class.

Arranging several images

For grouping several subfigures with captions within a single figure, there are several supporting packages you can choose from, outlined as follows:

- `subcaption` is a package for subfigures with subcaptions and belongs to the `caption` package. (If you use hyperlinks in a document, choose the `subcaption` package since this supports hyperlinks better. For hyperlinks, also see *Chapter 12, Enhancing Your Documents Further*.)

- `subfig` is a sophisticated package, supporting the inclusion of small figures. It takes care of positioning, labeling, and captioning within single floats.

- `subfigure` is still available for this purpose, but we can consider it obsolete since `subfig` has appeared.

Don't load two of these packages together. In general, loading two packages that serve the same purpose can lead to conflicts.

For aligning images, stacking images, or positioning them in a grid, there are explained examples in the *LaTeX Cookbook, Chapter 4, Working with Images.*

Letting text flow around images

Though it's a bit playful, you might wish to let the text flow around a figure. We can achieve this using the `wrapfig` package and its `wrapfigure` environments.

We will modify our previous example that embedded an image (see *Figure 5.3*). We would like the image to appear on the left side, accompanied by the body text on the right side, with the help of the following steps:

1. In our example code for *Figure 5.3*, additionally load the `wrapfig` package, as follows:

```
\documentclass[a5paper]{article}
\usepackage[english]{babel}
\usepackage{blindtext}
\usepackage{graphicx}
\usepackage{wrapfig}
\pagestyle{empty}
\begin{document}
```

2. Begin an unnumbered section, and place a `wrapfig` environment within some filler text, like this:

```
\section*{Text flowing around an image}
\blindtext
\begin{wrapfigure}{l}{4cm}
   \includegraphics[width=4cm]{ example-image}
   \caption{Test figure}
\end{wrapfigure}
\blindtext
\end{document}
```

3. Compile the document and take a look. You should see the following output:

Text flowing around an image

Hello, here is some text without a meaning. This text should show what a printed text will look like at this place. If you read this text, you will get no information. Really? Is there no information? Is there a difference between this text and some nonsense like "Huardest gefburn"? Kjift – not at all! A blind text like this gives you information about the selected font, how the letters are written and an impression of the look. This text should contain all letters of the alphabet and it should be written in of the original language. There is no need for special content, but the length of words should match the language.

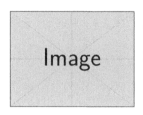

Figure 1: Test figure

Hello, here is some text without a meaning. This text should show what a printed text will look like at this place. If you read this text, you will get no information. Really? Is there no information? Is there a difference between this text and some nonsense like "Huardest gefburn"? Kjift – not at all! A blind text like this gives you information about the selected font, how the letters are written and an impression of the look. This text should contain all letters of the alphabet and it should be written in of the original language. There is no need for special content, but the length of words should match the language.

Figure 5.4 – Text flowing around an image

The `wrapfigure` environment has different parameters from the `figure` environment. We used just two of them. If you need more, here's the complete definition:

```
\begin{wrapfigure}[number of lines]{placement}[overhang]{width}
```

The first optional argument states the number of wrapped text lines. If omitted, this would be automatically calculated from the height. The second argument, `placement`, can be one of `r`, `l`, `i`, and `o` characters for the right, left, inner, or outer side, or the corresponding uppercase letters `R`, `L`, `I`, `O` with the same meaning, but allowing the figure to float. Only one character for specifying the option is allowed. The other optional argument, `overhang`, can set a width by which the figure should hang out into the margin; the default is `0` pt. The final—and mandatory—argument gives the `width` of the figure.

You can read more in the manual at `https://texdoc.org/pkg/wrapfig`.

Summary

In this chapter, we have learned how to include images in our document. We now know which file types we can use and how to place figures in our document.

LaTeX can generate a list of figures like a table of contents. We will deal with such lists in *Chapter 8, Listing Contents and References*.

As our figures are numbered, we can use these numbers to refer to them within the text. In *Chapter 7, Using Cross-References*, we will figure out how to do this, benefiting from LaTeX's built-in cross-referencing capabilities.

In the next chapter, we will work with tables, and we will see that table positioning is very similar to figure positioning.

6
Creating Tables

Scientific documents and others do not just contain plain text; they also present information and data in tables. We shall become familiar with that in this chapter.

In this chapter, we will learn how to perform the following:

- Using tab stops to write in columns
- Typesetting tables
- Adding captions to tables
- Using packages for further customization

Let's tackle these tasks. We will start by simply arranging text in columns.

Technical requirements

You need to have a LaTeX installation, or you can compile the example code online at `https://latexguide.org/chapter-06`.

The code is also available on GitHub: `https://github.com/PacktPublishing/LaTeX-Beginner-s-Guide-2nd-Edition-/tree/main/Chapter_06_-_Creating_Tables`.

In this chapter, we will use the following LaTeX packages: `array`, `booktabs`, `caption`, and `multirow`.

We will also briefly talk about these packages: color, colortbl, dcolumn, longtable, ltablex, ltxtable, microtype, ragged2e, rccol, rotating, siunitx, stabular, supertabular, tabularx, tabulary, xcolor, and xtab.

Using tab stops to write in columns

Remember the time of the typewriter and early word processing software? When we needed to line up some text in columns, we could use tab stops. LaTeX provides a similar way to easily align text in columns, namely, the tabbing environment.

We want to present a quick overview of LaTeX. We shall present one point on each line, aligned at words and colons, with the help of the following steps:

1. Begin a new document and open a tabbing environment:

    ```
    \documentclass{article}
    \begin{document}
    \begin{tabbing}
    ```

2. Write the text, set tab stops with \=, and end the line with \\:

    ```
    \emph{Info:} \= Software \= : \= \LaTeX \\
    ```

3. Add further lines, move to the next tab stop with \>, and again, end lines with \\:

    ```
    \> Author \> : \> Leslie Lamport \\
    \> Website \> : \> www.latex-project.org
    ```

4. Close the tabbing environment and end the document:

    ```
    \end{tabbing}
    \end{document}
    ```

5. Click the **Typeset** button to compile the document, and take a look at the output:

    > *Info:* Software : LaTeX
    >   Author   : Leslie Lamport
    >   Website : www.latex-project.org

    Figure 6.1 – Simply aligned text

The `tabbing` environment that we used begins a new line. We used three simple tags for markup:

- `\=` sets a tab stop. We could put several tab stops on a line. We usually do it in the first row.

- `\\` ends a row.

- `\>` goes to the next tab stop.

Aside from the first row, we can also use `\=` in another row to adjust a previously set tab stop. For example, if we already used two `\>` tags in a text line to go to two tab stops, a `\=` tag would put a (new or replaced) third tab stop.

At `https://latexguide.org/tabbing`, you can see several examples using these tags.

With `tabbing`, we can quickly produce columns containing left-aligned text. If the rows of the `tabbing` environment reached the end of a page, it would continue on the next page. So, `tabbing` is a very basic way to make tables crossing page breaks or even spanning over multiple pages.

But what if a column is too long, running over the tab stop? Let's see how to solve that.

In *Chapter 2, Formatting Text and Creating Macros*, we got to know a lot of font commands and declarations. We saw a table containing those commands and example output. Now we shall create such a table ourselves, as follows:

1. Begin a new document, like the one in *step 1* of our previous example, but also define a command for setting the header font:

```
\documentclass{article}
\newcommand{\head}[1]{\textbf{#1}}
\begin{document}
\begin{tabbing}
```

2. Write the first row's set of tab stops with `\=`, and use `\>` to move to the tab stops. Use the `\verb|...|` command to typeset the LaTeX commands:

```
\= \head{Command} \= \head{Declaration} \= \
head{Example}\\
\> \verb|\textrm{...}| \> \verb|\rmfamily| \> \rmfamily
text\\
```

```
    \> \verb|\textsf{...}| \> \verb|\sffamily| \> \sffamily
text\\
```

```
    \> \verb|\texttt{...}| \> \verb|\ttfamily| \> \ttfamily
text
```

3. End the `tabbing` environment and the document:

```
\end{tabbing}
```

```
\end{document}
```

4. Click on **Typeset** to compile the document, and examine the output:

Command Declaration Example

```
\textrm{...\rmfamily    text
\textsf{...\sffamily    text
\texttt{...\ttfamily    text
```

Figure 6.2 – Overlapping aligned text

5. As we can see, the tab stops are too narrow. We shall correct it. Create a new head row containing the tab stops, but this time, we will end the line with `\kill` to hide that line. Use filler text to specify the width between the tab stops, such as the longest text in the column. Complete it with further font commands. The tabbing code now looks like this:

```
\begin{tabbing}
    \= \verb|\textrm{...}| \= \head{Declaration} \=
        \head{Example}\kill
    \> \head{Command} \> \head{Declaration} \> \
head{Example}\\
    \> \verb|\textrm{...}| \> \verb|\rmfamily| \> \rmfamily
text\\
    \> \verb|\textsf{...}| \> \verb|\sffamily| \> \sffamily
text\\
    \> \verb|\texttt{...}| \> \verb|\ttfamily| \> \ttfamily
text
\end{tabbing}
```

6.   Compile again to get the final result:

Command	Declaration	Example
\textrm{...}	\rmfamily	text
\textsf{...}	\sffamily	text
\texttt{...}	\ttfamily	text

Figure 6.3 – Corrected aligned text

After we noticed that our tab stops had been set too narrow, we constructed a new first row containing the tab stops. It consists of words representing the widest entries of each column. To hide this additional row, we used the \kill command right at the end of the line; \kill at the end of a line causes this line to have no output.

Like in this example, the \verb|code| command typesets code "as it is" without interpreting commands within. Instead of |, we can choose any character as the delimiter. \verb cannot be used in arguments of commands including \section and \footnote, and not in table heads.

For longer, verbatim text, use the environment with the same name: verbatim.

There are further useful commands, especially if you work a lot with tabbed texts:

- \+ at the end of a line (before \\) moves the left margin of the subsequent lines one tab stop to the right. Use it twice, \+\+, to move it two tab stops to the right, and so on.

- \- at the end of a line moves the left margin of the subsequent lines one tab stop to the left. Also, here, \-\- would move two tab stops to the left. \- is basically for undoing a previous indentation made by \+.

- \< cancels the effect of a preceding \+ command for that line. It moves the left margin one tab stop to the left. We should only use it at the beginning of a line. Repeat it to move two tab stops to the left.

The mentioned commands already allow good use of the tabbing environment. We can find even more commands in the reference manual: https://latex2e.org/tabbing.

Inside tabbing environments, declarations are local to the current item. A following \=, \>, \\, or \kill command would stop the effect.

Also, tabbing environments cannot be nested.

That was a way to arrange text in columns easily. Now let's see how to build tables with separation lines and alignment.

Typesetting tables

We might need more complicated structures and formatting, such as centering in columns, dividing lines, or even nested structures. LaTeX provides the `tabular` environment for typesetting straightforward and complex tables.

We will now create a table of font family commands as in the previous example, but this time, we would like to make all entries in a column horizontally centered to each other. We will also add some horizontal lines to mark the border and the header of the table by following these steps:

1. Create a new document. Define a command for setting the font for the head row:

```
\documentclass{article}
\newcommand{\head}[1]{\textnormal{\textbf{#1}}}
\begin{document}
```

2. Begin a `tabular` environment. As a mandatory argument, provide `ccc`, standing for three centered columns:

```
\begin{tabular}{ccc}
```

3. Write the table head row, add & to separate column entries, and add \\ to end rows. Use \hline to insert horizontal lines:

```
\hline
\head{Command} & \head{Declaration} & \head{Output}\\
\hline
```

4. Continue with the table body and end the environment and the document. To typeset LaTeX commands, write \verb|\command|:

```
\verb|\textrm| & \verb|\rmfamily| & \rmfamily Example
text\\
\verb|\textsf| & \verb|\sffamily| & \sffamily Example
text\\
\verb|\texttt| & \verb|\ttfamily| & \ttfamily Example
text\\
\hline
\end{tabular}
\end{document}
```

5. Click on **Typeset** on the document to see the table:

Command	Declaration	Output
\textrm	\rmfamily	Example text
\textsf	\sffamily	Example text
\texttt	\ttfamily	Example text

Figure 6.4 – A simple table

In *step 2*, in the mandatory argument, we wrote a list of characters. Each character stands for a formatting option. As we used three characters, we've got three columns. c stands for centered alignment. Therefore, the entries of all columns have been centered.

In *steps 3* and *4*, column entries are separated with &, while \\ terminates a row. Don't end the last line with \\ unless you further wish to write a line below. It's also a good idea to align the ampersands in our source code to keep it readable.

Inside the column entries, you may use ordinary text as well as LaTeX commands. As in the tabbing environment, declarations are local to the curly cell, like if curly braces surrounded each cell's content.

Furthermore, tabular has an optional alignment argument just like minipage. So, the complete definition is as follows:

```
\begin{tabular}[position]{column specifiers}
   row 1 col 1 entry & row 1 col 2 entry ... & row 1 col n
entry\\
   ...
\end{tabular}
```

In the optional [position] argument, t means alignment at the top row, and b means alignment at the bottom row. The default is vertically centered alignment, c. This optional argument may come in handy if you would like to place two tables next to each other or within other text.

We will learn how to customize tables in the following sections, such as adding lines, aligning to left, right, or center, and spanning cells over multiple columns or rows.

Drawing lines in tables

Within `tabular`, we can use three types of lines:

- `\hline` draws a horizontal line over the whole width of the table.

- `\cline{m-n}` draws a horizontal line starting at the beginning of column m and ending at the end of column n. That syntax is required; if this line is only for one particular column, for example, only column 3, you should still write `\cline{3-3}`.

- `\vline` draws a vertical line over the full height and depth of the current row.

We will use `\hline` in the following sections.

Understanding formatting arguments

Of course, further formatting is possible. Have a look at this example table, where we add l, c, r, and p as arguments:

```
\begin{tabular}{|l|c|r|p{1.7cm}|}
  \hline
  left & centered & right & a fully justified paragraph cell\\
  \hline
  l & c & r & p\\
  \hline
\end{tabular}
```

This code would produce the following table:

left	centered	right	a fully justified paragraph cell
l	c	r	p

Figure 6.5 – A table with different alignments

The options understood by the `tabular` environment are as follows:

- l for left alignment.

- c for centered alignment.

- r for right alignment.

- p{width} for a "paragraph" cell of a certain width. If you place several p cells next to each other, they will be aligned at their top line. It's equivalent to using \parbox[t]{width} within a cell.

- @{code} inserts code instead of empty space before or after a column. The code can also be some text, or it could be left empty to avoid this space, such as @{}.

- | stands for a vertical line.

- *{n}{options} is equivalent to n copies of options, where n is a positive integer and options may consist of one or more column specifiers, including * as well.

> **Tip**
> It is strongly advised to avoid vertical lines in tables. Lines should subtly support your information, but they should not make reading difficult.

After loading the array package with \usepackage{array}, you may use some options, such as the following:

- m{width} is similar to \parbox{width}: the baseline is in the middle.

- b{width} is like \parbox[b]{width}: the baseline is at the bottom.

- !{code} can be used like | but inserts code instead of a vertical line. In contrast to @{...}, the space between columns will not be suppressed.

- >{code} can be used before an l, c, r, p, m, or b option, and inserts code right at the beginning of each entry of that column.

- <{code} can be used after an l, c, r, p, m, or b option, and inserts code at the end of the entry of that column.

This example shows loading array and using the effect of @{} and the p, m, and b alignment arguments:

```
\documentclass{article}
\usepackage{array}
\begin{document}
\begin{tabular}{@{}lp{1.2cm}m{1.2cm}b{1.2cm}@{}}
  \hline
  baseline & aligned at the top & aligned at the middle
  & aligned at the bottom\\
  \hline
```

```
\end{tabular}
\end{document}
```

The output table is as follows:

			aligned
		aligned	at the
baseline	aligned	at the	bottom
	at the	middle	
	top		

Figure 6.6 – A table with different vertical alignments

Look at the last column of *Figure 6.6* – the text is not aligned to the bottom of the table cell since option b means that the baseline of the cell text shall be the bottom line. Baselines are vertically aligned to be at the same level. So, to align text where the baseline is its bottom line with the other baselines, it has to move up. You can consider baselines as anchor lines, and all anchors are at the same height.

Increasing the row height

You may have noticed that horizontal lines nearly touch the letters in the cells, especially capital letters. The array package introduces a length called \extrarowheight. If it has a positive value, this will be added to the height of every row of the table.

The next example, following the very first example of this chapter, shows how to extend the row height in the highlighted line. Additionally, it shows the effect of further array options, as follows:

```
\documentclass{article}
\usepackage{array}
\setlength{\extrarowheight}{4pt}
\begin{document}
\begin{tabular}{@{}>{\itshape}ll!{:}l<{.}@{}}
  \hline
  Info:     & Software & \LaTeX\\
  & Author   & Leslie Lamport\\
  & Website  & www.latex-project.org\\
  \hline
\end{tabular}
\end{document}
```

The output is as follows:

Info:	Software	:	LaTeX.
	Author	:	Leslie Lamport.
	Website	:	www.latex-project.org.

Figure 6.7 – A stretched table

Here, we used `>{\itshape}` to change the font of a row to italic. `>{}` is often used to insert an alignment declaration such as `\centering`. Still, there's a pitfall: such declarations might change the internal meaning of `\\`, which is a shortcut for `\tabularnewline` within tables. But the `array` package offers a command to repair it. In such cases, just add `\arraybackslash`, as in the following example:

```
\begin{tabular}{>{\centering\arraybackslash}p{5cm}}
```

Otherwise, the content of paragraph cells stated by p, m, or b will be fully justified.

After a specific row, you can add vertical space with the optional argument of `\\`, such as `\\[10pt]`.

You may even stretch a whole table: the `\arraystretch` command contains a stretching factor with a default value of 1. Just redefine it. For example, `\renewcommand{\arraystretch}{1.5}` will increase the height of the rows by 50 percent. You could use it inside a group or an environment to keep the effect local.

Beautifying tables

Our tables still don't look as perfect as they look in good books. Particularly, the lines and their distances to the text might need improvement. The `booktabs` package comes to the rescue. After loading it, you can enhance the quality of your tables with new line commands replacing `\hline` and `\cline`.

We shall use the new commands introduced by `booktabs` with the help of the following steps:

1. In our previous example for *Figure 6.4*, load the `booktabs` package:

    ```
    \usepackage{booktabs}
    ```

2. Use `\toprule`, `\midrule`, and `\bottomrule` instead of `\hline`. Specify the thickness as an optional argument. The table becomes the following:

    ```
    \begin{tabular}{ccc}
        \toprule[1.5pt]
    ```

```
    \head{Command} & \head{Declaration} & \head{Output}\\
    \midrule
    \verb|\textrm| & \verb|\rmfamily| & \rmfamily Example
text\\
    \verb|\textsf| & \verb|\sffamily| & \sffamily Example
text\\
    \verb|\texttt| & \verb|\ttfamily| & \ttfamily Example
text\\
    \bottomrule[1.5pt]
\end{tabular}
```

3. Compile to see the difference:

Command	Declaration	Output
\textrm	\rmfamily	Example text
\textsf	\sffamily	Example text
\texttt	\ttfamily	Example text

Figure 6.8 – A stretched table

British typesetters call a line a rule. The booktabs developer chose this terminology for the new commands. These are their definitions:

-   \toprule[thickness] may be used to draw a horizontal line at the top of the table. If desired, a thickness may be specified, such as 1pt or 0.5mm.

-   \midrule[thickness] draws a horizontal dividing line between rows of a table.

-   \bottomrule[thickness] draws a horizontal line to finish off a table.

-   \cmidrule[thickness](trim){m-n} draws a horizontal line from column m to column n. (trim) is optional, like thickness. It could be (l) or (r) to trim the line at its left or right end. Write (lr) to trim at both ends. Even adding {width}, such as in (l{10pt}), is possible and specifies the trim width.

The booktabs package does not define vertical rules or lines. They are not advised anyway. The same applies to double rules. Neither vertical nor double lines are recommended. They are even widely considered to be bad typographic styles.

Consider using \toprule and the other line commands without optional arguments –
let's figure out how.

Adjusting lengths

We briefly introduced the \setlength command in the *Increasing the row height*
section of this chapter. Instead of specifying a line thickness with an optional argument to
\toprule, \midrule, \cmidrule, or \bottomrule, always omit it. Instead, set it
once for your whole document with \setlength in the preamble.

So, for example, after \usepackage{booktabs}, you can write the following:

```
\setlength{\heavyrulewidth}{1.5pt}
```

Now just use \toprule and \bottomrule without an argument, and they will always
be 1.5pt thick.

These are the lengths for the booktabs package that we can adjust:

- \heavyrulewidth for the thickness of the top and bottom lines.
- \lightrulewidth for the thickness of the middle lines with \midrule.
- \cmidrulewidth for the thickness of \cmidrule.
- \cmidrulekern for the trimming in \cmidrule.
- \abovetopsep is the space above the top rule; the default is 0pt.
- \belowbottomsep is the space below the bottom rule; the default is 0pt.
- \aboverulesep specifies the space above \midrule, \cmidrule, and
  \bottomrule.
- \belowrulesep is for the space below \midrule, \cmidrule, and
  \toprule.

Try to change the thickness of the lines. The lengths already have reasonable values, but
you may change them. So, the adjustment in your preamble would apply to all tables in
your document.

Spanning entries over multiple columns

We can group columns concerning the same subject by a common header. In such a case, we should merge two cells in the header. The \multicolumn command does this for us.

Regarding our example table, commands and declarations are both inputs, whereas the remaining column contains output. We shall emphasize that in our header as follows:

1. In our previous example, insert another header row. Use *{3}l to get three left-aligned columns. Put @{} before and after to remove inter-column space. Use \multicolumn to merge cells. Alter the column formatting argument and the middle rule. The changes are highlighted here:

```
\begin{tabular}{@{}*{3}l@{}}
    \toprule[1.5pt]
    \multicolumn{2}{c}{\head{Input}} &
    \multicolumn{1}{c}{\head{Output}}\\
    \head{Command} & \head{Declaration} & \\
    \cmidrule(r){1-2}\cmidrule(l){3-3}
    \verb|\textrm| & \verb|\rmfamily| & \rmfamily Example
text\\
    \verb|\textsf| & \verb|\sffamily| & \sffamily Example
text\\
    \verb|\texttt| & \verb|\ttfamily| & \ttfamily Example
text\\
    \bottomrule[1.5pt]
\end{tabular}
```

2. Compile and see the output:

Input		Output
Command	Declaration	
\textrm	\rmfamily	Example text
\textsf	\sffamily	Example text
\texttt	\ttfamily	Example text

Figure 6.9 – A table with merged cells

We used the \multicolumn command twice – once to merge two cells, and surprisingly, another time just for one cell. Let's first look at its definition:

```
\multicolumn{number of columns}{formatting options}{entry text}
```

The number of columns to be spanned may be a positive integer or just 1. The formatting options will be applied instead of the options specified in the tabular definition for this cell.

We took advantage of this when we used \multicolumn{1}{c}{...}, overriding the l option of the column with a c option to get just this cell centered.

The other change we made concerns \cmidrule. We used it instead of \midrule, together with the trimming argument, to get a gap between the input and the output column.

Inserting code column-wise

There are many more font commands that we would like to add to the table. Writing \verb|...| in each cell is tiresome. We shall exploit the >{...} feature of the array package to define the formatting of the entries once for the column.

We will modify the table definition to set our input columns in the typewriter font. At the same time, we will insert a column on the left, standing for our command type:

1. Extend the preamble of our example by defining a \normal command. It shall use \multicolumn to produce an l cell, no matter what the column formatting is:

    ```
    \documentclass{article}
    \usepackage{array}
    \usepackage{booktabs}
    \newcommand{\head}[1]{\textnormal{\textbf{#1}}}
    \newcommand{\normal}[1]{\multicolumn{1}{l}{#1}}
    \begin{document}
    ```

2. As \verb cannot be used in table headers, we shall use \ttfamily to get the typewriter font. We add \textbackslash so we won't repeat the long command phrase within the cells. Use *{2}>{...} to insert it twice. Then, add <{Example text} to the last column to save typing work:

    ```
    \begin{tabular}{@{}l*{2}{>{\ttfamily\textbackslash }l}l%
      <{Example text}@{}}
    \toprule[1.5pt]
    & \multicolumn{2}{c}{\head{Input}} &
    \multicolumn{1}{c}{\head{Output}}\\
    ```

3. We'll use the `\normal` command to avoid the typewriter formatting in the header:

```
& \normal{\head{Command}} & \normal{\head{Declaration}}
& \normal{}\\
\cmidrule(lr){2-3}\cmidrule(l){4-4}
```

4. Now we may continue listing the font command names:

```
Family & textrm & rmfamily & \rmfamily\\
       & textsf & sffamily & \sffamily\\
       & texttt & ttfamily & \ttfamily\\
\bottomrule[1.5pt]
\end{tabular}
\end{document}
```

5. Compile, and look at the result:

	Input		Output
	Command	Declaration	
Family	\textrm	\rmfamily	Example text
	\textsf	\sffamily	Example text
	\texttt	\ttfamily	Example text

Figure 6.10 – A table with column formatting commands

Using `>{\textbackslash\ttfamily}l` defines a left-aligned row, where each entry is preceded by a backslash and is switched to typewriter font. We wrote `*{2}{...}` to define two columns of this style. Because the example text has been inserted according to our table definition with `<{...}`, we just had to put the declarations into the last column without the text.

Spanning entries over multiple rows

We already know how to span text over several columns. But what if the text should cross over several rows? LaTeX doesn't define a command for this. However, the `multirow` package does. Let's now merge cells using the `multirow` package.

Before we complement the font table, we want to center the word "Family" vertically, that is, span this cell over three rows. This is how we do it:

1. In our previous example, additionally load the `multirow` package:

    ```
    \usepackage{multirow}
    ```

2. Replace the word `Family` with `\multirow{3}{*}{Family}`:

    ```
    \multirow{3}{*}{Family} & textrm & rmfamily & \rmfamily\\
    ```

3. Compile to see the small change:

	Input		Output
	Command	**Declaration**	
	\textrm	\rmfamily	Example text
Family	\textsf	\sffamily	Example text
	\texttt	\ttfamily	Example text

Figure 6.11 – Vertically merged cells

We used the `\multirow` command to span three rows. Its definition is as follows:

```
\multirow{number of rows}{width}{entry text}
```

The entry will span that `number of rows` from the row on which `\multirow` is used. If the number is negative, it will span the rows above.

You can specify a width or just write * for the natural width. If you set a width, LaTeX would wrap the text accordingly.

`multirow` understands further optional arguments for fine-tuning. The documentation at `https://texdoc.org/pkg/multirow` describes this.

Now that we know how to create tables, let's see how to add caption text.

Adding captions to tables

Especially with longer text, we would like to add captions and numbers to our tables. Numbering the tables allows easy referencing, whereas captions add information and tell the reader what the table is about. LaTeX has built-in features to achieve that.

Now it's time to complete our table. We shall list the remaining font commands. We'll use the first column to describe the category of the font commands: family, weight, shape, and so on. Then, we will add another column to show the effect of combining font commands.

To finish, we shall center the table and provide a number and a caption. To do that, we will put a `table` environment around our example table, use `\centering` inside it, and insert a `\caption` command at the end of the `table` environment. We will add more font commands and add another column at the right, containing more examples. Let's break it down into the following steps:

1. Start with the document's `article` class, and load the `array`, `booktabs`, and `multirow` packages:

    ```
    \documentclass{article}
    \usepackage{array}
    \usepackage{booktabs}
    \usepackage{multirow}
    ```

2. Define a macro for formatting the header cells and a macro for normal cells, which we want to be left-aligned:

    ```
    \newcommand{\head}[1]{\textnormal{\textbf{#1}}}
    \newcommand{\normal}[1]{\multicolumn{1}{l}{#1}}
    ```

3. Begin the document:

    ```
    \begin{document}
    ```

4. Now, we will create the table, center the content, and write up all the rows:

    ```
    \begin{table}
      \centering
      \begin{tabular}{@{}l*{2}{>{\textbackslash\ttfamily}l%
        l<{Example text}l@{}}
        \toprule[1.5pt]
        & \multicolumn{2}{c}{\head{Input}}
        & \multicolumn{2}{c}{\head{Output}}\\
        & \normal{\head{Command}}
        & \normal{\head{Declaration}}
        & \normal{\head{Single use}} & \head{Combined}\\
        \cmidrule(lr){2-3}\cmidrule(l){4-5}
        \multirow{3}{*}{Family} & textrm & rmfamily
        & \rmfamily & \\
        & textsf & sffamily & \sffamily& \\
        & texttt & ttfamily & \ttfamily& \\
    ```

```
    \cmidrule(lr){2-3}\cmidrule(lr){4-4}
    \multirow{2}{1.1cm}{Weight} & textbf & bfseries
    & \bfseries
    & \multirow{2}{1.8cm}{\sffamily\bfseries Bold and
      sans-serif}\\
    & textmd & mdseries & \mdseries & \\
    \cmidrule(lr){2-3}\cmidrule(lr){4-4}
    \multirow{4}{*}{Shape} & textit & itshape
    & \itshape & \\
    & textsl & slshape & \slshape &
    \multirow{2}{1.8cm}{\sffamily\slshape Slanted and
      sans-serif}\\
    & textsc & scshape & \scshape & \\
    & textup & upshape & \upshape  & \\
    \cmidrule(lr){2-3}\cmidrule(lr){4-4}
    Default & textnormal & normalfont & \normalfont & \\
    \bottomrule[1.5pt]
  \end{tabular}
  \caption{\LaTeX\ font selection}
\end{table}
```

5. End the document:

```
\end{document}
```

6. Compile, and our table is now ready:

| | Input | | Output | |
	Command	Declaration	Single use	Combined
Family	\textrm	\rmfamily	Example text	
	\textsf	\sffamily	Example text	
	\texttt	\ttfamily	Example text	
Weight	\textbf	\bfseries	**Example text**	**Bold and**
	\textmd	\mdseries	Example text	**sans-serif**
Shape	\textit	\itshape	*Example text*	
	\textsl	\slshape	*Example text*	*Slanted and*
	\textsc	\scshape	EXAMPLE TEXT	*sans-serif*
	\textup	\upshape	Example text	
Default	\textnormal	\normalfont	Example text	

Table 1: LaTeX font selection

Figure 6.12 – A table with a caption

We put the `tabular` environment in a `table` environment. It's used in this way together with the `\caption` command:

```
\begin{table}[placement options]
   table body
   \caption{table title}
\end{table}
```

The `table` environment is a floating environment, just like the `figure` environment that we saw in *Chapter 5, Including Images*. Unlike normal text, they might appear somewhere else other than what is defined by their position in the source code. The optional `placement` argument determines where the table might appear. However, LaTeX will position a table within the text to achieve good page breaks without too much empty space at the end of a page. We discussed floating environments in the previous chapter when we talked about the placement of graphics, and the same applies here, with the same `placement` arguments. Like with figures, `\begin{table}[htbp!]` is the most flexible choice.

`\caption` understands an optional argument as well. If you write `\caption[short text]{long text}`, then the short text will appear in a list of tables and long text in the document body. That's useful if you need very long descriptive captions.

Tables are automatically numbered. Let's talk about positioning and formatting in the following two sections.

Placing captions above

In typesetting, it's very common to place captions above tables instead of below. We can achieve this by writing `\caption` before the table body. However, LaTeX expects the caption to always be below, resulting in a cramped look to the table. There'll be too little space between the caption and the following table. So, you might wish to add some space, for instance, by entering `\vspace{10pt}` directly after a top caption.

Remember the `booktabs` package? If you begin tables with `\toprule`, just specify the `\abovetopskip` length, as in the following example:

```
\setlength{\abovetopsep}{10pt}
```

By putting this line into your preamble, `10pt` space would be added below the caption and above the top line of the table.

Customizing captions

By default, captions look like normal body text; there's no visual difference. Would you like to have a slight change in font size, different formatting of the label, some margins or indentation, or any other customization? The `caption` package is the answer to most needs.

By using a few options, you could enhance the visual appearance of all of your captions. Try the following:

```
\usepackage[font=small,labelfont=bf,margin=1cm]{caption}
```

This way, your captions will be smaller than normal text, the label with the number will be bold, and it will not be as wide as normal text. The package offers a lot of features, both for document-wide settings and fine-tuning. It's very well documented. So, have a look at its documentation. Either visit `https://texdoc.org/pkg/caption` or type `texdoc caption` at the command line.

There are various packages for table layout and appearance. In the next section, we will get to know such packages.

Using packages for further customizations

When typesetting tables, we may encounter further challenges. For example, we may need column width adjustment, page breaks within a table, color, to rotate a table, and get a specific alignment. In the following sections, we will have a look at additional packages for such purposes.

You can find example tables and links to the documentation at `https://latexguide.org/tables` for each of the following sections.

Auto-fitting columns to the table width

`l`, `c`, and `r` columns have the width of their content. For `p` columns, you specify the width. This way, it's hard to find out the actual width of the table. Wouldn't it be a good idea to specify the table width and let LaTeX decide how wide the columns may be? The `tabularx` package allows that. Using it looks as follows:

```
\usepackage{tabularx}
...
\begin{tabularx}{width}{column specifiers}
  ...
\end{tabularx}
```

The new `tabularx` environment requires an additional argument: the `width` of the table. It introduces a new column type, `X`. It behaves like `p` columns, but `X` columns use all available space. One `X` column would take all of the available space. If you use several `X` columns, they will share the space equally. So, you could write, for instance, the following:

```
\begin{tabularx}{0.6\textwidth}{lcX}
```

This way, you would get a table occupying 60 percent of the text width – a left-aligned and a centered column as wide as their content, and a paragraph column as wide as possible until 60 percent is reached.

Though it's easy to use, the `tabularx` documentation gives further examples, informs us about the derived types, and gives advice such as this: don't let `\multicolumn` entries cross any X column. Read the documentation at `https://texdoc.org/pkg/tabularx` or by typing `texdoc tabularx` at the command line.

There are two similar approaches:

- LaTeX provides a starred version of the `tabular` environment:

```
\begin{tabular*}{width}[position]{column specifiers}
```

The table adjusts to `width` by modifying the inter-column space. `tabularx` has been developed to satisfy this need in a more useful way.

- The `tabulary` package provides another sophisticated `tabular` environment taking the total width. It weights each column width according to the natural width of the widest cell in the column.

The `tabularx` package is an excellent choice for adjusting the table width to the text width.

Generating multi-page tables

All the `tabular` environments that we've got to know until now cannot cross page boundaries. The `tabbing` environment is an exception due to its different nature.

As tables might contain a lot of data, we need a solution. There are several packages:

- `longtable` provides an environment with the same name that's like a multi-page version of `tabular`. It provides commands to set table captions, continued captions, and special headers and footers when a page break occurs. It's probably the easiest way for multi-page tables and therefore it's the most popular. The package documentation describes all you need. In combination with the `booktabs` package, you will get excellent results. This is the most commonly used package.

- `ltxtable` provides a combination of `longtable` and `tabularx`.

- `ltablex` is another approach to combine the features of `longtable` and `tabularx`.

- `supertabular` offers another multi-page extension of the internally used `tabular` environment, providing optional table tails and heads where page breaks occur. It's recommended for two-column documents.

- `xtab` extends `supertabular`, and reduces some of its weaknesses.

- `stabular` implements a simple way to use page breaks in `tabular` without much fuss.

Next, let's see how to add color to our tables.

Coloring tables

We haven't even colored text yet, as this usually isn't what we do first with LaTeX. But of course, we can do this with text as well as with tables. For coloring text, use the `color` package or, better, use the `xcolor` extension. To color tables, use the `colortbl` package. We can combine all this by using the following:

```
\usepackage[table]{xcolor}
```

The package allows coloring columns, rows, single entries, and lines in many ways. The package documentation can tell you more.

Using landscape orientation

We can typeset very wide tables in landscape orientation. The `rotating` package offers an environment called `sidewaystable` that you could use instead of the `table` environment.

Both the table and caption would be rotated +/-90 degrees and placed on a separate page. The package provides further rotation-related environments and commands.

Aligning columns at the decimal point

Columns containing numbers are more readable when the entries are aligned at the decimal marker and perhaps at an exponent. Several packages support this:

- `siunitx` is primarily intended for typesetting values with units in a consistent way, according to scientific conventions. However, it provides a tabular column type for such decimal alignment of numbers.

- `dcolumn` offers a column type for aligning at a comma, a period, or another single character.

- `rccol` defines a column type where numbers are "right-centered," that is, they are centered concerning other entries but flushed right to each other. This way, corresponding digits are aligned along the column.

In contrast to `dcolumn` and `rccol`, the `siunitx` package is newer and very powerful.

Handling narrow columns

Text in very narrow columns might require special attention because justification is difficult if there's little space. Here's some advice:

- Have a look at the correct hyphenation. If necessary, improve it as we did in *Chapter 2, Formatting Text and Creating Macros*. TeX doesn't hyphenate the first word of a line, a box, or a table entry. So, a long word may cross the column boundary. To enable hyphenation, insert an empty word: write `\hspace{0pt}` directly at the beginning.

- Load `microtype` to improve justification. It shows the best effect in narrow columns.

- Full justification in p columns and the like may look bad because of big gaps. Consider using `>{\raggedright\arraybackslash}` for such columns.

- From the `ragged2e` package, using the `\RaggedRight` command can do even better and doesn't need `\arraybackslash`.

Use those suggestions to avoid big gaps between words.

Summary

In this chapter, we have learned how to create tables. Specifically, we dealt with putting text into columns, adding captions to tables, spanning columns and rows, using packages to auto-fit columns, and creating colored, landscape, and even multi-page tables.

We can open the documentation of every mentioned package by running `texdoc packagename` at the command line or by visiting `https://texdoc.org/pkg/packagename`.

LaTeX can generate a list of tables like a table of contents. We will deal with such lists in *Chapter 8, Listing Contents and References*.

Similar to figures, LaTeX numbers our tables automatically. We can use these numbers to reference the tables. *Chapter 7, Using Cross-References*, is dedicated to referencing, so we will turn to it now.

7
Using Cross-References

Our documents contain many numbered things, such as pages, sections, list items, figures, and tables. There's even more that we have not listed yet; for instance, if you would like to write mathematical text, you may use number equations, theorems, definitions, and many more.

We number things not just to count them but also to refer to them in other places of our document. For instance, in this chapter, if I wanted to point you towards the third figure, I would say "see Figure 7.3". LaTeX automatically enumerates figures for you. If you insert another figure, LaTeX will automatically adjust the numbering of all figures after it. But what happens with the references? Well, LaTeX can take care of all of our cross-references, which is the subject of this chapter.

In this chapter, we shall learn about the following:

- Setting labels and references
- Using advanced referencing
- Referring to labels in other documents
- Turning references into hyperlinks

Let's figure out how to do all this in the following sections.

Technical requirements

You can use a local LaTeX installation, or you can compile the example code online at `https://latexguide.org/chapter-07`.

The code is also available on GitHub: `https://github.com/PacktPublishing/ LaTeX-Beginner-s-Guide-2nd-Edition-/tree/main/Chapter_07_-_ Using_Cross-References`.

In this chapter, we will use the `cleveref` package and the `varioref` package.

We will also get to know the `fancyref`, `hyperref`, and `xr` packages.

Setting labels and references

To be able to refer to a certain point, we have to mark it with a label. The name of that label will serve us afterward for referencing.

We will now typeset a list of the most used packages for papers, according to a survey on `https://latex.org`. Through the `\label` command, we will mark items that we can later refer to with the `\ref` command, as shown here:

1. Create a new book document:

    ```
    \documentclass{book}
    \begin{document}
    ```

2. Start a chapter and a section, and place a label for this section:

    ```
    \chapter{Statistics}
    \section{Most used packages by LaTeX.org users}
    \label{sec:packages}
    ```

3. Continue with some text, including a footnote:

    ```
    The Top Five packages, used by LaTeX.org
    members\footnote{according to the 2021 survey on
    LaTeX.org\label{fn:project}}:
    ```

4. Write an enumerated list and put a label on a few items for referring to them:

    ```
    \begin{enumerate}
        \item graphicx\label{item:graphicx}
        \item babel
    ```

```
\item amsmath\label{item:amsmath}
\item geometry
\item hyperref
\end{enumerate}
```

5. Let's have another chapter with a label:

```
\chapter{Mathematics}
\label{maths}
```

6. Finish with some text, including references:

```
\emph{amsmath}, on position \ref{item:amsmath}
of the top list in section~\ref{sec:packages} on
page~\pageref{sec:packages}, is indispensable to
high-quality mathematical typesetting in \LaTeX.
\emph{graphicx}, on position \ref{item:graphicx},
is for including images. See also the footnote
\ref{fn:project} on page~\pageref{fn:project}.
\end{document}
```

7. Click on **Typeset** and have a look at the output. Page 1 starts with headings and a bullet list.

Chapter 1

Statistics

1.1   Most used packages by LaTeX.org users

The Top Five packages, used by LaTeX.org members[1]:

1. graphicx

2. babel

3. amsmath

4. geometry

5. hyperref

Figure 7.1 – First chapter

Page 1 ends with a footnote:

---

[1]according to the 2021 survey on LaTeX.org

Figure 7.2 – Footnote

Page 2 is empty since **Chapter 2** starts on a right-hand page, which is page 3:

Chapter 2

Mathematics

amsmath, on position **??** of the top list in section **??** on page **??**, is indispensable to high-quality mathematical typesetting in LaTeX. *graphicx*, on position **??**, is for including images. See also the footnote **??** on page **??**.

Figure 7.3 – Unresolved references

8. Do you see the question marks? The references are still missing. Compile again and compare the differences:

Chapter 2

Mathematics

amsmath, on position 3 of the top list in section 1.1 on page 1, is indispensable to high-quality mathematical typesetting in LaTeX. *graphicx*, on position 1, is for including images. See also the footnote 1 on page 1.

Figure 7.4 – Resolved references

We created cross-references with just three commands:

- `\label` marks the position.
- `\ref` prints the number of the element we refer to.
- `\pageref` prints the page number of that element.

Each command takes the name of the element as an argument. We can choose any name.

We had to compile twice because LaTeX needs one run to produce the references that LaTeX can read during the next compiler run. If LaTeX cannot resolve a reference, it prints two question marks instead.

Let's have a closer look at creating an anchor label and how to refer to it.

Assigning a label

The \label{name} command assigns the current position to the name label. Precisely, it does the following:

- If the \label command appears in ordinary text, the current sectional unit would be assigned, such as the chapter or the section.

- If the \label command is placed within a numbered environment, that environment would be assigned to the label.

So, we cannot label a section within a table environment. To avoid any problems because of possible unsuitable positioning, a good rule of thumb is to place the \label command right after the position that we would like to refer to. For instance, place it directly after the corresponding \chapter or after \section.

In the figure or table environments, \caption is responsible for the numbering. That's why \label has to be placed after \caption, not before.

Therefore, typical floating environments look like the following:

```
\begin{figure}[htbp!]
\centering
\includegraphics{filename}
\caption{Test figure}\label{fig:name}
\end{figure}
```

Or, we could do the following in the case of a table:

```
\begin{table}[htbp!]
\centering
\caption{table descripion}\label{tab:name}
\begin{tabular}{cc}
...
\end{tabular}
\end{table}
```

A label name may consist of letters, digits, or punctuation characters. Also, label names are case-sensitive.

If you write larger documents, the number of labels could become very high. Imagine a section dealing with fonts and a font table – how do we distinguish their labels? We could prefix them with the type of environment. It has become common practice to label figures with `fig:name`, tables with `tab:name`, sections with `sec:name`, with similar approaches in other cases.

In the following sections, we will see several ways to refer to labels.

Referring to a label

Once we set a label and give it a name, we may refer to that name. For this, we use `\ref{name}`. This command prints the number that belongs to `name`. We can even use it before the corresponding `\label` command appears in our code.

Even though it's that simple, it's powerful. Each time we compile a document, LaTeX checks the labels and reassigns the numbers, responding to all changes. If LaTeX notices that labels have been changed, it would inform you that a second compiler run is required to update the corresponding labels. If in doubt, compile twice.

Referring to a page

The `\pageref{name}` command works analogous to `\ref`, except that it prints the corresponding page number.

Would all the references stay correct if we changed the section and page numbers? Let's put it to the test! Insert a dummy section and a page break at the beginning of our chapter, highlighted here:

```
\chapter{Statistics}
\section{Introduction}
```

```
\newpage
\section{Most used packages by LaTeX.org users}
\label{sec:packages}
```

Click on **Typeset** once. LaTeX will compile it, but it will show a message:

LaTeX Warning: Label(s) may have changed. Rerun to get cross-references right.

That's what we shall do! **Typeset** a second time, and now all the numbers have been correctly adjusted to **section 1.2** and **page 2**:

> *amsmath*, on position 3 of the top list in section 1.2 on page 2, is indispensable to high-quality mathematical typesetting in LaTeX. *graphicx*, on position 1, is for including images. See also the footnote 1 on page 2.

Figure 7.5 – Automatically adjusted references

Using a reference, together with the page number reference, you may write the following:

```
See figure~\ref{fig:name} on page~\pageref{fig:name}.
```

As you know how to define a command, you could make such referencing easier:

```
\newcommand{\fullref}[1]{\ref{#1} on page~\pageref{#1}}
...
See figure~\fullref{fig:name}.
```

This way, you would get a complete reference such as *See Figure 4.2 on page 32*. However, if the reference, such as for a figure, appears on the same page, writing out the page number looks a bit odd. How can we avoid that? The `varioref` package provides a way. We will focus on advanced referencing such as this in the following sections.

Using advanced referencing

LaTeX helps with automating all kinds of references. It's not only limited to numbering. LaTeX can even automate naming and phrasing. We will dig deeper into that here.

Producing intelligent page references

The `varioref` package offers a command to add *on the preceding page, on the following page*, or the page number to a reference, depending on the context.

We will use the `varioref` commands to introduce variable references, `\vref`, and `\vpageref`, to achieve enhanced reference texts:

1. Open our current example from the *Setting labels and references* section. Add the `varioref` package to your preamble. Use the `nospace` package option, which ensures that `varioref` doesn't insert additional undesirable space before or after a reference:

```
\usepackage[nospace]{varioref}
```

2. Edit the content of the second chapter in our example code:

```
\emph{amsmath}, on position \vref{item:amsmath}
of the top list in section~\vref{sec:packages},
is indispensable to high-quality mathematical
typesetting in \LaTeX. \emph{graphicx}, on position
\vref{item:graphicx}, is for including images.
See also the footnote \vref{fn:project}, that is,
\vpageref{fn:project}.
```

3. Compile twice and look at the result:

amsmath, on position 3 on the facing page of the top list in section 1.2 on the preceding page, is indispensable to high-quality mathematical typesetting in LᴬTᴇX. *graphicx*, on position 1 on the facing page, is for including images. See also the footnote 1 on the preceding page, that is, on the facing page.

Figure 7.6 – An image at the bottom of the page

The `\vref` command checked the distance from the label of the referenced section. As the label is on the facing page (here, on the preceding page in a two-sided layout), `\vref` wrote **1.2 on the preceding page**.

`\vpageref` refers to **the facing page** at the end of the paragraph.

`\vref{name}` acts in the following way:

- If the reference and `\label{name}` are on the same page, it behaves exactly like `\ref`. The page number will not be printed.
- If the reference and the corresponding `\label` are on two successive pages, `\vref` prints the referred number and additionally *on the preceding page, on the following page,* or *on the facing page*. It will choose the latter if the document is two-sided, that is, if `\label` and the reference fall onto a double-page spread.
- Otherwise, it will print both `\ref` and `\pageref`.

`\vpageref` is equivalent to `\pageref` but behaves like `\vref` concerning the page reference.

`varioref` switches between phrasings to have a bit of variation. It can say *following page* or *next page*, *preceding page* or *previous page*, *this page* or *current page*. And in a double-page layout, it switches between *facing page* and *preceding page* or *next page*. With such variation, the text reads more naturally. You can see this alternating phrasing in *Figure 7.6*.

Even though `varioref` defines new commands, you may still use the standard `\ref` and `\pageref` commands.

Fine-tuning page references

If the label and reference are very close to each other, they would probably fall on the same page, but not necessarily. In such cases, we usually know if the label comes before or after the reference. `varioref` allows specifying an optional argument to `\vpageref`, as we can see here:

```
see the figure \vpageref[above]{fig:name}
```

This will print the following:

- *see the figure above*, if the figure is on the same page
- *see the figure on the page before*, if the figure is on the preceding page

Whereas with the following code, we will have a different output:

```
see the footnote \vpageref[below]{fn:name}
```

This will print the following:

- *see the footnote below*, if the footnote is on the same page
- *see the footnote on the following page*, if the footnote is on the next page

`\vpageref` understands two optional arguments. While in the first optional argument we can state a phrase if the label and reference fall on the same page, in the second optional argument, we can give a phrase for the case when the label and reference fall on different pages. So, we could even write the following:

```
see the \vpageref[above figure][figure]{fig:name}
```

This would print the following:

- *see the above figure*, if the figure is on the same page

- *see the figure on the previous page*, if the figure is on the preceding page

Sounds complicated? Well, your demands might increase over time, requiring more sophisticated features so that these features might come in handy someday.

Referring to page ranges

`varioref` offers two more commands:

- `\vpagerefrange[opt]{label1}{label2}`, where `label1` and `label2` denote a range (such as a sequence of figures from `fig:a` to `fig:c`). If both labels fall on the same page, the result is the same as with `\vpageref`. Otherwise, the output will be a range, such as *on pages 32-36*. `opt` would be used if both labels fall on the current page.

- `\vrefrange[opt]{label1}{label2}` is analogous to `\vref`: see figures `\vrefrange{fig:a}{fig:c}` may result in *see figures 4.2 to 4.4 on pages 36-37*.

Visit `https://latexguide.org/chapter-07` to see examples.

You can find more information regarding customization in the package manual. As usual, you can open it at the command prompt by typing `texdoc varioref` or by visiting `https://texdoc.org/pkg/varioref`.

Using automatic reference names

Tired of writing `figure~\ref{fig:name}` and `table~\ref{tab:name}` again and again? Wouldn't it be great if LaTeX knew what type is meant by `\ref{name}` and would automatically write the type name and number? What if we want to abbreviate, say, `fig.~\ref{fig:name}` in the whole document? The `cleverev` package eases the work. It automatically determines the type of cross-reference and the context in which it is used.

You could use `\cref` or `\Cref` instead of `\ref`; choose the latter if you wish to capitalize. The corresponding range commands are `\crefrange` and `\Crefrange`.

We shall rewrite our first example to refer using `cleveref`. To verify that the package acts well, we intentionally omit prefixes in the label names for `\label` and `\cref`, as shown here:

1. Modify our first example of this chapter in the following way. The modified lines are highlighted:

```
\documentclass{book}
\usepackage{cleveref}
\crefname{enumi}{position}{positions}
\begin{document}
\chapter{Statistics}
\label{stats}
\section{Most used packages by LaTeX.org users}
\label{packages}
The Top Five packages, used by LaTeX.org
members\footnote{according to the 2021 survey on
LaTeX.org\label{project}}:
\begin{enumerate}
  \item graphicx\label{graphicx}
  \item babel
  \item amsmath\label{amsmath}
  \item geometry
  \item hyperref
\end{enumerate}
\chapter{Mathematics}
\label{maths}
\emph{amsmath}, on \cref{amsmath} of the top list in
\cref{packages} of \cref{stats}, is indispensable to
high-quality mathematical typesetting in \LaTeX.
\emph{graphicx}, on \cref{graphicx}, is for
including images.
See also the \cref{project} on \cpageref{project}.
\end{document}
```

2. Click on **Typeset** twice, and check that references have the correct names:

amsmath, on position 3 of the top list in section 1.1 of chapter 1, is indispensable to high-quality mathematical typesetting in LaTeX. *graphicx*, on position 1, is for including images. See also the footnote 1 on page 1.

Figure 7.7 – Automated references

As we can see, we didn't need to specify which object we refer to. \cref always chooses the right name and the correct number for us. That's really useful.

We used the \crefname command to tell cleveref which name it should use for enumerated items. The definition of \crefname is as follows:

```
\crefname{type}{singular}{plural}
```

type may be one of chapter, section, figure, table, enumi, equation, theorem, or many other types we have not encountered yet. cleveref uses the singular version for single references and the plural version for multiple. If you need capitalized versions, use \Crefname. So, a typical use may be the following:

```
\crefname{figure}{fig.}{figs.}
\Crefname{figure}{Fig.}{Figs.}
```

Also, here, we can refer to ranges using these commands:

- \crefrange{label1}{label2} to refer to a range of references
- \cpagerefrange{label1}{label2} to refer to a page range

It will get clearer with an example. Let's add this line to our current example:

```
See \crefrange{graphicx}{amsmath} and \cpagerefrange{stats}
{maths}.
```

This gives us: *See positions 1 to 3 and pages 1 to 3.*

We can sum up the benefits as follows:

- We save a lot of typing.
- We could use arbitrary labels. The fancyref package does a similar job but relies on prefixes such as chap, fig, and tab.
- If we decide to change wordings, it could be done quickly by doing this once in the preamble, having the desired effect in the whole document.

However, it's recommended to use a prefix such as `fig:` or `sec:` to distinguish the kind of referenced object. This way, your code would become more understandable – that's why it's common practice.

Combining intelligent references with automatic naming

As `cleveref` fully supports `varioref`, you may use both to get the most out of them. `cleveref` redefines the commands of `varioref` to use `\cref` internally. So, you could use the good page referencing features of `varioref` together with the clever naming automation.

Just load `varioref` before `cleveref`, as shown here:

```
\usepackage{varioref}
\usepackage{cleveref}
```

Now, you may use `\vref`, `\cref`, `\ref`, or the other commands – whichever seems appropriate.

While `varioref` is helpful for referencing within a document, we can also use references to pages, sections, and so on in other documents. Let's take a closer look at this.

Referring to labels in other documents

If you write several related documents that refer to each other, you might want to use references to labels of another document. The package with the name `xr` (standing for external references) implements this. First, load the `xr` package:

```
\usepackage{xr}
```

If you need to refer to sections or environments in an external document, say, `doc.tex`, insert this command into your preamble:

```
\externaldocument{doc}
```

This enables you to additionally refer to anything that has been given a label in `doc. tex`. You may do this for several documents. If you need to avoid conflicts when an external document uses the same `\label` as the main document, declare a prefix using the optional argument of `\externaldocument`, which you can use to add a prefix. For example, we can use `D-` as a prefix:

```
\externaldocument[D-]{doc}
```

This way, all references from `doc.tex` would be prefixed by `D-`, and you could write `\ref{D-name}` to refer to `name` in `doc.tex`. Instead of `D-`, you may choose any prefix that transforms your labels such that they become unique.

In the next section, we will see how we can make references active, meaning clickable, so that a click will lead the reader to the labeled object.

Turning references into hyperlinks

PDF documents offer bookmarks and hyperlink capabilities. How about exploring that? There's an outstanding package that offers hyperlink support – the `hyperref` package.

Try it by loading `hyperref` right before `cleveref`. This order is essential for the references to work because `cleveref` detects whether `hyperref` has been loaded and makes the references to hyperlinks. Even without any options or commands, your document will be hyperlinked as much as possible because of the following:

- All references become hyperlinks. Click on any of those numbers to jump to the referred table, list item, section, or page.

- Each footnote marker is a hyperlink to the footnote text. Click it to jump there.

- If you insert `\tableofcontents`, you will get a bookmark list for the documents, chapters, and sections listed in a navigation bar of your PDF reader.

`hyperref` can do even more for you – linking index entries to text passages, back-referencing of bibliography entries, and more. You can finely customize the behavior using options such as, for instance, choosing the color or frames for hyperlinks. So, you should keep that valuable package in mind. In *Chapter 12, Enhancing Your Documents Further*, we shall return to this topic.

On the one hand, `hyperref` detects many other packages, such as `varioref`, and can turn their commands into hyperlinks; that's why we should load `hyperref` after most other packages. On the other hand, some exceptional packages, such as `cleveref`, detect `hyperref` functions and build on them – in such cases, we should load them after `hyperref`. So, if you combine `varioref`, `cleveref`, and `hyperref`, the package loading order should be as follows:

```
\usepackage[nospace]{varioref}
\usepackage{hyperref}
\usepackage{cleveref}
```

The `hyperref` package manual has a whole section about compatibility with other packages and the required loading order. Open it by entering `texdoc hyperref` at the command prompt or visit `https://texdoc.org/pkg/hyperref`. Most of the time, `hyperref` should be loaded last, with a few exceptions mentioned in the manual.

Summary

In this chapter, we learned how to reference chapters, sections, footnotes, and environments by their number or by the number of the corresponding page.

Using labels for referencing, we did not need to specify a number by ourselves; LaTeX determines the correct number of a page for us, or of a section, a footnote, or an environment.

We even got to know some clever ways of context-dependent referencing.

In the next chapter, we shall deal with lists, which consist mainly of references: tables of contents, lists of figures and tables, and bibliographies.

8
Listing Contents and References

LaTeX makes it very easy to create lists for many purposes. For example, we've seen that just the simple \tableofcontents command creates a nice-looking table of contents. It takes the entries from the headings and the numbers of the pages they fall on and produces a nice list.

A **table of contents** (**TOC**) and an index are handy for navigating within a book. Lists of tables and lists of figures are similarly helpful. Usually, an academic paper or a book requires a list of references for citations, a bibliography. Once you finish this chapter, you will know how to create such lists and how to customize them.

In this chapter, we will cover the following topics:

- Customizing the table of contents
- Generating an index
- Creating a bibliography
- Changing the headings

We will start with the contents.

Technical requirements

You can use a local LaTeX installation, or you can compile the example code online at `https://latexguide.org/chapter-08`.

The code is available on GitHub at `https://github.com/PacktPublishing/LaTeX-Beginner-s-Guide-2nd-Edition-/tree/main/Chapter_08_-_Listing_Contents_and_References`.

In this chapter, we will use LaTeX standard features and the `index` package.

Furthermore, we will briefly talk about the following packages: `biblatex`, `cite`, `hyperref`, `makeidx`, `minitoc`, `multitoc`, `natbib`, `titlesec`, `titletoc`, `tocbibind`, `tocloft`, and `url`.

You can find related examples in the *LaTeX Cookbook, Chapter 7, Contents, Indexes, and Bibliographies*, with code examples available on the book's website: `https://latex-cookbook.net/chapter-7`.

Customizing the table of contents

Besides just calling `\tableofcontents` to get a pre-designed list of contents, LaTeX provides basic ways to modify it. Let's use some.

We will create a document that we will use for customizing, and it will also be our working example for the following sections.

We will build the frame of a document containing some headings. We will modify the automatically created table of contents to be more nuanced and to contain additional entries.

In *Chapter 3, Designing Pages*, we saw the effect of `\tableofcontents`. LaTeX collected the entries from the headings. We will use headings down to the subsubsection level.

Later, we will extend the TOC further. We will manually add entries for some headings. Let's start with the base document:

1. Start a new `book` document:

   ```
   \documentclass{book}
   ```

2. Set the table of contents' depth value to 3 to include headings down to the subsubsection level:

   ```
   \setcounter{tocdepth}{3}
   ```

3. Begin the document:

```
\begin{document}
```

4. Print the table of contents at the beginning:

```
\tableofcontents
```

5. Write headings in all the levels you want. Use \addcontentsline or \addtocontents to add something to the TOC manually:

```
\part{First Part}
\chapter*{Preface}
\addcontentsline{toc}{chapter}{Preface}
\chapter{First main chapter}
\section{A section}
\section{Another section}
\subsection{A smaller section}
\subsubsection[Deeper level]{This section has an
even deeper level}
\chapter{Second main chapter}
\part{Second part}
\chapter{Third main chapter}
```

6. Finish with an appendix that has its own chapters:

```
\appendix
\cleardoublepage
\addtocontents{toc}{\bigskip}
\addcontentsline{toc}{part}{Appendix}
\chapter{Glossary}
\chapter{Symbols}
\end{document}
```

7. Click on **Typeset** to compile. The first page will show **Contents** but no entries.

8. Click on **Typeset** a second time. Now we can see the table of contents:

Contents

I   First Part   3

Preface   5

1   First main chapter   7
    1.1   A section   7
    1.2   Another section   7
          1.2.1   A smaller section   7
                  Deeper level   7

2   Second main chapter   9

II   Second part   11

3   Third main chapter   13

Appendix   15

A   Glossary   15

B   Symbols   17

Figure 8.1 – An example of a table of contents

We structured a document using several sectioning commands. LaTeX read all of our sectioning commands in the first run and created a file with the .toc extension. This file contains the commands and the titles for all entries in the table of contents. During the first run, that file didn't exist yet; thus, the TOC remained empty.

During the second run, the \tableofcontents command read the .toc file and printed the TOC.

In this example, we raised the depth of the TOC by one level. We added a chapter-like entry for the preface and inserted a part-like heading showing the beginning of the appendix, using \addcontentsline. Through \addtocontents, we inserted some space before the latter heading. In the following sections, we will look at these commands in detail and learn more about customizing.

Adjusting the depth of the TOC

These are the standard sectioning commands and their so-called TOC level:

- \part: -1 in the book and report classes, and 0 in the article class article
- \chapter: 0 (except in the article class, since there are no chapters with article)

- `\section`: 1
- `\subsection`: 2
- `\subsubsection`: 3
- `\paragraph`: 4
- `\subparagraph`: 5

In the book and `report` classes, LaTeX creates TOC entries until level 2, until the `\subsection` level. In the `article` class, LaTeX creates TOC entries until level 3 by default, that is, until the `\subsubsection` level. In a book, this means, for example, that `\subsubsection` doesn't generate a TOC entry. There is a variable representing the level, namely, `\tocdepth`. It's an integer variable, which we call a counter. To tell LaTeX to include subsubsections in the TOC, we would have to raise this counter. There are two basic ways to adjust a counter value:

- `\setcounter{name}{n}` specifies an integer value of n for the name counter.
- `\addtocounter{name}{n}` adds the integer value of n to the value of the name counter. To decrease a counter, choose a negative value for n.

Thus, the following command would ensure that even `\subparagraph` gives a TOC entry:

```
\setcounter{tocdepth}{5}
```

Using `\addcounter` instead, you may raise or lower the level without knowing its number.

In contrast to commands, counter names don't begin with a backslash.

Shortening entries

As you have already learned in *Chapter 3, Designing Pages*, you may choose a text for the TOC different from the heading in the body text. Each sectioning command understands an optional argument for the TOC entry, which is especially useful if you wish to use very long headings. Still, a shorter TOC entry would be sufficient. In our example, we did this by means of the following command:

```
\subsubsection[Deeper level]{This section has an even deeper
level}
```

The body text shows the long heading, while the TOC shows the short one. Titles printed at the top of the pages, called **running titles**, would use the short entry as well, as the space in headers is very limited.

Adding entries manually

Starred commands, such as \chapter* and \section*, don't produce a TOC entry. In our example, we did that manually by using this command:

```
\addcontentsline{file extension}{sectional unit}{text}
```

We can use this command in several contexts. The file extension could be the following:

- toc for the table of contents file

- lof for the list of figures file

- lot for the list of tables file

Alternatively, it could be any such extension of a file type known to LaTeX.

sectional unit determines the formatting of the entry. It specifies the chapter to create an entry that is formatted like a regular chapter entry, and similarly for other sectional units such as part, section, or subsection.

The third argument contains the text for the entry.

You may insert text or commands more directly with the help of the following command:

```
\addtocontents{file extension}{entry}
```

Contrary to \addcontentsline, the argument entry is written directly to the file without any additional formatting. You may choose any formatting you like.

We can also use the \addtocontents command for some customization, for example:

- \addtocontents{toc}{\protect\enlargethispage {\baselineskip}} extends the text height such that one additional line fits to the contents page.

- \addtocontents{toc}{\protect\newpage} causes a page break in the TOC. For instance, if the automatic page break happens after a chapter entry and before the following section entries, you might wish to force a page break already before the chapter entry.

- \addtocontents{toc}{\protect\thispagestyle{fancy}} changes the page style of the current TOC page to fancy. As the first page of a chapter is of the plain style by default, the first page of the TOC would be plain as well, even if you specified \pagestyle{fancy}. The \addtocontents{toc}{\protect \thispagestyle{fancy}} command overrides it.

Place such commands where they should be effective. To affect the first TOC page, place it at the beginning of your document. To cause a page break before a specific chapter, put it right before the corresponding \chapter call.

Creating and customizing lists of figures

As briefly mentioned in *Chapter 5, Including Images*, and in *Chapter 6, Creating Tables*, the two commands for creating lists of figures and tables are \listoffigures and \listoftables. Depending on the class, they produce a fine list of all captions together with the figure, the table number, and the corresponding page numbers. As with the TOC, LaTeX can do everything automatically. However, we may use the same techniques, such as with the TOC, to customize the other lists. Let's try that.

Suppose all our figures are diagrams. We will avoid using the term figure, and we will add a list of diagrams:

1. Open our current example. Add these lines to your preamble:

   ```
   \renewcommand{\figurename}{Diagram}
   \renewcommand{\listfigurename}{List of Diagrams}
   ```

2. Right after \tableofcontents, add the following:

   ```
   \listoffigures
   ```

3. Add a diagram somewhere in the first chapter:

   ```
   \begin{figure}
   \centering
   \fbox{Diagram placeholder}
   \caption{Enterprize Organizational Chart}
   \end{figure}
   ```

4. In the second part of the third chapter, we'd like to add network design diagrams. Let's mark that in the **list of figures (LOF)** and let the diagrams follow:

   ```
   \addtocontents{lof}{Network Diagrams: }
   \begin{figure}
   \centering
   \fbox{Diagram placeholder}
   \caption{Network overview}
   \end{figure}
   ```

```
\begin{figure}
\centering
\fbox{Diagram placeholder}
\caption{WLAN Design}
\end{figure}
```

5. Click on **Typeset** twice to get the document and the list:

List of Diagrams

1.1   Enterprize Organizational Chart   9

Network Diagrams:
3.1   Network overview   15
3.2   WLAN Design   16

Figure 8.2 – A list of diagrams

We renamed the figures and the list heading by redefining LaTeX macros. At the end of this chapter, you will get a list of names used by LaTeX classes that you may redefine.

As with the TOC, we used the `\addtocontents` command to insert a bold heading into the `.lof` file, where LaTeX collects the captions. It works similarly to the TOC.

Creating a list of tables

You already know that all you need to create and customize a **list of tables** (**LOT**) is the file where LaTeX collects the tables' captions and has the `.lot` extension. So, the first argument of `\addtocontents` would be `lot`. Everything works analogously, like `\listoftables`, `\tablename`, and `\listtablename`.

Using packages for customization

Besides the simple methods described, packages provide sophisticated features for customizing the TOC and the lists of figures and tables:

- `tocloft` gives extensive control over the typography of TOC, LOF, and **LOT**. You may even define new kinds of such lists.
- `titletoc` offers convenient handling of entries and is the companion to `titlesec`, an excellent package for customizing sectioning headings.
- `multitoc` offers a layout in two or more columns using the `multicol` package.

- `minitoc` can create small TOCs for each part, chapter, or section.

- `tocbibind` can automatically add a bibliography, index, TOC, LOF, and LOT to the table of contents. It's even capable of using numbered headings instead of the default unnumbered ones.

Use the `texdoc` command-line tool or visit `https://texdoc.org` to read the package documentation.

Now we know how to create lists of contents, tables, and figures that we usually put at the beginning of a document. Let's now continue with lists that come at the end of a document – a keyword index and a bibliography.

Generating an index

Extensive documents often contain an index. An index is a list of words or phrases and page numbers pointing to where we can find related material in the document. In contrast to a full-text search feature, the index provides selective pointers to relevant information.

When it's our turn to identify and mark the words for the index, LaTeX will collect this information and typeset the index.

Suppose our example contains information about an enterprise and its structure as well as its network structure and design. We will mark places in the text where these concepts occur. Finally, we will order LaTeX to typeset the index, as follows:

1. Go back to our example. In the preamble, load the `index` package and add the command to create the index:

   ```
   \usepackage{index}
   \makeindex
   ```

2. In the caption of our enterprise diagram, index this point with the keyword `enterprise`:

   ```
   \caption{\index{enterprise}Enterprise Organizational
   Chart}
   ```

3. In the third chapter, which contains our diagrams, index by the keyword `network`:

   ```
   \index{network}
   ```

4. Directly before \end{document}, create an entry for the index for the table of contents. To ensure that it shows the correct page number, end the page before it:

```
\clearpage
\addcontentsline{toc}{chapter}{Index}
```

5. In the following line, order LaTeX to typeset the index:

```
\printindex
```

6. If you're using TeXworks, choose **MakeIndex** instead of pdfLaTeX in the drop-down box next to the **Typeset** button. Then, click the **Typeset** button. If you use another editor, use its MakeIndex feature or type the following at the command prompt in the document directory:

```
makeindex documentname
```

7. Switch back to pdfLaTeX. Click on **Typeset**, and look at the last page:

Index

enterprise, 9

network, 15

Figure 8.3 – An index

We loaded the index package, which improves LaTeX's built-in indexing capabilities.

Alternatively, you could use the makeidx package, which is part of standard LaTeX. The \makeindex command prepares the index. Both commands belong to the preamble, so should be placed before \begin{document}.

The \index command takes just one argument, namely, the word or the phrase to be indexed. It writes this phrase into a file with the .idx extension. If you look into this file, you will find lines such as the following:

```
\indexentry {enterprise}{9}
\indexentry {network}{15}
```

These stand for the index entries and the corresponding page numbers.

The external `makeindex` program takes that `.idx` file and produces a `.ind` file. The latter consists of LaTeX code for the index creation. Specifically, it contains the index list environment together with the items and appears as follows:

```
\begin{theindex}
\item enterprise, 9
\indexspace
\item network, 15
\end{theindex}
```

More complex indexes may contain subitems, page ranges, and references to other items. Let's see how to produce such an index. At the book's website at `https://latexguide.org/chapter-08`, you can find fully compilable code containing example commands that we will get to know in the following sections. You can try them out directly on the web page.

Defining index entries and subentries

We have already created simple index entries with the following command:

```
\index{phrase}
```

We can produce subentries by specifying the main entry followed by the subentry, separated by an exclamation mark, for example:

```
\index{network!overview}
```

Also, subentries may have subentries; just use another `!` symbol, for example:

```
\index{enterprise!organization}
\index{enterprise!organization!sales}
\index{enterprise!organization!controlling}
\index{enterprise!organization!operation}
```

This is possible up to three levels.

Specifying page ranges

If several pages deal with the same concept, you may specify a page range for the index entry. Suffix the entry with | (where the range starts, and add |) where it ends. At the beginning of the `network` chapter, add | (as follows:

```
\index{network|(}
```

While, at the end of this chapter, add |) as follows:

```
\index{network|)}
```

This results in an entry of the form **Network, 15-17**.

Using symbols and macros in the index

`makeindex` sorts the entries alphabetically. If you would like to include symbols in the index, for example, Greek letters, chemical formulas, or math symbols, you may encounter the problem of integrating them into the sorting. For this purpose, \index understands a sort key. Use this key as a prefix for the entry, separated by the @ symbol, for instance:

```
\index{Gamma@$\Gamma$}
```

Using macros for index entries is generally not recommended. The macro name, including the backslash, would determine the sorting, although the macro would be expanded in the index. Imagine you've got a \group macro that stands for TeX Users Group, defined like this:

```
\newcommand{\group}{\TeX\ Users Group}
```

If you write the following, then the TeX Users Group entry would be treated like \group in the sorting and won't appear among the entries beginning with T:

```
\index{\group}
```

However, you could repair such issues by adding a sort key as a prefix, such as here:

```
\index{TeX@\group}
```

Similarly, you can indicate how words with special characters will be sorted. Here, the word *schön* will be sorted like the word *schon*:

```
\index{schon@sch\"{o}n}
```

As the symbols |, @, and ! have special meanings within index entries, we need to take an extra step to print them as their original symbol meaning. That's an example of how we can print them:

```
\index{exclamation ("!)!loud}
```

We can print the symbols |, @, and ! in the index by quoting them, using a preceding ".

Referring to other index entries

Different words may stand for the same concept. For such cases, it's possible to add a cross-reference to the main phrase without a page number. Adding the code |see{entry list} achieves that, for example:

```
\index{wireless|see{WLAN}}
\index{WLAN}
```

As such, references don't print a page number, so their position in the text doesn't matter. You could collect them in one place of your document.

Fine-tuning page numbers

If an index entry refers to several pages, you might want to emphasize a specific page number to indicate it as the primary reference. You could define a command for emphasizing as follows:

```
\newcommand{\main}[1]{\emph{#1}}
```

And, for the index entry, add a pipe symbol and the command name:

```
\index{WLAN|main}
```

Thus, LaTeX emphasizes the corresponding page number. Simply writing \index{WLAN|emph} or \index{WLAN|texbf} is possible as well. However, defining your own macro is more consistent—remember the concept of separating form and content.

Designing the index layout

If we extend our example document with the example commands mentioned in the previous sections, \printindex gives us this layout, containing subentries, ranges, references, and emphasized entries:

Index

TEX Users Group sorted wrong, 17

enterprise, 9
    organization, 9
      controlling, 9
      operation, 9
    sales, 9
exclamation (!)
    loud, 17

Γ, 17

network, 15–17
    overview, 15

schön, 17

TEX Users Group sorted correctly,
    17

wireless, *see* WLAN
WLAN, *17*

Figure 8.4 – A more complex index

LaTeX provides some index styles called latex (the default), gind, din, and iso. To use another style, specify it using the -s option of the makeindex program, for example:

```
makeindex -s iso documentname
```

If you compile after this call, the index layout changes to the following:

Index

TEX Users Group sorted wrong . 17
enterprise 9
    organization 9
      controlling 9
      operation 9
    sales 9
exclamation (!)
    loud 17
Γ 17
network 15–17
    overview 15
schön 17
TEX Users Group sorted correctly
    17
wireless . . . . *see* WLAN
WLAN *17*

Figure 8.5 – An index with the iso style

You could even define your own styles. To learn more about indexing and `makeindex`, use `texdoc` at the command prompt:

```
texdoc index
```

For more information about the `makeindex` tool, use the following command:

```
texdoc makeindex
```

Or, visit the documentation online at `https://texdoc.org/pkg/index` or `https://texdoc.org/pkg/makeindex`.

Although it seems natural to generate the index while writing the document, this might lead to inconsistencies in the index. It's first recommended to finish writing and then to work out what should appear in the index.

Our next list topic is printing the list references, that is, the bibliography.

Creating a bibliography

Scientific documents in particular commonly contain a list of references or a bibliography. We will work out how to typeset a bibliography and how to refer to its entries.

Using LaTeX's standard features, we will create a small list of references containing a book and an article by Donald E. Knuth, the creator of TeX. In our body text, we will refer to both:

1. Create a new document as follows:

```
\documentclass{article}
\begin{document}
\section*{Recommended texts}
To study \TeX\ in depth, see \cite{DK86}.
For writing math texts, see \cite{DK89}.
\begin{thebibliography}{8}
\bibitem{DK86} D.E. Knuth, \emph{The {\TeX}book}, 1986
\bibitem{DK89} D.E. Knuth, \emph{Typesetting Concrete
Mathematics}, 1989
\end{thebibliography}
\end{document}
```

2. Click on **Typeset** and examine the output:

Recommended texts

To study TEX in depth, see [1]. For writing math texts, see [2].

References

[1] D.E. Knuth, *The TEXbook*, 1986

[2] D.E. Knuth, *Typesetting Concrete Mathematics*, 1989

Figure 8.6 – A list of references

We used an environment called `thebibliography` to typeset the list of references, which is similar to a description list as we've seen in *Chapter 4, Creating Lists*. Each item on this list has got a key. For the purpose of citing in the body text, we referred to that key using the `\cite` command. Let's look at these commands in detail.

Using the standard bibliography environment

LaTeX's standard environment for bibliographies has the following form:

```
\begin{thebibliography}{widest label}
\bibitem[label]{key} author, title, year etc.
\bibitem...

...

\end{thebibliography}
```

Each item is specified using the `\bibitem` command. This command requires a mandatory argument determining the key. We may simply refer to this key with `\cite{key}` or `\cite{key1,key2}`. `\cite` accepts an optional argument stating a page range, for example, `\cite[p.\,18--20]{key}`. You may choose a label by means of the optional argument of `\bibitem`. If we did not state a label, LaTeX would number the items consecutively in square brackets, as we've seen in *Figure 8.6*.

Using labels, the environment could look as follows:

```
\begin{thebibliography}{Knuth89}
\bibitem[Knuth86]{DK86} D.E. Knuth, \emph{The {\TeX}book}, 1986
\bibitem[Knuth89]{DK89} D.E. Knuth, \emph{Typesetting Concrete
Mathematics}, 1989
\end{thebibliography}
```

And the corresponding output is this:

Recommended texts

To study TEX in depth, see [Knuth86]. For writing math texts, see [Knuth89].

References

[Knuth86] D.E. Knuth, *The TEXbook*, 1986

[Knuth89] D.E. Knuth, *Typesetting Concrete Mathematics*, 1989

Figure 8.7 – A list of references

As you can see, LaTeX adjusted the output of \cite to the new labels automatically. The cite package offers compressed and sorted lists of numerical citations, such as [2,4-6], and further formatting options for in-text citations.

The mandatory item of the environment should contain the widest label for the alignment of the items. So, for instance, if you have more than 9 but fewer than 100 items, you may write two digits into the argument.

Using bibliography databases with BibTeX

Manually creating the bibliography is laborious. Especially if you use references in several documents, it would be beneficial to use a database and let a program generate the bibliography for you. This sounds more complicated than it actually is. Let's try this.

We will create a separate database file containing the references of our previous example. We will modify our example to use that database. To make this database usable, we have to call the external program called **BibTeX**:

1. Create a new document. Begin by writing the entry for the TeXbook:

```
@book{DK86,
author = "D.E. Knuth",
title = "The {\TeX}book",
publisher = "Addison Wesley",
year = 1986
}
```

2. For the next entry, that is, the article, we will specify even more fields:

```
@article{DK89,
author = "D.E. Knuth",
title = "Typesetting Concrete Mathematics",
```

```
journal = "TUGboat",
volume = 10,
number = 1,
pages = "31--36",
month = apr,
year = 1989
}
```

3. Save the file and give it the name `example.bib`. Open our example document and modify it as follows:

```
\documentclass{article}
\begin{document}
\section*{Recommended texts}
To study \TeX\ in depth, see \cite{DK86}. For writing
math texts,
see \cite{DK89}.
\bibliographystyle{alpha}
\bibliography{example}
\end{document}
```

4. Click on **Typeset** one time with pdfLaTeX. If you're using TeXworks, choose BibTeX instead of pdfLaTeX, present in the drop-down box next to the **Typeset** button, and then click on **Typeset**. If you are writing with another editor, use its BibTeX option or type at the command prompt in the document directory as follows:

```
bibtex documentname
```

5. Click on **Typeset** twice with pdfLaTeX. Here's the result:

Recommended texts

To study TEX in depth, see [Knu86]. For writing math texts, see [Knu89].

References

[Knu86] D.E. Knuth. *The TEXbook*. Addison Wesley, 1986.

[Knu89] D.E. Knuth. Typesetting concrete mathematics. *TUGboat*, 10(1):31–36, April 1989.

Figure 8.8 – A bibliography based on a database file

We created a text file containing all bibliography entries. In the next section, we will look at its format in depth. Our document chose a style called `alpha`, which sorts entries according to the author's name and uses a shortcut consisting of `author` and `year` as the label. Then we told LaTeX to load the bibliography file called `example`. The `.bib` extension has been added automatically.

Afterward, we called the external program BibTeX. This program knows from the example `.tex` file that `example.bib` has to be translated. Thus, out of this `.bib` file, it creates a `.bbl` file containing a LaTeX `thebibliography` environment and the final entries.

Finally, we had to compile twice, to ensure that all the cross-references are correct.

Though we need some more steps to generate the bibliography, there are also benefits – we don't need to fine-tune each entry. We can easily switch between styles. We can then reuse the `.bib` file.

So, let's look at the `.bib` file format. It supports various entry types, such as `book` and `article`. Furthermore, these entries contain fields such as `author`, `title`, and `year`. Let's first look at the supported fields, and afterward, we will talk about the different kinds of entries.

Looking at the BibTeX entry fields

Here's a list of the standard fields. Some fields are common, some are rarely used—we will just list them in alphabetical order, following the BibTeX documentation:

- `address`: Usually, the address of the publisher. At least for small publishers, this information might be useful.
- `annote`: An annotation not used by the standard bibliography styles. Other styles or macros might use this.
- `author`: The name(s) of the author(s).
- `booktitle`: The title of a book if you cite a part of it. You can also use the `title` field instead.
- `chapter`: A chapter number.
- `crossref`: The key of the database entry being cross-referenced.
- `edition`: The edition (first, second, and suchlike) of a book. Commonly, it is capitalized.
- `editor`: The name(s) of the editor(s).

- `howpublished`: The way of publishing, especially if it's unusual. Capitalize the first word.

- `institution`: This could be a sponsoring institution.

- `journal`: A journal name; you may use common abbreviations.

- `key`: Used for alphabetizing, cross-referencing, and labeling if the author's information is missing. Don't confuse it with the key used in the `\cite` command, which corresponds to the beginning of the entry.

- `month`: The month in which the work was published or written if it's not yet published. Usually, a three-letter abbreviation is used.

- `note`: Any additional useful information. Capitalize the first word.

- `number`: The number of a journal or another kind of work in a series.

- `organization`: This can be a sponsoring organization.

- `pages`: A page number or range of page numbers, such as 12-18 or 22+.

- `publisher`: The name of the publisher.

- `school`: Could be the name of the school where the document was written.

- `series`: The name of a series of books or its number in a multi-volume set.

- `title`: The title of the work.

- `type`: The type of the publication.

- `volume`: The volume of a journal or multi-volume book.

- `year`: The year of the publication or the year when it was written if it hasn't been published yet. Generally, four numerals are used, such as 2010. You may use any fields possibly supported by other styles and ignored by standard styles.

You can read the BibTeX documentation by typing `texdoc bibtex` at the command line or visiting `https://texdoc.org/pkg/bibtex`.

Referring to Internet resources

Today, we often refer to online sources. To put internet addresses into BibTeX fields, use the `\url` command of the `url` or `hyperref` package, for example:

```
howpublished = {\url{https://latex.org}}
```

Some styles offer a `url` field that formats the content as URL implicitly, so we don't need to use the `\url` command there.

Understanding BibTeX entry types

Firstly, you decide which entry type you want to add, and then you fill in the fields. Different types may support various fields. Some fields are required, some are optional and may be omitted, and some are simply ignored when the style doesn't support it.

Usually, the name of the entry tells you its meaning. These are the standard entry types and their required and optional fields, according to the BibTeX reference:

Type	Required fields	Optional fields
article	author, title, journal, year	volume, number, pages, month, note
book	author or editor, title, publisher, year	volume or number, series, address, edition, month, note
booklet	title	author, howpublished, address, month, year, note
conference	author, title, booktitle, year	editor, volume or number, series, pages, address, month, organization, publisher, note
manual	title	author, organization, address, edition, month, year, note
mastersthesis	author, title, school, year	type, address, month, note
misc	none	author, title, howpublished, month, year, note
phdthesis	author, title, school, year	type, address, month, note
proceedings	title, year	editor, volume or number, series, address, month, organization, publisher, note
techreport	author, title, institution, year	type, number, address, month, note
unpublished	author, title, note	month, year

Figure 8.9 – BibTeX entry types and fields

Have a look at the BibTeX reference for more details by typing the following at the command prompt:

```
texdoc bibtex
```

Alternatively, you can visit `https://texdoc.org/pkg/bibtex`.

If no other entry fits, choose `misc`. For the type, it doesn't matter if you use capitals or small letters; `@ARTICLE` is understood the same as `@article`. As the example shows, entries have the following form:

```
@entrytype{keyword,
fieldname = {field text},
fieldname = {field text},
...
}
```

Use braces around `field text`. Straight quotes instead, as in `"field text"`, are also supported. For numbers, you may omit the braces.

Some styles change the capitalization, which might lead to undesired lowercase letters. To protect letters or words from becoming lowercase, put additional braces around them. Preferably do it around a word instead of just the letter to keep ligatures and for spacing improvement. For example, `{WAL}` looks better than `{W}AL`, because in a standard text flow, LaTeX moves an **A** closer to a preceding **W**. Separating braces hampers LaTeX's micro-typographic improvements.

Choosing the bibliography style

Standard styles are as follows:

- `plain`: Arabic numbers are used for the labels, sorted according to the names of the authors. The number is written in square brackets, which also appear with `\cite`.

- `unsrt`: There's no sorting. All entries appear like they were cited in the text. Otherwise, it looks like `plain`.

- `alpha`: Sorting is realized according to the names of the authors; the labels are shortcuts comprising the author's name and the year of publication. Also, square brackets are used here.

- abbrv: This is like `plain`, but first names and other field entries are abbreviated. The style should be chosen after `\begin{document}` and before `\bibliography`. You may write `\bibliographystyle` right before `\bibliography` to keep it together.

There are more styles available in TeX distributions and on the Internet. For instance, the `natbib` package provides styles and the capability to cite in a nice author-year scheme. This package further adds some fields, such as `ISBN`, `ISSN`, and `URL`.

You could give the `natbib` package a try and use its `plainnat`, `abbrvnat`, and `unsrtnat` styles, for instance:

```
\usepackage{natbib}
\bibliographystyle{plainnat}
```

These lines would change our example as follows:

- `natbib` reimplemented the `\cite` command and offers variations to it, with the main purpose of supporting author-year citations. It works with most other available styles.

- `natbib` introduces the citation command, `\citet`, for textual citations, and the `\citep` command for parenthetical citations. There are starred variants that print the full author list, and optional arguments that allow the addition of text before and after.

Check out the documentation if you would like to benefit from this excellent package. As usual, type `texdoc natbib` at the command line or visit `https://texdoc.org/pkg/natbib`.

The `biblatex` package provides a complete reimplementation of the bibliographic features offered by BibTeX and LaTeX. `biblatex` doesn't require learning the BibTeX language and it works with a program called `biber`, which replaces BibTeX. In the *LaTeX Cookbook, Chapter 7, Contents, Indexes, and Bibliographies*, you can read a well-explained step-by-step example involving `biblatex` and `biber`.

Listing references without citing

BibTeX takes only those references from the database that are cited in the text and prints them out. However, you may specify keys for references, which should appear nevertheless. Just write the following for a single reference:

```
\nocite{key}
```

Or, write the following to list the complete database:

```
\nocite{*}
```

Make sure to remove `\nocite{*}` in the final version of the document if you don't want to have references in the bibliography that you never cited in the document.

Now that we know how to create such tables, lists, indexes, and bibliographies, let's have a final look at how to customize them.

Changing the headings

As in our diagram example in *Figure 8.2*, if you don't like the heading **Contents**, you could easily change it. LaTeX stores the text of the heading in the `\contentsname` text macro. So, just redefine it as follows:

```
\renewcommand{\contentsname}{Table of Contents}
```

Here's a list of such macros and their default values:

- `\contentsname`: Contents
- `\listfigurename`: List of figures
- `\listtablename`: List of tables
- `\bibname`: Bibliography (in the `book` and `report` classes)
- `\refname`: References (in the `article` class)
- `\indexname`: Index

Furthermore, as promised, here's a list of other macros for names used by LaTeX, with their default values:

- `\figurename`: Figure
- `\tablename`: Table

- `\partname`: Part

- `\chaptername`: Chapter

- `\abstractname`: Abstract

- `\appendixname`: Appendix

This is not really surprising! Using name macros is especially useful when you write in another language. For instance, the `babel` package takes a language option and redefines all those name macros according to the chosen language.

However, they are also useful when choosing abbreviations such as **Fig.** or different phrasing, such as **Appendices** instead of **Appendix**.

Summary

In this chapter, we dealt with many kinds of lists. Specifically, we learned about generating and customizing the table of contents, lists of figures and tables, producing an index pointing to relevant information for keywords and phrases, and creating bibliographies, both manually and using a bibliography database.

These lists will guide you to the information that you are looking for. They aren't just for listing and summarizing. That's why the headings of the list of figures and the list of tables usually don't appear in the TOC, as they directly follow the TOC. Sometimes, there's even the strange requirement to list the table of contents within itself. If you are not sure about a design or a requirement, have a look at a good book in your particular field to see what exemplary tables of contents, lists, and indexes might look like.

In the next chapter, we will look at scientific writing in depth.

9
Writing Math Formulas

At the beginning of this book, in *Chapter 1*, *Getting Started with LaTeX*, we promised that LaTeX offers excellent quality for mathematical typesetting. Now it's time to prove this. By the end of this chapter, you will be able to write beautiful mathematical texts.

To benefit from LaTeX's math capabilities, we shall now deal with the following:

- Writing basic formulas
- Typesetting multi-line formulas
- Exploring the wealth of math symbols
- Building math structures

That's a tremendous undertaking—let's tackle it!

Technical requirements

You can use a local LaTeX installation, or you can compile the example code online at `https://latexguide.org/chapter-09`.

The code is available on GitHub: `https://github.com/PacktPublishing/LaTeX-Beginner-s-Guide-2nd-Edition-/tree/main/Chapter_09_-_Writing_Math_Formulas`.

In this chapter, we will use the following packages: `amsmath`, `amssymb`, `geometry`, `latexsym`, and `upgreek`.

Furthermore, we will briefly discuss these packages: `amsthm`, `dsfont`, `graphicx`, `mathtools`, `ntheorem`, `siunitx`, `xits`, and `zapfino`.

You can find further code examples in *Chapter 10, Advanced Mathematics* of *LaTeX Cookbook* with compilable code on that book's website at `https://latex-cookbook.net/chapter-10`.

Writing basic formulas

LaTeX offers three writing modes:

- **Paragraph mode**: The text is typeset as a sequence of words in lines, paragraphs, and pages. That's what we used in the previous chapters.

- **Left-to-right mode**: The text is a sequence of words, but LaTeX typesets it from left to right without breaking the line. For instance, the argument of \mbox will be typeset in this mode; so \mbox prevents hyphenation.

- **Math mode**: Here, LaTeX treats letters as math symbols. That's why they're typeset in italics, which is common practice for variables. A lot of symbols can only be used in math mode. Such symbols are roots, sum signs, relation signs, math accents, arrows, and various delimiters, such as brackets and braces. LaTeX ignores space characters between letters and symbols. Instead, the spacing depends on the type of symbols—spacing of relation signs is different from spacing of opening or closing delimiters. All math expressions require this mode.

Now we shall enter the math mode for the first time.

Our first math text shall deal with the solutions of quadratic equations. We will typeset formulas with constants, variables, superscripts for the square, and subscripts for the solutions. The solution itself needs a root symbol. Finally, we will use cross-references to formulas. That's quite a challenge, so let's break it down into the following steps:

1. Start a new document. For now, we don't need any packages:

```
\documentclass{article}
```

```
\begin{document}
\section*{Quadratic equations}
```

2. State the quadratic equation with its conditions. Use an equation environment for it. Surround small pieces of math within text using \ (and \) :

```
The quadratic equation
\begin{equation}
  \label{quad}
  ax^2 + bx + c = 0,
\end{equation}
where \( a, b \) and \( c \) are constants and
\( a \neq 0 \), has two solutions for the variable
\( x \):
```

3. Use another equation for the solutions. The command for a square root is \sqrt. The command for a fraction is \frac:

```
\begin{equation}
  \label{root}
  x_{1,2} = \frac{-b \pm \sqrt{b^2-4ac}}{2a}.
\end{equation}
```

4. Let's introduce the discriminant and discuss case zero. To get an unnumbered displayed equation, we surround the formula with \ [and \]:

```
If the \emph{discriminant} \( \Delta \) with
\[
  \Delta = b^2 - 4ac
\]
is zero, then the equation (\ref{quad}) has a double
solution:
(\ref{root}) becomes
\[
  x = - \frac{b}{2a}.
\]
\end{document}
```

5. Click on **Typeset** to compile the document. The equation references are unresolved in the first run and look like (**?**). Compile again to let LaTeX resolve them, and look at the result:

Quadratic equations

The quadratic equation

$$ax^2 + bx + c = 0, \tag{1}$$

where a, b and c are constants and $a \neq 0$, has two solutions for the variable x:

$$x_{1,2} = \frac{-b \pm \sqrt{b^2 - 4ac}}{2a}. \tag{2}$$

If the *discriminant* Δ with

$$\Delta = b^2 - 4ac$$

is zero, then the equation (1) has a double solution: (2) becomes

$$x = -\frac{b}{2a}.$$

Figure 9.1 – An example of a mathematical text

Just as we said in *Chapter 1*, *Getting Started with LaTeX*, writing formulas also looks a lot like programming. We build formulas from commands; there are commands with arguments, such as for roots and fractions, and simple commands for symbols, such as for Greek letters. Most symbols have to be within a math environment and don't work within regular text. However, this chapter will help you master it, and the results are worth the effort.

The `equation` environment created a displayed formula. This formula has been horizontally centered, and LaTeX added some vertical space before and after. Furthermore, these formulas are consecutively numbered.

However, \ [... \] and \ (... \) are also, in reality, environments. Let's look more closely for further details in the next sections.

Embedding math expressions within text

LaTeX provides the math environment for in-text formulas:

```
\begin{math}
    expression
\end{math}
```

Since it's very trying to write this environment for each small expression or symbol, LaTeX offers an alias, which does the same:

```
\(
    expression
\)
```

You may also write it without line breaks, such as \(expression \).

A third way is by using a shortcut, coming from TeX: $ expression $.

A disadvantage of the latter is that the commands for beginning and ending the math environment are the same, which may easily lead to errors. However, it's much easier to type, which may be the reason why it's still popular among LaTeX users.

Writing formulas inline saves space and allows fluent explanations. This is recommended for short math expressions within the text.

Displaying formulas

For displayed formulas, which have to be centered, LaTeX offers the displaymath environment:

```
\begin{displaymath}
    expression
\end{displaymath}
```

The effect of this environment is that when the paragraph ends, some vertical space follows it, then the centered formula is displayed, which is again followed by the vertical space. As this math environment takes care of the spacing, don't leave empty lines before and after it. This would cause additional vertical space because of the extra paragraph breaks.

Also, for this environment, there's a shortcut. Here, it's with square brackets, instead of parentheses as in the previous section:

```
\[
    expression
\]
```

In this case, putting the \[and \] shortcuts on separate lines commonly improves the code readability.

Do not use the similar `$$ expression $$` TeX low-level command that you may see elsewhere for displayed formulas, as this has issues with LaTeX, such as incorrect vertical spacing.

Formulas in the displayed style are more prominent – they are centered and have additional space before and after. Choose the style that is optimal for the readability of your text.

> **Note**
>
> For the rest of this chapter, all pieces of code will use math mode. Either we will explicitly use a math environment or assume that we are already in math mode for short code snippets.

Numbering equations

Equations and formulas, in general, may be numbered. However, this applies only to displayed formulas. The `equation` environment is responsible for this:

```
\begin{equation}
  \label{key}
  expression
\end{equation}
```

It looks similar to `displaymath`, but it's numbered this time. The number will be displayed in parentheses on the right side of the equation, as we can see in *Figure 9.1*.

Adding subscripts and superscripts

As exponents and indexes are frequently used, there are concise commands for typesetting them.

An underscore _ gives an index or subscript:

```
{expression}_{subscript}
```

A caret ^ produces an exponent or superscript:

```
{expression}^{superscript}
```

As we see here, we use braces to define the relevant part of the expression.

Subscripts and superscripts may be nested. If you use both subscripts and superscripts in the same expression, the order of ^ and _ doesn't matter. In the case of single letters, numerals, or symbols, you can omit the braces. Let's look at an example:

```
\[ x_1^2 + x_2^2 = 1, \quad 2^{2^x} = 64 \]
```

This gives us the output:

$$x_1^2 + x_2^2 = 1, \quad 2^{2^x} = 64$$

Figure 9.2 – Subscripts and superscripts

You can also notice that the exponent at the higher level is smaller than the exponent at the lower level. When we nest subscripts or superscripts, the inner font size becomes smaller.

Using operators

Trigonometric functions, logarithmic functions, and other analytic and algebraic functions are commonly written with upright Roman letters. Simply typing log would otherwise look like a product of the three variables: l, o, and g. There are commands for many common functions or so-called **operators**. Here's an alphabetical list of the predefined ones:

\arccos, \arcsin, \arctan, \arg, \cos, \cosh, \cot, \coth, \scs, \deg, \det, \dim, \exp, \gcd, \hom, \inf, \ker, \lg, \lim, \liminf, \limsup, \ln, \log, \max, \min, \Pr, \sec, \sin, \sinh, \sup, \tan, \tanh

We can write the modulo function in two ways – either by using \bmod for a binary relation or by using \pmod{argument} for a modulo expression in parentheses.

Some operators support subscripts, which are set in displayed formulas below the operator as follows:

```
\[ \lim_{n=1, 2, \ldots} a_n \qquad \max_{x<X} x \]
```

The output is as follows:

$$\lim_{n=1,2,\ldots} a_n \qquad \max_{x<X} x$$

Figure 9.3 – Operators with subscripts

Superscripts would be set above the operator.

When operators are used inline within text, like this:

```
Within text, we have \( \lim_{n=1, 2, \ldots} a_n \)
and \( \max_{x<X} x \).
```

The output is different:

$$\text{Within text, we have } \lim_{n=1,2,\ldots} a_n \text{ and } \max_{x<X} x.$$

Figure 9.4 – Subscripts

That's to avoid a wide spacing between text lines.

In addition, *Figure 9.30* and *Figure 9.31* show the positioning and size of subscripts and superscripts for operators.

Taking roots

Our first example code in this chapter, contained a square root: \sqrt{value}. As there are higher-order roots, this command accepts an optional argument for the order. The complete definition is as follows:

```
\sqrt[order]{value}
```

Roots may be nested. We can see it in this example:

```
\sqrt[64]{x} = \sqrt{\sqrt{\sqrt{\sqrt{\sqrt{\sqrt{x}}}}}}
```

The output is as follows:

$$\sqrt[64]{x} = \sqrt{\sqrt{\sqrt{\sqrt{\sqrt{\sqrt{x}}}}}}$$

Figure 9.5 – Nested roots

LaTeX adjusts the size of the root symbol automatically to the height and the width of the value expression. That's why outer roots are bigger than inner roots.

Writing fractions

Within text formulas, you may just write / to denote fractions, such as \((a+b)/2 \). For larger fractions, there's the \frac command:

```
\frac{numerator}{denominator}
```

Here is an example:

```
\[ \frac{n(n+1)}{2} \quad \frac{\frac{\sqrt{x}+1}{2}-x}{y^2} \]
```

The output is as follows:

$$\frac{n(n+1)}{2} \quad \frac{\frac{\sqrt{x}+1}{2}-x}{y^2}$$

Figure 9.6 – Fractions and nested fractions

LaTeX adjusts the separation line automatically to the maximum width of the numerator and denominator.

Writing Greek letters

Mathematicians like to use Greek letters, for instance, to denote constants. To get a lowercase Greek letter, write the name with a backslash for the command. Here are the lowercase Greek letters with their corresponding LaTeX commands:

α \alpha	ζ \zeta	λ \lambda	π \pi	ϕ \phi
β \beta	η \eta	μ \mu	ρ \rho	χ \chi
γ \gamma	θ \theta	ν \nu	σ \sigma	ψ \psi
δ \delta	ι \iota	ξ \xi	τ \tau	ω \omega
ϵ \epsilon	κ \kappa	o o	υ \upsilon	

Figure 9.7 – Lowercase Greek letters

For some letters, variants are available:

ε \varepsilon	ϖ \varpi	ς \varsigma
ϑ \vartheta	ϱ \varrho	φ \varphi

Figure 9.8 – Alternative variants for some Greek letters

As the `omicron` looks like an o, there's no command for it. It's similar to most uppercase Greek letters, which are like Roman letters. For example, there's no \Alpha or \Beta; just type A or B instead. The uppercase Greek letters, which look different from Roman letters are produced as follows:

Γ \Gamma	Λ \Lambda	Σ \Sigma	Ψ \Psi
Δ \Delta	Ξ \Xi	Υ \Upsilon	Ω \Omega
Θ \Theta	Π \Pi	Φ \Phi	

Figure 9.9 – Uppercase Greek letters

You can see that lowercase Greek letters are typeset in italics, and uppercase Greek letters are written upright. That selection comes from the traditional writing style in mathematics. The frugality of having only italic lowercase letters and a limited amount of upright Greek letters comes from space limitations in character tables in the early time of TeX.

If you would like to have upright Greek letters, you may write \usepackage{upgreek} and use the following commands:

α \upalpha	ζ \upzeta	λ \uplambda	π \uppi	φ \upphi
β \upbeta	η \upeta	μ \upmu	ρ \uprho	χ \upchi
γ \upgamma	θ \uptheta	ν \upnu	σ \upsigma	ψ \uppsi
δ \updelta	ι \upiota	ξ \upxi	τ \uptau	ω \upomega
ε \upepsilon	κ \upkappa	o \mathrm{o}	υ \upupsilon	

Figure 9.10 – Upright lowercase Greek letters

The following variants are available:

ε \upvarepsilon	ϖ \upvarpi	σ \upvarsigma
ϑ \upvartheta	ρ \upvarrho	φ \upvarphi

Figure 9.11 – Alternative upright variants for some Greek letters

The upright Greek letters are taken from the Euler font and not from the default Computer Modern fonts.

Writing script letters

For the 26 uppercase letters A, B, C, …, Z, there's a calligraphic shape, produced by \mathcal:

```
\[ \mathcal{A}, \mathcal{B}, \mathcal{C}, \ldots, \mathcal{Z}
\]
```

This is how they look:

$$\mathcal{A}, \mathcal{B}, \mathcal{C}, \ldots, \mathcal{Z}$$

Figure 9.12 – Calligraphic letters

There are packages offering different calligraphic fonts, such as `zapfino` and `xits`.

Producing an ellipsis

You already know `\ldots` means a low ellipsis. It also works in math mode. We use the low ellipsis mainly between letters and commas. Between operation and relation symbols, writing a centered ellipsis is common practice. Furthermore, a matrix may require a diagonal or a vertical ellipsis. Here's how we can produce them:

...	`\ldots`	$\ddots$	`\ddots`
$\cdots$	`\cdots`	$\vdots$	`\vdots`

Figure 9.13 – Ellipsis in various positions

For a diagonal ellipsis in the other direction, you can use `\reflectbox{$\ddots$}`. The `\reflectbox` command requires `\usepackage{graphicx}` in your preamble.

Changing the font, style, and size

In *Chapter 2*, *Formatting Text and Creating Macros*, we learned to modify the common text font. We can use further commands to change the font style in math mode:

Command	Used package	Example
`\mathrm{...}`		roman 123
`\mathit{...}`		*italic 123*
`\mathsf{...}`		sans − serif 123
`\mathbb{...}`	amsfonts	$\mathbb{ABC}$
`\mathbbm{...}`	bbm	$\mathbb{CRQZ}1$
`\mathds{...}`	dsfont	$\mathbb{CRQZ}1$
`\mathfrak{...}`	eufrak	$\mathfrak{ABC}$ 123
`\mathnormal{...}`		*normal*

Figure 9.14 – Math font commands

So, for example, once you added `\usepackage{dsfont}` to your document preamble, you can use the `\mathds{Z}` command to get a double-stroke letter Z.

Though letters in math mode are italic, they are considered separate as symbols, resulting in a different spacing than an italic word. For instance, in math mode, `fi` may be the product of the variables `f` and `i` but not the ligature `fi`. Compare these two versions:

```
\(Definition\) and \textit{Definition}
```

This gives us the following:

$$Definition \text{ and } \mathit{Definition}$$

Figure 9.15 – Plain math writing versus italic text

The version on the right is definitely better.

Also, `\textit` treats arguments as text in italic math font; that's not the text font. Regarding text within formulas, please read the *Inserting text into formulas* section later in this chapter.

If you wish to switch to bold typeface for a complete math expression, you can use the `\boldmath` declaration before the expression, that is, outside math mode. The `\unboldmath` declaration switches back to the standard typeface. Also the latter is used outside math mode.

To make parts of a formula bold, you can switch to left-to-right mode with the `\mbox` command and use `\boldmath` in its argument.

Four math styles are available, which determines the kind of typesetting and the font size:

- `\textstyle`: Letters and symbols are written as within in-text formulas.
- `\displaystyle`: Letters and symbols are written as they would be in displayed formulas.
- `\scriptstyle`: This uses a smaller font size for subscripts and superscripts.
- `\scriptscriptstyle`: This uses a much smaller font size for the nested script style.

`\textstyle` differs from `\displaystyle` in mainly two ways – with `\textstyle`, variable-sized symbols are smaller, and subscripts and superscripts are usually placed beside the expression instead of below and above, respectively. Otherwise, the font size is the same.

LaTeX switches the style automatically. If you write a simple exponent, it will be typeset in script style with smaller font size.

You may force the desired style using one of the four commands listed here. So, for instance, you can insert \displaystyle into a formula, so even within the text, it would appear like in a displayed formula: bigger fraction and bigger sum signs. Furthermore, subscripts are placed below, and superscripts are placed above. Note – this increases the line spacing.

Customizing displayed formulas

Two document class options modify the way the formulas are displayed:

- fleqn for *flush left equations*: LaTeX will align all displayed formulas at the left margin.

- leqno for *left equation numbers*: All numbered formulas would get the numbers on the left side instead of the right.

Often, formulas are not displayed just standalone. We may encounter situations where the following applies:

- A formula is too long to fit on one line.

- Several formulas are listed row by row.

- An equation is to be transformed step by step.

- A chain of inequalities spans over more than one line.

- Several formulas are to be aligned at relation symbols.

We may also encounter similar situations where we have to write multi-line formulas, often with some kind of alignment. The amsmath package offers specialized environments for nearly every such need, which will be our next section's topic.

Typesetting multi-line formulas

We shall use the amsmath package to typeset a very long formula and a system of equations:

1. Start a new document on A6 paper size to have a smaller text width, so we can see what happens with line breaks without typing super long formulas:

```
\documentclass{article}
\usepackage[a6paper]{geometry}
```

2. Load the amsmath package, and begin the document:

```
\usepackage{amsmath}
\begin{document}
```

3. Use the multline environment to span a long equation over three lines. End the lines with a double backslash \\, except the last one:

```
\begin{multline}
    \sum = a + b + c + d + e \\
            + f + g + h + i + j \\
            + k + l + m + n
\end{multline}
\end{document}
```

4. Click on **Typeset** to compile, and look at the formula:

$$\sum = a + b + c + d + e$$
$$+ f + g + h + i + j$$
$$+ k + l + m + n \quad (1)$$

Figure 9.16 – A formula spanning three lines

5. Now we handle a system of equations. Use the gather environment to add these equations. Again, end lines with \\ except the last one:

```
\begin{gather}
    x + y + z = 0 \\
        y - z = 1
\end{gather}
```

6. Compile again, and look at the equations:

$$x + y + z = 0 \tag{2}$$
$$y - z = 1 \tag{3}$$

Figure 9.17 – A system with two equations

7. Commonly, equation systems are aligned at the equal sign. Let's do this. Use the ampersand symbol & to mark the point that we wish to align:

```
\begin{align}
    x + y + z &= 0 \\
        y - z &= 1
\end{align}
```

8. Compile again; now the equations are aligned as desired:

$$x + y + z = 0 \qquad (4)$$

$$y - z = 1 \qquad (5)$$

Figure 9.18 – A system with two aligned equations

Because we loaded the amsmath package, we have access to several multi-line math environments. Each line in such an environment is ended by \\, except the last one. Otherwise, if we add \\ to the last line, LaTeX would think another line has been started and would also number it, even if the line is empty.

The alignment depends on the environment. Here's a list of the amsmath multi-line environments:

- multline: The first line is left-aligned, the last line is right-aligned, and all others are centered.

- gather: Each line is centered.

- align: Use & to mark a symbol where you want to align the formulas. Use another & to end a column if you need several aligned columns.

- flalign: This is similar to align with more than one column, but the columns are flush to the left and the right margin, respectively.

- alignat: This allows alignment at several places, where each has to be marked by &.

- split: Similar to align, but within another math environment.

- aligned, gathered, and alignedat: Used for an aligned block within a math environment. This can either be displayed math or inline math.

Numbering can be adjusted as follows.

Numbering rows in multi-line formulas

In multi-line math environments, each line is numbered like an ordinary equation. If you wish to suppress the numbering of a line, write \notag before the end of the line.

If you would like to have a particular style of numbering, such as a symbol or name as a tag for a formula, you can use the \tag command, such as \tag{$\star$} to mark it with a star, or \tag{name} for tagging it as **(name)**.

Use a starred variant such as align* or gather* if you would like to avoid numbering altogether.

Inserting text into formulas

To insert some text into a formula, standard LaTeX provides the \mbox command. amsmath offers further controls:

- \text{words} inserts text within a math formula. The size is adjusted according to the current math style; \text produces smaller text within subscripts or superscripts.
- \intertext{text} suspends the formula, then prints the text in a separate paragraph, then the multi-line formula is resumed, keeping the alignment. Use it for longer text.

These commands are good when you would like to use text within math environments.

Let's now look into mathematical symbols.

Exploring the wealth of math symbols

Let's go beyond writing variables and basic math operators. We may need many symbols for particular purposes: relation signs, unary and binary operators, function-like operators, sum and integral symbols and variants of the latter, arrows, and many more. LaTeX and additional packages offer thousands of symbols for many purposes.

So, let's look at some math symbols and the commands for producing them. We shall cover many standard LaTeX symbols; the latexsym package provides some additional symbols. Even more symbols are accessible using, for instance, the amssymb package.

Binary operation symbols

Besides plus and minus, there are a few more operations:

		Standard LaTeX				
II	\amalg	∘	\circ	⊖	\ominus	⋆ \star
∗	\ast	∪	\cup	⊕	\oplus	× \times
◯	\bigcirc	†	\dagger	⊘	\oslash	◁ \triangleleft
▽	\bigtriangledown	‡	\ddagger	⊗	\otimes	▷ \triangleright
△	\bigtriangleup	⋄	\diamond	±	\pm	⊎ \uplus
•	\bullet	÷	\div	\	\setminus	∨ \vee
∩	\cap	∓	\mp	⊓	\sqcap	∧ \wedge
·	\cdot	⊙	\odot	⊔	\sqcup	≀ \wr
		latexsym				
⊴	\unlhd	⊵	\unrhd	▷	\rhd	◁ \lhd

Figure 9.19 – Binary operation symbols

You need to have \usepackage{latexsym} in your document preamble to be able to use the symbols in the last row here.

Binary relation symbols

Values of expressions might be equal, in which case you just need an equal sign =, but there are other possible relations. For example, they may be congruent, parallel, or they might have any other relation:

			Standard LaTeX				
≈	\approx	≡	\equiv	≺	\prec	≻	\succ
≍	\asymp	⌢	\frown	≼	\preceq	≽	\succeq
⋈	\bowtie	|	\mid	∝	\propto	⊢	\vdash
≅	\cong	⊨	\models	∼	\sim		
⊣	\dashv	∥	\parallel	≃	\simeq		
≐	\doteq	⊥	\perp	⌣	\smile		
			latexsym				
		⋈	\Join				

Figure 9.20 – Binary relation symbols

You can negate any relation by inserting \not before it. So, for *not equivalent*, use \not \equiv to create a crossed-out \equiv symbol.

Inequality relation symbols

If expressions are not equal, we can describe the inequality in different ways:

$\geq$ \geq	$\gg$ \gg	$\leq$ \leq	$\ll$ \ll	$\neq$ \neq

Figure 9.21 – Inequality relation symbols

Here, \neq looks precisely like what you get when you write \not=, as in the previous section.

Subset and superset symbols

For comparing sets and expressing relations between them, there are many symbols:

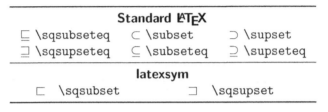

Standard LaTeX		
$\sqsubseteq$ \sqsubseteq	$\subset$ \subset	$\supset$ \supset
$\sqsupseteq$ \sqsupseteq	$\subseteq$ \subseteq	$\supseteq$ \supseteq
latexsym		
$\sqsubset$ \sqsubset		$\sqsupset$ \sqsupset

Figure 9.22 – Subset and superset symbols

Also, here you can use \not to negate such a set relation.

Arrows

LaTeX provides us with lots of different arrows:

Standard LaTeX		
$\downarrow$ \downarrow	$\Longleftarrow$ \Longleftarrow	$\Rightarrow$ \Rightarrow
$\Downarrow$ \Downarrow	$\longleftrightarrow$ \longleftrightarrow	$\searrow$ \searrow
$\hookleftarrow$ \hookleftarrow	$\Longleftrightarrow$ \Longleftrightarrow	$\swarrow$ \swarrow
$\hookrightarrow$ \hookrightarrow	$\longmapsto$ \longmapsto	$\uparrow$ \uparrow
$\leftarrow$ \leftarrow	$\longrightarrow$ \longrightarrow	$\Uparrow$ \Uparrow
$\Leftarrow$ \Leftarrow	$\Longrightarrow$ \Longrightarrow	$\updownarrow$ \updownarrow
$\leftrightarrow$ \leftrightarrow	$\mapsto$ \mapsto	$\Updownarrow$ \Updownarrow
$\Leftrightarrow$ \Leftrightarrow	$\nwarrow$ \nwarrow	
$\longleftarrow$ \longleftarrow	$\rightarrow$ \rightarrow	
latexsym		
$\leadsto$ \leadsto		

Figure 9.23 – Arrows

Arrows are used for implications, maps, or descriptive expressions.

Harpoons

There are special arrows called harpoons:

↽ \leftharpoondown	⇁ \rightharpoondown	⇌ \rightleftharpoons
↼ \leftharpoonup	⇀ \rightharpoonup	

Figure 9.24 – Harpoons

Harpoons are used, for example, in chemical reaction formulas.

Symbols derived from letters

Some letter-like symbols are used in math:

Standard LaTeX				
⊥ \bot	∀ \forall	$\imath$ \imath	∋ \ni	⊤ \top
ℓ \ell	ℏ \hbar	∈ \in	∂ \partial	℘ \wp
∃ \exists	ℑ \Im	$\jmath$ \jmath	ℜ \Re	

latexsym
℧ \mho

Figure 9.25 – Symbols derived from letters

Mathematicians will probably often use \in, \forall, and \exists in statements.

Miscellaneous symbols

Here are more LaTeX symbols that do not match the aforementioned categories:

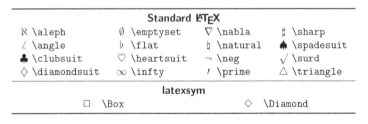

Standard LaTeX			
ℵ \aleph	∅ \emptyset	∇ \nabla	♯ \sharp
∠ \angle	♭ \flat	♮ \natural	♠ \spadesuit
♣ \clubsuit	♡ \heartsuit	¬ \neg	√ \surd
◇ \diamondsuit	∞ \infty	′ \prime	△ \triangle

latexsym		
□ \Box		◇ \Diamond

Figure 9.26 – Additional LaTeX symbols

The Comprehensive LaTeX Symbol List lists about 15,000 symbols sorted into categories. If you need to search for a symbol, have a look at this document. As usual, with TeX Live, you could open this document by using the following code at the command prompt:

```
texdoc symbols
```

Or visit `https://texdoc.org/pkg/symbols` to read that list of symbols.

Handwritten symbol recognition is a different and fascinating approach. You draw a symbol with the mouse (or with your finger on a touchscreen), and the software tries to recognize the symbol and tells you the code for it. Let's have a quick look:

1. Visit `https://detexify.kirelabs.org`.

2. Draw into the white box. It doesn't matter if it's a shaky mouse sketch, like this:

Figure 9.27 – Handwritten symbol

3. After a few seconds, you get suggestions for symbols and the corresponding code:

Figure 9.28 – Symbol and code suggestions

Detexify also offers a name search feature. Click the **symbols** button at the top, enter a phrase into a filter, and Detexify will show symbols and commands that match that phrase.

Writing units

If you use units in text, they should not look like variables. For example, m for meters should not look exactly like a variable m. Similarly, s may stand for seconds, but not for a variable s. A typographical convention is to use an upright font shape for units, while variables are written in italics. Furthermore, it's common to use a thin space between the value and the dimension. So, for 10 meters, you may write `10\,\mathrm{m}`. However, this is very time-consuming. That's why the `siunitx` package has been developed, which supports correct and consistent typesetting of units. It requires reading some documentation before you can use it, but it's worth the effort. Run `texdoc siunitx` at the command prompt or visit `https://texdoc.org/pkg/siunitx`.

Variable sized operators

For sums, products, and set operations, we can use operator symbols that are variable in size: they are bigger in display style and smaller in text style.

$\bigcap$ \bigcap	$\bigotimes$ \bigotimes	$\bigwedge$ \bigwedge	$\prod$ \prod
$\bigcup$ \bigcup	$\bigsqcup$ \bigsqcup	$\coprod$ \coprod	$\sum$ \sum
$\bigodot$ \bigodot	$\biguplus$ \biguplus	$\int$ \int	
$\bigoplus$ \bigoplus	$\bigvee$ \bigvee	$\oint$ \oint	

Figure 9.29 – Variable sized operators

Let's see what this means in text style:

```
\(
    \int_a^b \! f(x) \, dx = \lim_{\Delta x \rightarrow 0}
    \sum_{i=1}^{n} f(x_i) \,\Delta x_i
\)
```

This code gives us the following:

$$\int_a^b f(x)\, dx = \lim_{\Delta x \to 0} \sum_{i=1}^{n} f(x_i)\, \Delta x_i$$

Figure 9.30 – Inline text style equation

And this is the same equation in displayed style:

```
\[
    \int_a^b \! f(x) \, dx = \lim_{\Delta x \rightarrow 0}
    \sum_{i=1}^{n} f(x_i) \,\Delta x_i
\]
```

This time we get the following:

$$\int_a^b f(x)\, dx = \lim_{\Delta x \to 0} \sum_{i=1}^{n} f(x_i)\, \Delta x_i$$

Figure 9.31 – Displayed style equation

As we see, the symbols are significantly bigger in displayed style.

Variable sized delimiters

Delimiters such as parentheses, brackets, and braces can vary in size. The following are such LaTeX delimiters:

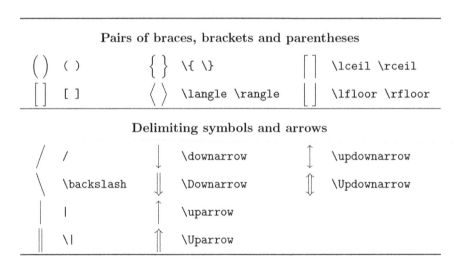

Figure 9.32 – Variable sized delimiters

If you write \left or \right before such a delimiter, its size will be automatically matched to the size of the inner expression. We have to use these size macros in pairs. To match a pair, if you don't wish to have a second delimiter, use \left. or \right. to get an invisible delimiter on one side.

Automatically self-adjusting delimiters are useful for bigger composed math terms, such as matrices, so let's look into this next.

Building math structures

Variables and constants are simple. But there are more complex objects, such as binomial coefficients, vectors, and matrices. We shall figure out how to typeset such structures.

Let's begin with simple arrays.

Creating arrays

For arranging math expressions within a surrounding expression, there's the `array` environment. We use it exactly like a `tabular` environment. However, it requires math mode, and all of its entries are made using math mode as well.

For example, we can use variable-sized parentheses around an array:

```
\[
  A = \left(
    \begin{array}{cc}
      a_{11} & a_{12} \\
      a_{21} & a_{22}
    \end{array}
  \right)
\]
```

This produces a matrix:

$$A = \left(\begin{array}{cc} a_{11} & a_{12} \\ a_{21} & a_{22} \end{array} \right)$$

Figure 9.33 – A simple array

There are specific commands for matrices.

Typesetting matrices

The `amsmath` package provides us with many special matrix environments. A standard matrix can be typeset by the `pmatrix` environment:

```
\documentclass{article}
\usepackage{amsmath}
```

```
\begin{document}
\[
  A = \begin{pmatrix}
    a_{11} & a_{12} \\
    a_{21} & a_{22}
  \end{pmatrix}
\]
\end{document}
```

The following is the output:

$$A = \begin{pmatrix} a_{11} & a_{12} \\ a_{21} & a_{22} \end{pmatrix}$$

Figure 9.34 – A simple matrix

You may notice that the parentheses are closer to the matrix entries than in the array example in the previous section. That tighter layout comes from the amsmath style.

These are amsmath matrix environments and their delimiters:

- matrix: no delimiters
- pmatrix: parentheses ( )
- bmatrix: square brackets [ ]
- Bmatrix: braces { }
- vmatrix: ||
- Vmatrix: || ||
- smallmatrix: no delimiters – can be added if needed, more compact

The compact smallmatrix environment is useful for matrices within regular text.

Writing binomial coefficients

We could write binomial coefficients and matrices using an array together with delimiters. However, the amsmath package provides shorter commands, for instance, \binom for binomial coefficients:

```
\binom{n}{k} = \frac{n!}{k!(n-k)!}
```

The result is as follows:

$$\binom{n}{k} = \frac{n!}{k!(n-k)!}$$

Figure 9.35 – A binomial coefficient in an equation

That's a more straightforward syntax for such small expressions compared to arrays or matrices.

Underlining and overlining

\overline puts a line above its argument:

```
\overline{\Omega}
```

This gives us the following:

$$\overline{\Omega}$$

Figure 9.36 – An overlined omega symbol

The counterpart is \underline.

It doesn't always have to be a line; braces are popular too. The commands for using braces are \underbrace and \overbrace.

```
N = \underbrace{1 + 1 + \cdots + 1}_n
```

This results in the following:

$$N = \underbrace{1 + 1 + \cdots + 1}_{n}$$

Figure 9.37 – An underbrace below an expression

A subscript to an underbrace is written below, a superscript to an overbrace is placed above.

Setting accents

In *Chapter 2*, *Formatting Text and Creating Macros*, we've already seen how to write accents in text mode. For math mode, we need different commands. We can apply them to any letter. Here's the list of math accents using the lowercase letter *a* as an example:

$\acute{a}$ \acute{a}	$\check{a}$ \check{a}	$\grave{a}$ \grave{a}	$\tilde{a}$ \tilde{a}
$\bar{a}$ \bar{a}	$\ddot{a}$ \ddot{a}	$\hat{a}$ \hat{a}	$\vec{a}$ \vec{a}
$\breve{a}$ \breve{a}	$\dot{a}$ \dot{a}	$\mathring{a}$ \mathring{a}	

Extensible

$\widehat{abc}$ \widehat{abc}	$\widetilde{abc}$ \widetilde{abc}

Figure 9.38 – Various math accents

The **extensible accents** are also called **wide accents**. They fit the width of their argument.

Putting a symbol above or below another one

Besides the array environment, there are amsmath commands to stack expressions directly:

- \underset{expression below}{expression} puts an expression below another, using the subscript size below.
- \overset{expression above}{expression} puts an expression above another, using the subscript size above.

This is an example of how we can use these commands:

```
\underset{\circ}{\cap} \neq \overset{\circ}{\cup}
```

The preceding code gives us the following:

$$\underset{\circ}{\cap} \neq \overset{\circ}{\cup}$$

Figure 9.39 – Putting a symbol above or below another one

Another handy command is \stackrel{expression above}{relation}. See the following formula, for example:

```
X \stackrel{\text{def}}{=} 0
```

It gives us the following:

$$X \stackrel{\text{def}}{=} 0$$

Figure 9.40 – Text above a relation symbol

`\stackrel` puts an expression above a relation sign.

Writing theorems and definitions

LaTeX provides environments for theorems, definitions, and the like. Returning to our very first example in this chapter, we could use the `\newtheorem` command to define a **Theorem** environment `thm` as follows:

```
\newtheorem{thm}{Theorem}
```

Then, we can declare a **Definition** environment. Let's call it `dfn` here:

```
\newtheorem{dfn}[thm]{Definition}
```

We can use an optional argument referring to an existing environment (here, `thm`). Then this new environment uses the same counter as that already existing environment. In our case here, this means that after *Theorem 1* follows *Definition 2*.

We can use these environments in this simple way as follows:

```
\begin{dfn}
  A quadratic equation is an equation of the form
  \begin{equation}
    \label{quad}
    ax^2 + bx + c = 0,
  \end{equation}
  where \( a, b \) and \( c \) are constants and \( a \neq 0
\).
\end{dfn}
\begin{thm}
  A quadratic equation (\ref{quad}) has two solutions for the
  Variable \( x \):
  \begin{equation}
    \label{root}
```

```
      x_{1,2} = \frac{-b \pm \sqrt{b^2-4ac}}{2a}.
   \end{equation}
\end{thm}
```

Take a look at the output:

Definition 1 *A quadratic equation is an equation of the form*

$$ax^2 + bx + c = 0, \tag{1}$$

where a, b and c are constants and $a \neq 0$.

Theorem 2 *A quadratic equation (1) has two solutions for the Variable x:*

$$x_{1,2} = \frac{-b \pm \sqrt{b^2 - 4ac}}{2a}. \tag{2}$$

Figure 9.41 – A definition and a theorem

In the output, such environments are numbered and labeled **Definition** and **Theorem**, respectively. In *Chapter 11, Developing Large Documents*, when we prepare large documents, we will use this to create a complete document containing definitions, theorems, and lemmas.

There are two special packages offering much more flexibility:

- `amsthm` provides several styles, allows fine customization, and includes a proof environment.

- `ntheorem` does similar work but handles traditional *quod erat demonstrandum* (*what was to be shown*) end marks for proofs in a better way.

If you would like to use such environments, look at their documentation and compare the relevant features to decide which package is the best for you. As usual, execute `texdoc amsthm` and `texdoc ntheorem` at the command prompt, or visit `https://texdoc.org/pkg/amsthm` and `https://texdoc.org/pkg/ntheorem`.

Choose one of those closely related packages; don't load both.

Further tools for writing mathematics

Take a look at all the mathematics typesetting options in `amsmath` by entering `texdoc amsmath` at the command line or visit `https://texdoc.org/pkg/amsmath`.

The `mathtools` package extends `amsmath`. If you need a particular feature and cannot find it, neither in standard LaTeX nor in `amsmath`, look at `mathtools`. Here are some of its features:

- Tools for fine-tuning math typesetting, for example, more compact superscript styles

- Aligning limits of consecutive operators vertically

- Adjusting the width of operators

- Better control over tags – modifying their appearance and only showing tags for equations that have been referenced

- Extensible symbols – more arrows along with the ability to adjust their width automatically; also offers extensible brackets and braces to be set under or over expressions

- New math environments for more flexible matrices, cases, improved multi-line formulas, and arrows between aligned formulas

- Less spacing for shorter intertext

- Declaration of paired delimiters

- Additional symbols such as a vertically centered colon, along with combinations of relation symbols with colons and shortcuts for auto-sized parentheses

- Techniques such as spreading lines in multi-line formulas, setting left subscripts and superscripts, typesetting math within italicized text, and producing multi-line fractions

Have a look at the documentation of this valuable package and find out which commands can be applied to achieve the styles and alignments listed here. Open it by running `texdoc mathtools` at the command prompt or go to `https://texdoc.org/pkg/mathtools`.

In *Chapter 10, Advanced Mathematics*, in the *LaTeX Cookbook*, you can find a lot of examples showing enhancements with the `mathtools` package. Visit `https://latex-cookbook.net/tag/mathematics/` to see and run examples online that include fine-tuning math formulas, automatic line breaking in equations, plotting functions, and drawing diagrams and geometry pictures.

Summary

Now we can write complex math formulas, and we've got the necessary tools to write scientific texts. We worked with the `amsmath` package, which provides us with many features tailored to traditional mathematical typesetting.

We can now fine-tune math expressions, align and number equations, and use various math symbols from symbol fonts. In the next chapter, we will also work with fonts, in general.

10
Using Fonts

The text's base font determines the appearance of your text significantly. You may choose a font that's especially clear and readable for a long piece of writing or a fancy calligraphic font for a greeting card. Your job application letter might use a very clear and serious font, whereas a mathematical article requires fonts with a lot of symbols and a text font that fits well with them.

Until now, we have been covering the logical properties of fonts. Although we have always used the LaTeX standard font, we switched, for instance, from roman to sans-serif, or typewriter, and learned how to make text bold, italicized, or slanted in *Chapter 2, Formatting Text and Creating Macros*. However, we never deviated from the standard set of fonts.

In this chapter, we will cover the following topics:

- Using comprehensive font bundles
- Using specific font families
- Using arbitrary fonts

While we will inspect the text appearance, we will also look at the design of math formulas when fonts support math symbols.

As this book is printed and electronically distributed with bitmap images, you will not see the original LaTeX quality in the font samples in this chapter. Visit `https://latexguide.org/chapter-10` to see the fonts in original LaTeX and PDF quality. We will see the font examples in a larger size to easily highlight the fine details and differences.

Let's start with an example. This will be the basis of our work with fonts throughout this chapter.

Technical requirements

You can use a local LaTeX installation, or you can compile the example code online at `https://latexguide.org/chapter-10`.

The code is available on GitHub: `https://github.com/PacktPublishing/LaTeX-Beginner-s-Guide-2nd-Edition-/tree/main/Chapter_10_-_Using_Fonts`.

In this chapter, we will use the following packages: `arev`, `beramono`, `bookman`, `calligra`, `charter`, `cmbright`, `concmath`, `concrete`, `courier`, `fontenc`, `fouriernc`, `helvet`, `inconsolata`, `kerkis`, `kmath`, `kpfonts`, `kurier`, `lmodern`, `mathdesign`, `miama`, `newcent`, `newpx`, `newpxmath`, `newtx`, `newtxmath`, `sfmath`, and `unicode-math`.

In addition, we will briefly discuss these packages: `cm-super`, `inputenc`, and `sansmath`.

You can find other and advanced code examples in the *LaTeX Cookbook, Chapter 3, Adjusting Fonts*, with compilable code at the book's website: `https://latex-cookbook.net/chapter-3`.

Using comprehensive font bundles

We start with the most extensive font bundles. To test fonts, we may use a **pangram**. This word has a Greek origin: *pan gramma* means *every letter*. It stands for a sentence that uses every letter of the alphabet. Thus, a pangram is very convenient for displaying fonts.

We will print out a very famous pangram phrase using the **Latin Modern** font family. Latin Modern is very similar to the default LaTeX font called **Computer Modern**. However, Latin Modern contains a lot of additional characters, most of them being accented characters. Because of this advantage and its very high quality, we can consider it as the successor to the standard font. Let's see how it looks in various font families and shapes, and with a math formula:

1. Start a new document:

    ```
    \documentclass{article}
    ```

2. Create a macro for the pangram with additional numerals. It will have one argument, which will be our font family or shape selection command. We will add a paragraph break at the end, as shown:

    ```
    \newcommand{\pangram}[1]{{#1 The quick brown fox
    jumps over the lazy dog. 1234567890\par}}
    ```

3. Load the fontenc package and choose T1 font encoding:

    ```
    \usepackage[T1]{fontenc}
    ```

4. Load the lmodern package to get the Latin Modern font:

    ```
    \usepackage{lmodern}
    ```

5. Begin the document and choose a large font size so that we can see the details clearly:

    ```
    \begin{document}
    \large
    ```

6. Now we use our \pangram macro several times with different font settings:

    ```
    \pangram{\rmfamily}
    \pangram{\sffamily}
    \pangram{\ttfamily}
    \pangram{\itshape}
    \pangram{\slshape}
    ```

7. To get a math font example, we use the code that we wrote for *Figure 9.29* in *Chapter 9, Writing Math Formulas*:

    ```
    \[
       \int_a^b \! f(x) \, dx = \lim_{\Delta x \rightarrow 0}
       \sum_{i=1}^{n} f(x_i) \,\Delta x_i
    \]
    \end{document}
    ```

8. Click on **Typeset** to compile, and then look at the font examples:

The quick brown fox jumps over the lazy dog. 1234567890
The quick brown fox jumps over the lazy dog. 1234567890
The quick brown fox jumps over the lazy dog.   1234567890
The quick brown fox jumps over the lazy dog. 1234567890
The quick brown fox jumps over the lazy dog. 1234567890

$$\int_a^b f(x)\,dx = \lim_{\Delta x \to 0} \sum_{i=1}^{n} f(x_i)\,\Delta x_i$$

Figure 10.1 – Latin Modern font examples

In our \pangram macro, we had another pair of curly braces. In our argument { { ... } }, the outer curly brace contains the argument to \newcommand, and the inner curly braces embrace our commands to restrict the effect of the font command.

> **Note**
>
> The \pangram macro is just a small demonstration macro for us, so we won't have to repeat the demo sentence for each font family. In your everyday documents, load the font package and just write your text. If needed, you can switch between font families such as \sffamily, \ttfamily, or \rmfamily.

In *step 3*, we chose a **font encoding**. Technically, encodings are mappings of character codes to symbols of the font. For Western European languages and English, the T1 font encoding is highly recommendable. It's also known as **Cork encoding** because it was developed in the city of Cork in Ireland during a TeX user group conference. The default LaTeX font encoding is called OT1. Compared to OT1, the T1 encoding has larger encoding tables that significantly improve accented characters' internal handling.

For example, with the default historic LaTeX encoding, the accented character ö is composed of the glyph o and dots, to be printed in the PDF file. With T1, an ö is a single glyph of the current font. Thus, LaTeX can also properly apply hyphenation rules to the words containing accented characters. The search feature of a PDF reader also works with those characters, and copying and pasting from the PDF file also works fine. With default OT1 encoding, copying and pasting the character ö would result in dots and an o.

> **Tip**
>
> If you notice a decrease in default font quality with `T1` encoding, your installation may be missing fonts. In that case, install the `cm-super` package using the package manager, or switch to one of the fonts that we see in the following sections.

While this is output encoding, you may also encounter the term **input encoding**. Modern operating systems and editors support **UTF8** –**Unicode** – an industry standard for text encoding that extends the ASCII code. LaTeX directly supports UTF8, so we won't need to do anything. So, if you encounter the `inputenc` package in older books or code on the internet, you may omit it.

Now, we will take a look at some good fonts with examples. All of them supports `T1` encoding, so before you load a font, use the following command:

```
\usepackage[T1]{fontenc}
```

In the following sections, we will explore the different fonts.

Latin Modern – a replacement for the standard font

Latin Modern has been designed to look like the default LaTeX font, but the encoding has been improved, and it has also received some more fine-tuning. Latin Modern contains many diacritic characters, whereas, with Computer Modern, such characters are built from letters and accents.

Latin Modern has 72 text fonts and 20 math fonts under the hood to work with all font families, shapes, and weights.

In *Figure 10.1*, we saw how it looks.

Kp-Fonts – another extensive set of fonts

Th **Kp-Fonts** collection from the Johannes Kepler project provides serif, sans-serif, and monospaced fonts as well as mathematics symbol fonts in different shapes and weights. Even bold extended and combinations such as slanted serif small caps are present.

Just load the package to use those fonts:

```
\usepackage{kpfonts}
```

The previous example will change to the following:

> The quick brown fox jumps over the lazy dog. 1234567890
> The quick brown fox jumps over the lazy dog. 1234567890
> The quick brown fox jumps over the lazy dog.   1234567890
> *The quick brown fox jumps over the lazy dog. 1234567890*
> *The quick brown fox jumps over the lazy dog. 1234567890*

$$\int_a^b f(x)\,dx = \lim_{\Delta x \to 0} \sum_{i=1}^{n} f(x_i)\,\Delta x_i$$

Figure 10.2 – Kepler font examples

Kp-Fonts offers light versions with the same font metrics. The light versions might look nice in print, but that light appearance might not be perfect for reading on screen.

To switch to the light font set, load the package with the `light` option:

```
\usepackage[light]{kpfonts}
```

The look will be different now:

> The quick brown fox jumps over the lazy dog. 1234567890
> The quick brown fox jumps over the lazy dog. 1234567890
> The quick brown fox jumps over the lazy dog.   1234567890
> *The quick brown fox jumps over the lazy dog. 1234567890*
> *The quick brown fox jumps over the lazy dog. 1234567890*

$$\int_a^b f(x)\,dx = \lim_{\Delta x \to 0} \sum_{i=1}^{n} f(x_i)\,\Delta x_i$$

Figure 10.3 – Kepler font as a light version

Now, let's look at specialized font packages that come with a single style.

Using specific font families

We will explore many more TeX fonts that are special in their own way. We will use our `\pangram` macro from the previous section with the corresponding family command for testing.

Serif fonts

A small line or stroke attached to a larger stroke in a letter or symbol is called a **serif**. A font regularly using such serifs is called a serif font, or a serif typeface.

The default serif font is called **Computer Modern Roman**. Latin Modern provides a very similar font, and you already know the Kp-Fonts serif font. Other packages specialize in serif fonts, and we will now look at some of them.

Times Roman

The `newtx` package defines a **Times** text font and a matching math font.

It's split into two parts, so they can be used independently, such as when you would like to have a different math font. That's why we load it in this way:

```
\usepackage{newtxtext}
\usepackage{newtxmath}
```

With `\pangram{\rmfamily}` and our math formula, we get the following:

The quick brown fox jumps over the lazy dog. 1234567890

$$\int_a^b f(x)\,dx = \lim_{\Delta x \to 0} \sum_{i=1}^n f(x_i)\,\Delta x_i$$

Figure 10.4 – A Times Roman font

As you can see, Times is a very narrow font suitable for multi-column text as in newspapers, but not so recommended for single-column text. Wide text lines would be less readable.

Palatino

The `newpx` package defines a Palatino text font and a matching math font. This package consists of two parts for independent use, so we load it in this way:

```
\usepackage{newpxtext}
\usepackage{newpxmath}
```

This gives us the following:

The quick brown fox jumps over the lazy dog. 1234567890

$$\int_a^b f(x)\,dx = \lim_{\Delta x \to 0} \sum_{i=1}^{n} f(x_i)\,\Delta x_i$$

Figure 10.5 – A Palatino font

We can see that Palatino is considerably wider than Times.

Charter

Charter is similar to the default Computer Modern font but a bit heavier. We load it as shown:

```
\usepackage{charter}
```

For proper math support, load the `mathdesign` package with the `charter` option instead of loading `charter` directly:

```
\usepackage[charter]{mathdesign}
```

This results in the following:

The quick brown fox jumps over the lazy dog. 1234567890

$$\int_a^b f(x)\,dx = \lim_{\Delta x \to 0} \sum_{i=1}^{n} f(x_i)\,\Delta x_i$$

Figure 10.6 – Charter and mathdesign fonts

> **Text fonts for the mathdesign package**
>
> In addition to `charter`, `mathdesign` can load the **Utopia** font by means of `\usepackage[utopia]{mathdesign}` and the **Garamond** font by means of `\usepackage[garamond]{mathdesign}`.

New Century Schoolbook

The `newcent` package provides this easy-to-read serif typeface, **New Century Schoolbook**:

```
\usepackage{newcent}
```

For a suitable math font, you may wish to load the **Fourier** math fonts:

```
\usepackage{fouriernc}
```

Here they are together:

The quick brown fox jumps over the lazy dog. 1234567890

$$\int_a^b f(x)\,dx = \lim_{\Delta x \to 0} \sum_{i=1}^n f(x_i)\,\Delta x_i$$

Figure 10.7 – New Century Schoolbook and Fourier fonts

nc in the fouriernc package stands for *New Century* because it's set up for being used together.

Concrete Roman

The **Concrete Roman** font may not look perfect on screen but offers high quality in print. Just load the concrete package:

```
\usepackage{concrete}
```

Also, for Concrete Roman, there's a matching math font package, called concmath:

```
\usepackage{concmath}
```

These give us the following:

The quick brown fox jumps over the lazy dog. 1234567890

$$\int_a^b f(x)\,dx = \lim_{\Delta x \to 0} \sum_{i=1}^n f(x_i)\,\Delta x_i$$

Figure 10.8 – Concrete Roman font with math support

With the upright integral sign and the non-serif summation sign, Concrete Roman looks distinctive.

Bookman

Bookman is an old-style serif font, provided by the bookman package, loaded by the following command:

```
\usepackage{bookman}
```

The **Kerkis** font is an extension of bookman with math support, meaning that you can load this instead:

```
\usepackage{kmath}
\usepackage{kerkis}
```

We get the following:

The quick brown fox jumps over the lazy dog. 1234567890

$$\int_a^b f(x)\, dx = \lim_{\Delta x \to 0} \sum_{i=1}^{n} f(x_i)\, \Delta x_i$$

Figure 10.9 – Kerkis, aka Bookman, with math support

An even more enhanced Bookman version is available under the name **TeX Gyre Bonum**. This one, though, especially with math support, is better used as an OpenType font. In the last section of this chapter, *Using arbitrary fonts*, we will deal with this.

Font names

Same or similar fonts can have very different names. That's often for legal reasons, as the font names can be protected, but the design can be used.

Sans-serif fonts

Sans-serif fonts are simply fonts where no serifs are used. They may look straighter and clearer and are a good choice for slide presentations.

They don't appear as heavy as serif fonts when they are bold. That's why they may be a good choice for headings, but many believe that running text with traditional serifs is much more readable.

That's the reason why **KOMA-Script** classes use a serif font in the document body text and a sans-serif font for the headings by default.

If required, the main body font could be rendered sans-serif by means of this command:

```
\renewcommand{\familydefault}{\sfdefault}
```

We already know that Latin Modern and Kp-Fonts provide sans serif fonts. Let's now take another look at some specific sans-serif fonts.

Arev

Arev is a sans-serif font designed for slide presentations. The name means Vera backward, as it extends the **Vera Sans** font, which is derived from the **Frutiger** font. Arev adds math support. Load it by means of the following command:

```
\usepackage{arev}
```

Text and math become the following:

The quick brown fox jumps over the lazy dog. 1234567890

$$\int_a^b f(x)\,dx = \lim_{\Delta x \to 0} \sum_{i=1}^n f(x_i)\,\Delta x_i$$

Figure 10.10 – Arev, a Frutiger-like font

Note that integral and summation signs still show serifs, as this is very common.

Computer Modern Bright

CM Bright has been derived from Computer Modern Sans Serif to have a lighter font. The `cmbright` package provides this font together with a light typewriter font and a sans-serif math font. Load it by means of the following command:

```
\usepackage{cmbright}
```

The output of our sample code will be as follows:

The quick brown fox jumps over the lazy dog. 1234567890

$$\int_a^b f(x)\,dx = \lim_{\Delta x \to 0} \sum_{i=1}^n f(x_i)\,\Delta x_i$$

Figure 10.11 – Computer Modern Bright font

If you compare it with other sans serif fonts, it's less intrusive. It would be good not to match it with a heavier serif font because of the different weights.

Kurier

Some sans-serif fonts appear to look similar, but you can see differences in detail – look at the Kurier font in *Figure 10.12*, for example, at the letter g and the math symbols. Load it by means of the following command:

```
\usepackage{kurier}
```

We get math support by using the `math` option:

```
\usepackage[math]{kurier}
```

Compiling our example code gives us the following:

The quick brown fox jumps over the lazy dog. 1234567890

$$\int_a^b f(x)\, dx = \lim_{\Delta x \to 0} \sum_{i=1}^n f(x_i)\, \Delta x_i$$

Figure 10.12 – The Kurier font

In this case, we have even integral and summation signs without serifs.

Helvetica

The classical sans-serif font **Helvetica** is simple and clean. You probably know a descendant made by Microsoft: **Arial**. Load the font this way:

```
\usepackage{helvet}
```

Use the `scaled` option if the font looks too big, especially when used together with a serif font. For instance, to get it a bit smaller, you can write the following:

```
\usepackage[scaled=0.95]{helvet}
```

Helvetica doesn't provide direct math support, but the `sfmath` package comes to the rescue:

```
\usepackage{sfmath}
```

If you add the `sfmath` package to your document preamble, the current sans-serif text font will also be used within math formulas. Load it after other font packages, so it has a chance to detect the font. Further explanations with examples, more options, and an alternative approach with the `sansmath` package can be found in *Chapter 3, Adjusting Fonts*, in the *LaTeX Cookbook*.

Loading `helvet` and `sfmath` as in this section results in the following output:

The quick brown fox jumps over the lazy dog. 1234567890

$$\int_a^b f(x)\, dx = \lim_{\Delta x \to 0} \sum_{i=1}^{n} f(x_i)\, \Delta x_i$$

Figure 10.13 – Helvetica example

At the `sfmath` author's home page, `https://dtrx.de/od/tex/sfmath.html`, you can find further information.

Typewriter fonts

Typewriter fonts, a.k.a. **monospaced** fonts, are widely used for source codes, as in this book. We will look at three of them.

Courier

Courier is a very wide-running typewriter font. We can load it by means of the following command:

```
\usepackage{courier}
```

Then, with `\ttfamily` or `\texttt`, we will get the following:

```
The quick brown fox jumps over the lazy dog.  1234567890
```

Figure 10.14 – The Courier font

If that looks too big compared to your standard document font, you can load the `couriers` package (s for scaled) with a scaled option, such as:

```
\usepackage[scaled=0.95]{couriers}
```

This gives us the Courier font with 95% of its original size.

Inconsolata

Inconsolata is a very nice, monospaced font designed for source code listings. It is easy to read and not as wide as Courier. Load it by means of the following command:

```
\usepackage{inconsolata}
```

The output proves that monospaced fonts can be beautiful:

```
The quick brown fox jumps over the lazy dog. 1234567890
```

Figure 10.15 – The Inconsolata font

In contrast to Courier, it is sans-serif. It also works with a `scaled` option.

Bera Mono

Bera Mono is another sans-serif typewriter font. Use it by means of the following command:

```
\usepackage{beramono}
```

This is how it looks:

```
The quick brown fox jumps over the lazy dog.  1234567890
```

Figure 10.16 – The Bera Mono font

Here, also you can specify a `scaled` option.

Calligraphic fonts

Calligraphic fonts are **script typefaces** with fluid strokes similar to handwriting. Let's pick two beautiful handwriting fonts for a closer look.

Calligra

We load the font as usual:

```
\usepackage{calligra}
```

For switching to the font, we can use the `\calligra` command in the text. As we know about local switching commands, that font will be valid until a surrounding environment or group { ... } ends. It also works with our `\pangram` macro, such as:

```
\pangram{\calligra}
```

This prints the following:

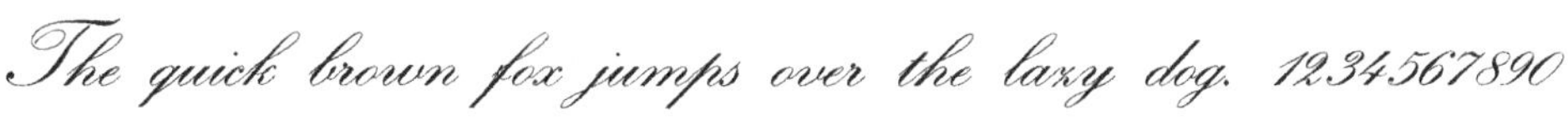

The quick brown fox jumps over the lazy dog. 1234567890

Figure 10.17 – The Calligra handwritten font

Capital letters and letters with descenders look exceptionally playful.

Miama Nueva

Miama Nueva writes beautiful ascenders and descenders. Load it by means of the following command:

```
\usepackage{miama}
```

Then, the \fmmfamily command switches to that font. Again, use it within a group { … } or an environment if you would like to limit the font to just a piece of text. We can use our \pangram macro again:

```
\pangram{\fmmfamily}
```

The writing is a pleasure to read:

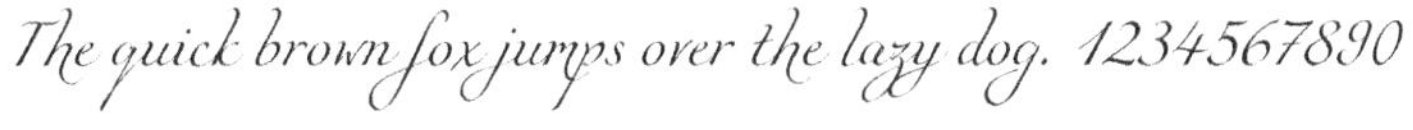

The quick brown fox jumps over the lazy dog. 1234567890

Figure 10.18 – The Miama Nueva handwritten font

Miama Nueva is very charming, for example, on invitation cards for weddings.

Exploring the whole world of LaTeX fonts

Probably the best place to browse LaTeX fonts is **The LaTeX Font Catalogue**. You can visit it online at https://www.tug.org/FontCatalogue/. The catalog aims to present all freely available fonts for LaTeX. It is based on TeX Live. It shows visual examples and the required code, along with further useful information. Just choose a category, browse a visual preview, and click on a font to see some examples, usage, and code.

There are additional fonts you can use – that's where we will be going now.

Using arbitrary fonts

Arbitrary is a bit broadly worded, but the meaning is valid as today, we can choose among many thousands of fonts that were not even prepared for LaTeX. That may be operating system fonts, TrueType fonts, or modern OpenType fonts.

Let's use some fonts that are available on a Microsoft Windows 10 computer.

Selecting the main font

We can either open **Settings** / **Fonts** via the Windows start menu or look into the folder C:\Windows\Fonts to see the installed fonts. The **Segoe UI** font appears available with several names, so let's choose **Segoe UI Semilight**. We will see whether it's hard to use:

1. Start a new document:

   ```
   \documentclass{article}
   ```

2. Load the fontspec package because it provides us with font selection commands:

   ```
   \usepackage{fontspec}
   ```

3. Choose the main font:

   ```
   \setmainfont{Segoe UI Semilight}
   ```

4. Write the document body with some large text:

   ```
   \begin{document}
   \large
   The quick brown fox jumps over the lazy dog. 1234567890
   \end{document}
   ```

5. Now we enter a new way: choose either **LuaLaTeX** or **XeLaTeX** as the compiling engine. In TeXworks, this is a drop-down list right next to the Typeset button, as shown here:

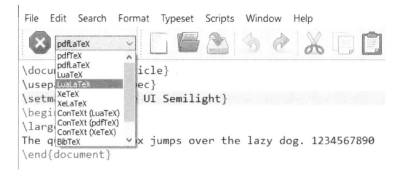

Figure 10.19 – Selecting LuaLaTeX

6. Click on **Typeset** to compile, and see what we get:

The quick brown fox jumps over the lazy dog. 1234567890

Figure 10.20 – Segoe UI Semilight from Microsoft Windows 10

That font selection was quite easy: loading one package, using one command. Let's now do it with multiple fonts in a document.

Selecting multiple font families

We can look for further already installed fonts on Windows. We can do that again either via **Settings / Fonts** in the Windows Start menu or by looking in the C:\Windows\Fonts folder. This time, we will choose the following:

- Cambria as the primary font that we want to be serif
- Segoe UI as the sans-serif font
- Lucida Console as the typewriter font
- Cambria Math as the serif math font

All are just Windows-installed fonts.

So, let's create a document that displays all these four fonts:

1. Start a new document and enter our \pangram macro again for easier testing:

```
\documentclass{article}
\newcommand{\pangram}[1]{{#1 The quick brown fox
jumps over the lazy dog. 1234567890\par}}
```

2. Load the fontspec package and the unicode-math package. The latter is for selecting the math font, as shown:

```
\usepackage{fontspec}
\usepackage{unicode-math}
```

3. Set the fonts as we planned at the beginning of this section. We use an optional argument that automatically scales the fonts, so their lowercase letter height matches the main font lowercase letter heights, as follows:

```
\setmainfont{Cambria}
\setsansfont{Segoe UI}[Scale=MatchLowercase]
\setmonofont{Lucida Console}[Scale=MatchLowercase]
\setmathfont{Cambria Math}[Scale=MatchLowercase]
```

4. Then, write a test document body again to view the available fonts:

```
\begin{document}
\large
\pangram{\rmfamily}
\pangram{\sffamily}
\pangram{\ttfamily}
\[
    \int_a^b \! f(x) \, dx = \lim_{\Delta x \rightarrow 0}
    \sum_{i=1}^{n} f(x_i) \,\Delta x_i
\]
\end{document}
```

5. Keep **LuaTeX** or **XeLaTeX** selected as the compiler. Click on **Typeset** and take a look:

The quick brown fox jumps over the lazy dog. 1234567890
The quick brown fox jumps over the lazy dog. 1234567890
The quick brown fox jumps over the lazy dog. 1234567890

$$\int_a^b f(x)\,dx = \lim_{\Delta x \to 0} \sum_{i=1}^{n} f(x_i)\,\Delta x_i$$

Figure 10.21 – Various Microsoft Windows fonts

We got Cambria as the default document font, and whenever we switch to sans-serif, we get Segoe UI, and when we write code listings in typewriter font, Lucida Console is chosen. Also, math formulas are now printed in Cambria Math instead of the default Computer Modern font. This easy font selection is actually quite an evolution in LaTeX, and it's worth considering **LuaLaTeX** or **XeLaTeX** just because of the extended font support. Both support OpenType and Truetype fonts, which do not yet work with **pdfLaTeX**.

XeLaTeX has been developed with a focus on using system fonts directly, which was impossible with **pdfLaTeX**. **LuaLaTeX** started by adding the Lua language as a scripting engine to LaTeX, and it also got better font support over time. Without dealing with their advanced features, we can simply choose one of them when it comes to fonts where we don't have a package for use with **pdfLaTeX**.

Summary

Now we can use different text and math fonts. Our documents no longer need to look like simple default font LaTeX articles or books.

We learned about installing and choosing font sets and specific fonts and made a survey of good font packages. For some advanced font tasks with ready-to-use examples, you can take a look at *Chapter 3*, *Adjusting Fonts*, in the *LaTeX Cookbook*.

Now, let's go back from fonts to LaTeX, and we will learn how to develop and manage larger documents in the next chapter.

11
Developing Large Documents

The first chapter of this book claimed that LaTeX handles large documents easily. When you create extensive documents, you will notice that LaTeX keeps on doing its job reliably. For the computer, it doesn't matter how the source code is formatted. But for you, as the developer, it's essential to keep your source document manageable. After all, it may consist of hundreds of pages with thousands of lines.

By the end of this chapter, we will be able to handle a big document project with several files, a title page, and separately numbered front matter and back matter parts.

In this chapter, we will learn about the following:

- Splitting the input
- Creating front and back matter
- Designing a title page
- Working with templates

That's a big step forward on the way to writing a thesis, a book, or an extensive report.

Let's begin by building a document based on several files.

Technical requirements

You can use a local LaTeX installation, or you can compile the example code online at `https://latexguide.org/chapter-11`.

The code is available on GitHub at `https://github.com/PacktPublishing/LaTeX-Beginner-s-Guide-2nd-Edition-/tree/main/Chapter_11_-_Developing_Large_Documents`.

In this chapter, we will use the following packages: `amsmath`, `amsthm`, `babel`, `blindtext`, `fontenc`, `geometry`, `lmodern`, `microtype`, `natbib`, and `tocbibind`.

We will also briefly look at the `pdfpages` and `titling` packages.

Splitting the input

Divide and conquer—this could be our motto now. We will figure out how to break down a document into several sub-documents. Thus, while we are writing, we will be able to manage a huge project consisting of many chapters in separate files.

Firstly, we will separate settings and body text by swapping out the preamble. Secondly, we will write chapters in separate files and include them afterward.

We will begin to write a detailed document regarding equations and equation systems. The result should be in the style of a thesis or a book. We can use the last example of *Chapter 9, Writing Math Formulas*, where we dealt with theorems concerning equations.

We will create several files, step by step:

1. Create a new document. Inside this, load all the packages and specify the options, like we did in our preambles in the previous chapters. Use all the beneficial packages that we have already learned about:

```
\usepackage[english]{babel}
\usepackage[T1]{fontenc}
\usepackage{lmodern}
\usepackage{microtype}
\usepackage{natbib}
\usepackage{tocbibind}
\usepackage{amsmath}
\usepackage{amsthm}
\newtheorem{thm}{Theorem}[chapter]
```

```
\newtheorem{lem}[thm]{Lemma}
\theoremstyle{definition}
\newtheorem{dfn}[thm]{Definition}
```

2. Save this document under the name `preamble.tex`.

3. Start another new document and copy the contents of the `Equations` chapter in the theorem example of the *Writing theorems and definitions* section of *Chapter 9, Writing Math Formulas*:

```
\chapter{Equations}
\section{Quadratic equations}
\begin{dfn}
   A quadratic equation is an equation of the form
   \begin{equation}
      \label{quad}
      ax^2 + bx + c = 0
   \end{equation}
   where \( a, b \) and \( c \) are constants
   and \( a \neq 0 \).
\end{dfn}
```

4. Save this document under the name `chapter1.tex`.

5. Create another document for the next chapter, write the chapter heading and some more, including a few sections. Save it as `chapter2.tex`:

```
\chapter{Equation Systems}
\section{Linear Systems}
. . .
\section{Non-linear Systems}
. . .
```

6. Now we will construct the top-level document. Create another file called `equations.tex`. This one starts with the `\documentclass` command and lists the preamble and the chapters for inclusion:

```
\documentclass{book}
\input{preamble}
\begin{document}
```

```
\tableofcontents
\include{chapter1}
\include{chapter2}
\end{document}
```

7. Compile the document twice. Remember that this action is necessary to get the table of contents. For now, check the contents to check that everything is in its correct place:

Contents

Contents   **1**

1   Equations   **3**
  1.1   Quadratic equations   3

2   Equation Systems   **5**
  2.1   Linear Systems   5
  2.2   Non-linear Systems   5

Figure 11.1 – Table of contents

We constructed a top-level document that we called equations.tex. It's tempting just to call it main.tex, or something similar. However, as this filename determines the name of the resulting PDF document, we chose a meaningful name.

This is the framework of our project. It's an ordinary LaTeX document, but we reduced it as much as possible and used two commands to import external .tex files:

- \input reads in another file, just as if we had typed it.

- \include also reads in an external file but automatically inserts \clearpage before and after.

The latter offers more to you, so let's have a closer look—we will treat the simpler \input command first.

Including small pieces of code

The simplest command to read in a file is as follows:

```
\input{filename}
```

When LaTeX encounters this command, it reads in the file with the name `filename`, exactly as if its contents have been typed at that point. Accordingly, the LaTeX compiler processes all commands in this file. You can even nest `\input`—this command may be used inside an included file.

If the filename doesn't have an extension, LaTeX assumes the extension `.tex`, so it inserts `filename.tex`. You may also specify a path, relative or absolute. As a backslash begins a command, use slashes / instead of backslashes \ in path names.

Using relative path names makes moving and copying a project more manageable.

Use `\input` if you wish to put your preamble into a separate file. Besides keeping your root document clean, a separate preamble can easily be copied and adjusted for use in another document.

However, simply splitting and inputting is not yet considered document management. For instance, though you could comment out selected `\input` lines for partial compilation, the numbering of pages, sections, and so on may be ruined, and cross-referencing to omitted document parts would fail.

There's a better way—so let's look at the `\include` command.

Including bigger parts of a document

When it comes to including one or more pages, this command proves to be useful:

```
\include{filename}
```

The argument is treated the same way as `\input`. However, there are some important differences:

- `\include` implicitly starts new pages. `\include{filename}` behaves like this:

```
\clearpage
\include{filename}
\clearpage
```

- This makes `\include` useful for page ranges such as chapters or sections. One consequence is that you may use `\include` only after `\begin{document}`.

- `\include` cannot be nested. You could still use `\input` within included documents, though it might not be a good idea to complicate the structure further.

- Most importantly, `\include` supports a mechanism for choosing which parts of the document you wish to compile—so we come to another command, namely, `\includeonly`.

Let's see how `\includeonly` works.

Compiling parts of a document

Such a partial document, intended for `\input` or `\include`, cannot be compiled standalone: you need a root document that specifies the document class.

However, once you swapped out parts of the document using `\include` while compiling your root document, you may specify which parts are included by this command:

```
\includeonly{file list}
```

We can use `\includeonly` only in the preamble, in other words, before `\begin{document}`.

The argument may be a comma-separated list of filenames. If a file, `name.tex`, is not specified within this argument, `\include{name}` would not insert this file but behave like `\clearpage` instead. This allows the exclusion of chunks or whole chapters from compiling. If you work on a huge document, this speeds up compilation if you choose to include just your current chapter while keeping the labels and references of the excluded chapter this way.

You may notice that LaTeX produces an `.aux` file for each `.tex` file included. LaTeX still reads in all those `.aux` files containing information such as chapter and page numbers. Of course, the included files need to be compiled at least once. This way, cross-referencing the numbering of pages, chapters, sections, and so on will remain intact even if you temporarily exclude the chapters.

Try it out—add the following:

```
\includeonly{chapter2}
```

Add it to your preamble in `equations.tex` and compile. The result will be just the second chapter keeping the correct numbering. Take a look at the output here with Acrobat Reader:

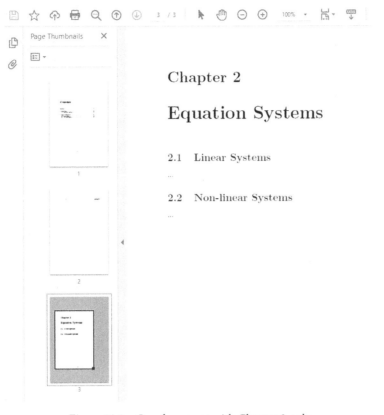

Figure 11.2 – Our document with Chapter 2 only

At the top of *Figure 11.2*, you can see **3/3** pages instead of 5 pages in the first example of the current chapter. On the left side, you see three pages as thumbnails, and the third page is our **Chapter 2**. On the right side, you see **Chapter 2**, with the correct page number **5** at the bottom. This shows us that **Chapter 1** is not included here, but only **Chapter 2**, as we desired. Also, the page numbers are still the same as they are in the full document, while the original chapter and section numbers are also unchanged.

Compiling time is significantly shorter if you work on a huge document with many chapters and use \includeonly to include just a single chapter that you are working on.

Finally, just comment the latter command out to typeset your complete document when you finish your work.

Of course, you can use \include without \includeonly just for splitting a large document into files.

Let's now return to the structure of a bigger document.

Creating front and back matter

In contrast to reports, books often begin with introductory material such as copyright information, a foreword, acknowledgments, or a dedication. This part, including the title page and the table of contents, is called the **front matter**.

At the end, a book might include an afterword and supporting material such as a bibliography and an index. This part is called the **back matter**.

The book class and some other classes, such as scrbook and memoir, support this kind of sectioning directly. Often, desired consequences of this sectioning are differences in the numbering of pages and chapters. Let's see how it works.

Our book will begin with a dedication. The front matter will consist of the table of contents, lists of tables and figures, and a dedication. All the pages of the front matter will be numbered with Roman numerals. Finally, we add an appendix providing supplementary proofs, which we like to present outside the main chapters:

1. Create a file, dedication.tex:

    ```
    \chapter{Dedication}
    This book is dedicated to one of the greatest
    mathematicians of all time: Carl Friedrich Gauss.
    Without him, this book wouldn't have been possible.
    ```

2. Create a file, proofs.tex:

    ```
    \chapter{Proofs}
    ...
    ```

3. Extend the main file, equations.tex, by means of the highlighted lines:

    ```
    \documentclass{book}
    \input{preamble}
    \begin{document}
    \frontmatter
    \include{dedication}
    \tableofcontents
    \listoftables
    \listoffigures
    \mainmatter
    \include{chapter1}
    \include{chapter2}
    ```

```
\backmatter
\include{proofs}
\nocite{*}
\bibliographystyle{plainnat}
\bibliography{example}
\end{document}
```

4. As you can see in the last highlighted line, we re-used the example.bib file from *Chapter 8, Listing Contents and References*. Click on **Typeset** to compile, run BibTeX, and compile again. Check out the numbering within the table of contents:

Contents

Dedication   i

Contents   iii

List of Tables   v

List of Figures   vii

1   Equations   1
    1.1   Quadratic equations   1

2   Equation Systems   3
    2.1   Linear Systems   3
    2.2   Non-linear Systems   3

Proofs   5

Figure 11.3 – Table of contents of a complex document

We saw that LaTeX printed the page number of the contents page in Roman numerals. This applies to all front-matter pages. Further, all the chapters in the front and back matter are unnumbered even though we did not use the starred command, \chapter*.

For this, the three commands – \frontmatter, \mainmatter, and \backmatter, are responsible. They start a new page and modified both the page and chapter numbering in the following way:

- \frontmatter: Pages are numbered with lowercase Roman numerals. Chapters generate a table of contents entry but don't get a number.

- \mainmatter: Pages are numbered with Arabic numerals. Chapters are numbered and produce a table of contents entry.

- \backmatter: Pages are numbered with Arabic numerals. Chapters generate a table of contents entry but don't get a number.

Like the book class, the scrbook and memoir classes provide the same commands with very similar behavior.

A large document usually starts with a title page. We will now see how to produce a title page in LaTeX.

Designing a title page

We can quickly create a good-looking title page using \maketitle, as we did in *Chapter 2, Formatting Text and Creating Macros*. Document classes usually offer this command to generate a suitable pre-formatted title page. Alternatively, you could use a titlepage environment to design its layout freely. So, let's design a nice title page for our book of equations.

In *Chapter 2, Formatting Text and Creating Macros*, we have already used some formatting commands, such as \centering, and font size and shape commands, such as \Huge and \bfseries, to format a title. We will do it similarly within a titlepage environment:

1. Create a file, title.tex, with the following content:

```
\begin{titlepage}
\raggedleft
{\Large The Author\\[1in]}
{\large The Big Book of\\}
{\Huge\scshape Equations\\[.2in]}
{\large Packed with hundreds of examples and solutions\\}
\vfill
{\itshape 2011, Publishing company}
\end{titlepage}
```

2. Add this line right after `\frontmatter`:

```
\include{title}
```

3. Our final book will be in A5 format, and so will the title page. Therefore, let's add that to the preamble:

```
\usepackage[a5paper]{geometry}
```

4. Click on **Typeset** to compile. Now we've got a title page:

The Author

The Big Book of

EQUATIONS

Packed with hundreds of examples and solutions

2011, Publishing company

Figure 11.4 – A title page

The `titlepage` environment typesets its contents on a separate page. Although this title page will be numbered like any other page, the page number won't be printed on that page.

Within this environment, we used some basic LaTeX font commands to modify the font size and shape. By grouping with curly braces, we limited those commands. Line breaks such as `\\[.2in]` cause some more space before the following line. `\vfill` inserts a flexible vertical space, which stretches as much as possible to fill the page. This way, we put the last line off to the end of the page.

Note that this page has the same page dimensions as the other pages in the document. That means, in a double-sided book, that it's a right-hand page. Thus, you may notice the unequal left and right margins, which might look undesirable, especially if your title is in the center. However, the explanation is simple: this title page is intended to be an inner title, not the cover page. The inner title page is, of course, a right-hand page.

A cover page is a different thing. Such a page should be one-sided, and thus it should have equal left and right margins. A cover page is often produced as a standalone document, printed out separately. For an electronic document, you may use the `pdfpages` package. Refer to the *Including whole pages* section in *Chapter 5, Including Images*, or the *Combining PDF files* section in *Chapter 8, Getting the Most Out of the PDF*, in the *LaTeX Cookbook*.

The `titling` package offers features to create sophisticated title pages. To get some ideas on how title pages may be designed, you could look at *Some Examples of Title Pages*, by Peter Wilson, available from `texdoc titlepages` and at `https://texdoc.org/pkg/titlepages`.

A document framework consisting of files, headings, title page, and style settings is called a template. We will learn how to use templates in the next section.

Working with templates

When we develop a document, we specify the document class, choose meaningful packages and options, and create a frame for the content. To repeat these steps for each document would be too laborious.

If we plan to write several documents of the same type, we may create a template. This could be a `.tex` file containing the following:

- A declaration of a suitable document class together with a set of meaningful options

- Routinely used packages and packages that are most eligible for our document type

- A predefined layout for the header, footer, and body of the text

- Self-made macros to facilitate our work

- A framework of sectioning commands, where we fill in the headings and the body text

- Or a framework containing `\include` or `\input` commands, for which we create the body text chunks later on

As we improve our LaTeX knowledge, such templates might grow and become better and more sophisticated. Many users publish their elaborate templates on the internet. Many universities, institutes, journals, and publishers do the same, offering templates for documents such as theses, papers, journal articles, and books, meeting their requirements.

You will find a carefully curated collection of templates, arranged by document types such as theses, reports, letters, and presentations, accompanied by sample output, in a template gallery at `https://latextemplates.com`.

You may download a template and start to fill in your text. Alternatively, you could start a document with a predefined template offered by your editor. Let's try that first.

LaTeX editors often provide templates to start with. TeXworks offers some as well. So, we will test this feature. Let's take one, open it, modify it, and compile it:

1. In the TeXworks main menu, click on **File** and then on **New from template**. A window will open, allowing you to choose a template:

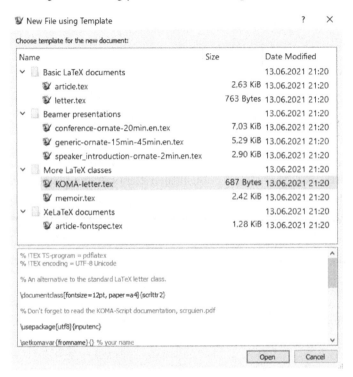

Figure 11.5 – TeXworks template selection

2. In the lower part of the window, you can read the template's source. Here's an example of KOMA-Script (KOMA-letter.tex):

```
% !TEX TS-program = pdflatex
% !TEX encoding = UTF-8 Unicode
% An alternative to the standard LaTeX letter class.
\documentclass[fontsize=12pt, paper=a4]{scrlttr2}
% Don't forget to read the KOMA-Script documentation,
% scrguien.pdf
\setkomavar{fromname}{} % your name
\setkomavar{fromaddress}{Address \\ of \\ Sender}
```

```
\setkomavar{signature}{} % printed after the \closing
\renewcommand{\raggedsignature}{\raggedright} % make
% the signature ragged right
\setkomavar{subject}{} % subject of the letter
\begin{document}
\begin{letter}{Name and \\ Address \\ of \\ Recipient}
\opening{} % eg. Hello
\closing{} %eg. Regards
\end{letter}
\end{document}
```

3. Click on **Open**. Fill in the gaps and edit the filler text of the example:

```
\documentclass[fontsize=12pt, paper=a4]{scrlttr2}
\setkomavar{fromname}{My name} % your name
\setkomavar{fromaddress}{Street, City}
\setkomavar{signature}{Name} % printed after the \closing
\setkomavar{subject}{Invoice 1/2021} % subject of the
letter
\setkomavar{place}{Place}
\setkomavar{date}{January 1, 2021}
\begin{document}
\begin{letter}{Customer Name\\ Street No. X \\ City \\
Zipcode}
    \opening{To whom it may concern} % eg. Hello
    Text follows \ldots
    \bigskip
    \closing{With kind regards} %eg. Regards
\end{letter}
\end{document}
```

4. Compile the document. Have a look at our test letter:

My name
Street, City

My name, Street, City

Customer Name
Street No. X
City
Zipcode

Place, January 1, 2021

Invoice 1/2021

To whom it may concern

Text follows ...

With kind regards

Name

Figure 11.6 – A letter document

That was easy! We just opened the template and modified the filler text. By reading the KOMA-Script documentation, we can learn that the `\setkomavar` command is for specifying values for template parameters such as `name`, `address`, and `subject`. We used that to declare `date` and `place` as well.

Once we have written our personal data into this template, we may save that for later use instead of typing our address for each letter.

The KOMA-Script documentation (`texdoc scrguien`) describes the features of this `letter` class well. Using this, you would be able to create your professional-looking letter template for business use.

Imagine putting a job application letter created with the LaTeX layout and fonts together with the `microtype` package next to an application letter produced with some other word processing software. Which one will create a better impression?

While looking for LaTeX templates, code, and tips on the internet, you will find a lot of information and code. This code might be outdated, and this information might be obsolete.

When you develop your own template, you would probably like to be sure to use the best packages, options, and solutions available today. How can you be sure?

Both questions can be answered by studying `l2tabu`. This is the common shortcut for *An essential guide to LaTeX2e usage*, a document focusing on obsolete commands and packages, demonstrating the most common and severe mistakes that LaTeX users tend to make. As LaTeX has developed over many years, some packages and techniques are still available and described in online resources, but they may no longer be recommendable. Read this guide. It will help you to evaluate templates and code found on the internet, and ensure that you produce optimal code yourself.

Just type `texdoc l2tabuen` at the command prompt or visit `https://texdoc.org/pkg/l2tabuen`.

To test a template, you may use the `blindtext` package and its commands, `\blindtext` and `\Blinddocument`. The `\blindtext` command generates a paragraph of dummy text, and the `\Blinddocument` command generates dummy content for a big document, including sections and lists. That will demonstrate the output quality of a template. When using this package, we should load the `babel` package with a language option, for example, just with a basic minimal article template:

```
\documentclass{article}
\usepackage[english]{babel}
\usepackage{blindtext}
\begin{document}
\begin{abstract}
```

```
\blindtext
\end{abstract}
\Blinddocument
\end{document}
```

That gives us a document starting like this:

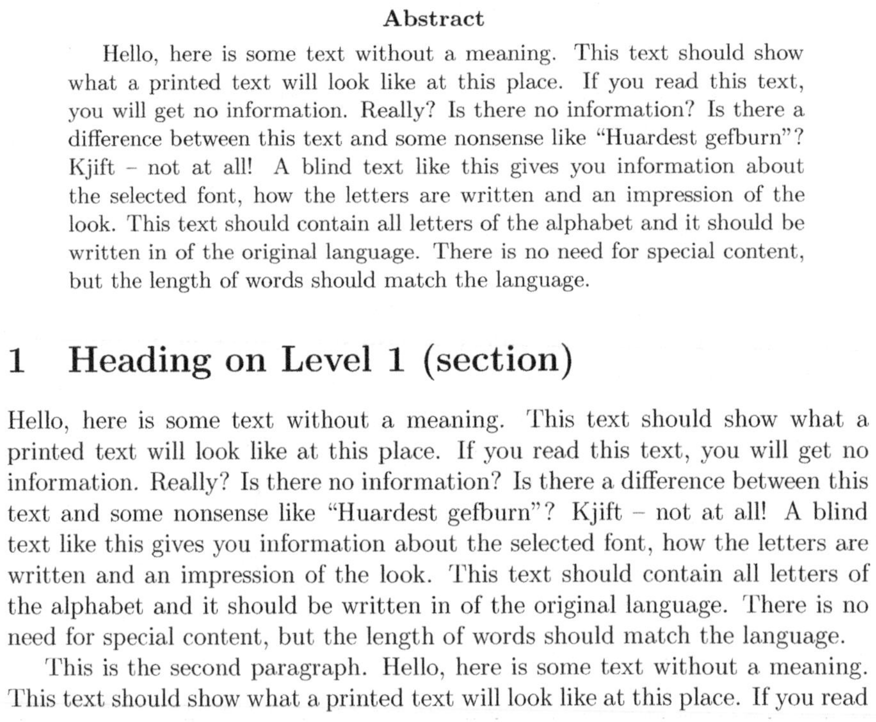

Abstract

Hello, here is some text without a meaning. This text should show what a printed text will look like at this place. If you read this text, you will get no information. Really? Is there no information? Is there a difference between this text and some nonsense like "Huardest gefburn"? Kjift – not at all! A blind text like this gives you information about the selected font, how the letters are written and an impression of the look. This text should contain all letters of the alphabet and it should be written in of the original language. There is no need for special content, but the length of words should match the language.

1   Heading on Level 1 (section)

Hello, here is some text without a meaning. This text should show what a printed text will look like at this place. If you read this text, you will get no information. Really? Is there no information? Is there a difference between this text and some nonsense like "Huardest gefburn"? Kjift – not at all! A blind text like this gives you information about the selected font, how the letters are written and an impression of the look. This text should contain all letters of the alphabet and it should be written in of the original language. There is no need for special content, but the length of words should match the language.

This is the second paragraph. Hello, here is some text without a meaning. This text should show what a printed text will look like at this place. If you read

Figure 11.7 – An article with dummy text

If you use TeXworks, as we did in the previous example, you can choose from some ready-to-use templates or download a template from `https://latextemplates.com`. However, if you work online with `https://overleaf.com`, you have even more choices. Basically, you can click on **New Project** and choose one of several basic templates:

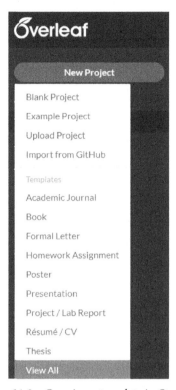

Figure 11.8 – Opening a template in Overleaf

If you click on **View All**, you can browse a comprehensive catalog:

Figure 11.9 – The Overleaf template catalog

The Overleaf template collection contains several thousand templates ready to use for filling in your text. A lot of them are contributed by institutions and users. Quality may vary, but you can see screenshots of contents or titles while browsing and try out those templates yourself.

We can enter keywords such as the document type, university or college name, features, or package names in the **Search** bar.

We can click on **Open as Template** and will get a compilable document with some filler text. That allows us to try out 10 templates in around 10 minutes until we find the perfect one for us.

Summary

The techniques we learned in this chapter will help us to develop and maintain bigger projects. Though enthusiastic users prefer LaTeX to write small documents, many people learn LaTeX because they plan to write longer texts such as a thesis. However, splitting documents and the use of templates are useful for small pieces of writing as well, such as for letters—just think of the header, footer, and address fields.

In this chapter, we created and managed large documents consisting of several files, including front and back matter and a separate title page.

Now that we can develop and handle large documents, we will see how to improve them further in the next chapter.

12
Enhancing Your Documents Further

By now, you're capable of writing structured documents in fine typographical quality, and you can meet high expectations for classic publications such as books, journal articles, or a university thesis.

Perhaps you would like to publish your PDF documents online. Such electronic documents or e-books usually require navigation such as hyperlinks and a bookmark index.

This chapter shall provide us with the tools for such enhancements. We shall figure out how to perform the following:

- Using hyperlinks and bookmarks
- Designing headings
- Coloring our documents

Let's implement this by using LaTeX packages that are dedicated to these subjects.

Technical requirements

You can use a local LaTeX installation, or you can compile the example code online at https://latexguide.org/chapter-12.

The code is available on GitHub: https://github.com/PacktPublishing/LaTeX-Beginner-s-Guide-Second-Edition/tree/main/Chapter_12_-_Enhancing_Your_Documents_Further.

In this chapter, we will use the following packages: bm, colortbl, hyperref, titlesec, and xcolor. Since we're going to continue working with the code of the previous chapter, we require the same packages as in *Chapter 11, Developing Large Documents*.

We will also briefly look at the bookmark package.

Using hyperlinks and bookmarks

There's a sophisticated package called hyperref that does nearly all basic hyperlinking automatically. Let's check it out.

Adding hyperlinks

We shall load the hyperref package and inspect its effect:

1. Open the preamble.tex file, which we used in the previous chapter. At the end, add this line:

   ```
   \usepackage{hyperref}
   ```

2. Save this document under the same name.

3. Open our *Book of Equations* from the previous chapter; we called it equations.tex.

4. Compile the document twice without making any changes. Let's see how the document now appears; here, we can see red boxes indicating hyperlinks:

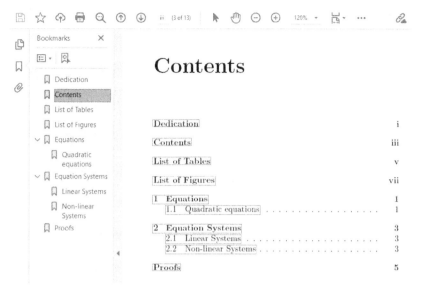

Figure 12.1 – A table of contents with hyperlinks and bookmarks

Cross-references, such as references to equation numbers, also have red boxes:

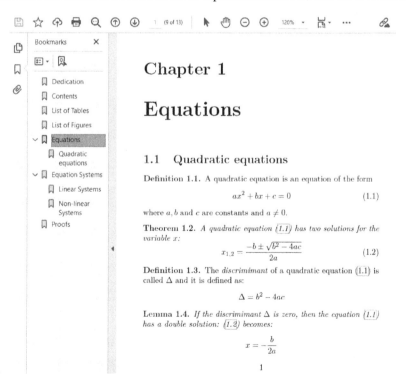

Figure 12.2 – References to equations with hyperlinks

By just loading the `hyperref` package, our document has significantly changed:

- We got a **Bookmarks** bar, which allows us to navigate through the document easily.
- Each entry in the table of contents has become a hyperlink to the beginning of the corresponding chapter. Hyperlinks are highlighted by red borders.
- All cross-references have become hyperlinks.

This is an excellent improvement for electronic versions of our documents.

The red boxes will not appear on paper when we print the document; they are only for electronic navigation. The same applies to the bookmarks.

If you don't like the default appearance of the hyperlinks with red borders, it can easily be changed by editing the options to `hyperref`. Let's try this next.

Customizing hyperlinks

Here, we shall pass options to `hyperref` affecting the way it emphasizes hyperlinks:

1. Open the `preamble.tex` file again. This time, specify the options for `hyperref`:

   ```
   \usepackage[colorlinks=true,linkcolor=red]{hyperref}
   ```

2. Save this document, go to the main `equations.tex` document, and compile it twice. The table of contents has changed:

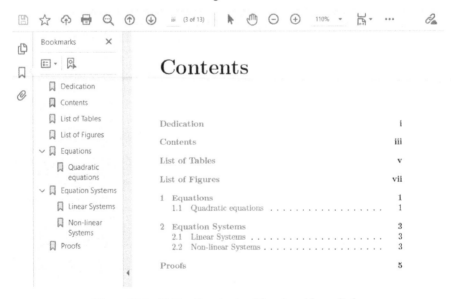

Figure 12.3 – Table of contents with colored hyperlinks

Instead of frames, we now have a red color for emphasized hyperlinks. Unlike the boxes, we can see the color in a printed document.

hyperref offers ways to set up these options. The first one we used is the following:

```
\usepackage[key=value list]{hyperref}
```

Alternatively, we could just write \usepackage{hyperref} and set the options afterward:

```
\hypersetup{key=value list}
```

Our example would do the same with the following:

```
\hypersetup{colorlinks=true,linkcolor=red}
```

We can also combine these methods.

We will look at a selection of particularly useful options. For the following options, you can choose either true or false. If you don't specify, hyperref selects the default value, which is shown in parentheses here:

- draft: Turns all hypertext options off (false).
- final: Turns all hypertext options on (true).
- debug: Prints extra diagnostic messages into the log file (false).
- backref: Adds backlinks to the bibliography, that is, links from bibliography items back to citations in the text (false).
- hyperindex: Adds links to page numbers in the index (true).
- hyperfootnotes: Converts footnote markers into hyperlinks (true).
- hyperfigures: Adds hyperlinks to figures (false).
- linktocpage: In the **table of contents (TOC)**, **list of figures (LOF)** and **list of tables (LOT)**, hyperrefs adds links to page numbers instead of to the text (false).
- frenchlinks: Uses small caps for links instead of color (false).
- bookmarks: Writes bookmarks for the PDF reader navigation (true).
- bookmarksopen: Shows all bookmarks in an expanded view when the PDF is opened (false).

- `bookmarksnumbered`: Includes the section number in bookmarks (false).

- `colorlinks`: Writes links and anchors in color, depending on the type of link, such as page references, URLs, file references, and citations, instead of printing a border around links (false).

When you use the `colorlinks` option, you can choose the color you want by link type, as in the following list. Again, the default value is in parentheses:

- `linkcolor`: Color of general links (red)

- `citecolor`: Color for citations of bibliography items (green)

- `urlcolor`: Color for website addresses, that is, URLs (magenta)

- `filecolor`: Color for links to files (cyan)

There are many more options for customizing link borders, the PDF page size, anchors, bookmark appearance, and the PDF page display style. The `hyperref` documentation lists them all. Just type `texdoc hyperref` at the command line or visit `https://texdoc.org/pkg/hyperref`.

> **Hiding links**
>
> If you want to disable all link highlighting, such as for printing on paper, just give the `hidelinks` option without value. Then, links will be invisible without a border and color, like regular text.

Some text options allow us to specify the metadata of PDF files, such as the author's name, title, and keywords. You can see this information if you inspect the document properties with the PDF reader. This is even more beneficial as internet search engines can find and classify your PDF document according to this meta information. If you publish on the internet, this improves the chances of readers finding your publication.

That's why we will now add PDF metadata to our *Book of Equations* from *Chapter 11, Developing Large Documents*. Besides choosing sensible keywords, we will set the title and the author's name. During development, why not choose the great mathematician to whom we dedicated our book? So, let's do it:

1. Open the `preamble.tex` file and add the following lines:

```
\hypersetup{pdfauthor={Carl Friedrich Gauss},
    pdftitle={The Big Book of Equations},
    pdfsubject={Solving Equations and Equation Systems},
    pdfkeywords={equations,mathematics}}
```

2. Save that file. Go to the main `equations.tex` document and click on **Typeset** to compile.

3. Let's inspect the **Document Properties**. So, if you are using Acrobat Reader, click on the **File** menu and then on **Properties**:

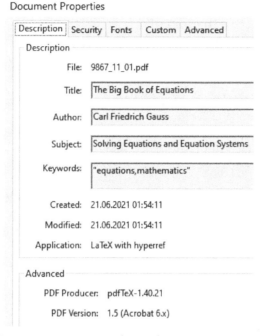

Figure 12.4 – PDF metadata in document properties

That was easy. We provided all the document properties using `hyperref` options; we just had to enclose each entry in curly braces.

The most used meta information options are as follows:

- `pdftitle`: Sets the title
- `pdfauthor`: Sets the author
- `pdfsubject`: Sets the subject
- `pdfcreator`: Sets the creator
- `pdfproducer`: Sets the producer
- `pdfkeywords`: Sets keywords

As `hyperref` redefines many other packages' commands to add hyperlink functionality, we have to load it after those packages.

> **hyperref loading order**
>
> A good rule of thumb is to load the `hyperref` package as the last
> package in your preamble. A few packages are exceptions to that rule;
> namely, `algorithm`, `amsrefs`, `bookmark`, `chappg`, `cleveref`,
> `glossaries`, `hypernat`, `linguex`, `sidecap`, and `tabularx`
> are known to be exceptions. For more information, see `https://`
> `latexguide.org/hyperref`.

There are further ways of adding hyperlinks and bookmarks that we will now see.

Creating hyperlinks manually

As `hyperref` already creates links for nearly all kinds of references, it's rarely necessary
to create links by yourself. But of course, it's possible. `hyperref` provides user
commands for that:

- `\href{URL}{text}` turns text into a hyperlink that points to the URL, the
  website address.

- `\url{URL}` prints the URL and links it.

- `\nolinkurl{URL}` prints the URL without linking it.

- `\hyperref{label}{text}` changes the text into a hyperlink that links to the
  place where the `label` has been set, thus to the same place `\ref{label}` would
  point to.

- `\hypertarget{name}{text}` creates a target name for potential hyperlinks
  with `text` as the anchor.

- `\hyperlink{name}{text}` turns `text` into a hyperlink that points to the
  target `name`.

Sometimes you might just need an anchor, for instance, if you use `\addcontentsline`,
which creates a hyperlinked TOC entry, but there hasn't been a sectioning command
setting the anchor. The TOC entry would point to the previously set anchor, thus to the
wrong place.

The \phantomsection command comes to the rescue; it just sets an anchor like \hypertarget{}{} would do. It's mostly used this way for creating a TOC entry for the bibliography while linking to the correct page, as follows:

```
\cleardoublepage
\phantomsection
\addcontentsline{toc}{chapter}{\bibname}
\bibliography{name}
```

So, we may consider \phantomsection as an invisible \section anchor. The following \addcontentsline command then refers to that anchor.

Creating bookmarks manually

Your bookmarks panel might already be full of chapters and section entries. But what if you wish to add bookmarks by yourself? You can do that as follows.

\pdfbookmark[level]{text}{name} creates a bookmark with text at the optionally specified level. The default level is 0. Treat name just like with the \label command; it should be unique because it stands for the internal anchor.

You can also create bookmarks relative to the current level:

- \currentpdfbookmark{text}{name} puts a bookmark at the current level.
- \belowpdfbookmark{text}{name} creates a bookmark one level deeper.
- \subpdfbookmark{text}{name} increases the level and creates a bookmark at that deeper level.

The bookmark package offers more features for customizing bookmarks, such as choosing the font style and color. You can read about it by running texdoc bookmark at the command line or at https://texdoc.org/pkg/bookmark.

Using math formulas and special symbols in bookmarks

Due to PDF restrictions, we cannot use math and special symbols within PDF bookmarks. This might cause a problem, for instance, in sectioning commands with math symbols in their title or font commands, which would be passed to the bookmark. There's a solution, though, and that's this command:

```
\texorpdfstring{string with TeX code}{pdf text string}
```

It returns the argument depending on the context to avoid such problems. It can be used like this:

```
\section{The equation
   \texorpdfstring{$y=x^2$}{y=x\texttwosuperior}}
```

That may come in handy.

If you load hyperref with the unicode option, you could use Unicode text characters in bookmarks, such as here:

```
\section{\texorpdfstring{$\gamma$}{\textgamma} radiation}
```

Let's quickly see how these commands work in a small sample document. Here it goes:

```
\documentclass{article}
\usepackage{bm}
\usepackage[colorlinks=true,psdextra,unicode]{hyperref}
\begin{document}
\pdfbookmark[1]{\contentsname}{toc}
\tableofcontents
\pdfbookmark[1]{Abstract}{abstract}
\begin{abstract}
\centering
Sample sections follow.
\end{abstract}
\section{The equation
   \texorpdfstring{$y=x^2$}{y=x\texttwosuperior}}
\section{\texorpdfstring{$\gamma$}{\textgamma} radiation}
\section[\texorpdfstring{Let $\int\sim\sum$ for
   $n\rightarrow\infty$}
   {Let \int\sim\sum\ for n\rightarrow\infty}]
   {Let $\bm{\int\sim\sum}$ for $\bm{n\rightarrow\infty}$}
\end{document}
```

As highlighted in the preceding code, the \section command does these three things:

- It prints the section heading. This time, we used the \bm command from the bm package to get a bold math font. Compare it with the other headings.

- It puts the section name into the table of contents.

- It creates a bookmark with Unicode text symbols as replacements for math symbols. We loaded `hyperref` with the `unicode` option and the `psdextra` option, which allows math symbols in bookmarks.

We get this output with bookmarks:

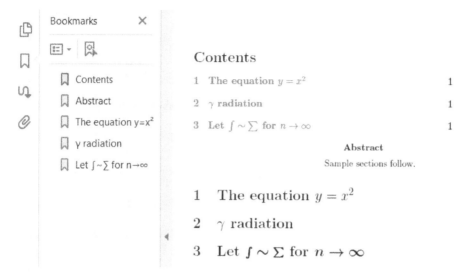

Figure 12.5 – Math formulas in bookmarks

> **Note**
>
> In the first argument to `\texorpdfstring`, we used $...$ for the math mode. However, in the second argument to `\texorpdfstring`, we omitted $...$ intentionally since that will be Unicode text, not math font glyphs.

While math formulas in headings and bookmarks may not be a good idea anyway, we see that we have ways to get it done if we really need it.

In the next section, we will deal with the appearance of headings.

Designing headings

In *Chapter 2, Formatting Text and Creating Macros*, we encountered the problem of customizing headings. There has to be a consistent way to modify the font of headings, their spacing, and their numbering for the whole document. Fortunately, there's a handy package for that, and it's called `titlesec`. We shall use it now to design chapter and section headings.

We'll return to the example that we used in this chapter. Our goal is to create headings with this appearance:

- Centered titles
- Smaller font size
- Less space above and below
- With a sans serif font, which is a good choice for bold headings

Let's start:

1. Open the `preamble.tex` file, which we have already used in this chapter. Insert this line to load the `titlesec` package:

```
\usepackage{titlesec}
```

2. Add this command to specify the layout and font of the chapter headings:

```
\titleformat{\chapter}[display]
    {\normalfont\sffamily\Large\bfseries\centering}
    {\chaptertitlename\ \thechapter}{0pt}{\Huge}
```

3. Now, define the section heading by calling the `\titleformat` command again:

```
\titleformat{\section}
    {\normalfont\sffamily\large\bfseries\centering}
    {\thesection}{1em}{}
```

4. Add this line to adjust the chapter heading's spacing:

```
\titlespacing*{\chapter}{0pt}{30pt}{20pt}
```

5. Save `preamble.tex` and compile the main `equation.tex` document. Let's see how the headings have changed:

Chapter 1

Equations

1.1   Quadratic equations

Definition 1.1. A quadratic equation is an equation of the form

$$ax^2 + bx + c = 0 \tag{1.1}$$

where a, b and c are constants and $a \neq 0$.

Figure 12.6 – Centered headings

In *step 1*, we loaded the `titlesec` package, which provides a comprehensive interface for customizing headings of parts, chapters, sections, and even smaller sectioning parts down to subparagraphs.

In *step 2*, we chose a display style, which means that numbering and the actual title use separate lines. Firstly, we used `\normalfont` to switch to the base font, to be on the safe side. With `\sffamily`, we switched to a sans serif font, chose the size and weight, and finally, declared that the complete heading shall be centered.

In *step 3*, everything is very similar to *step 2*; we just omitted `[display]` to get the number and title on the same line.

To understand the remaining arguments, have a look at the `\titleformat` definition:

```
\titleformat{cmd}[shape]{format}{label}{sep}{before}[after]
```

The meaning of the arguments is as follows:

- `cmd` stands for the sectioning command that we redefine, that is, `\part`, `\chapter`, `\section`, `\subsection`, `\subsubsection`, `\paragraph`, or `\subparagraph`.

- `shape` specifies the paragraph shape. The effects of the possible values are as follows:

  - `display` puts the label into a separate paragraph.

  - `hang` creates a hanging label like in standard sections and is the default option.

  - `runin` produces a run-in title like `\paragraph` does by default.

- `leftmargin` sets the title into the left margin.

- `rightmargin` puts the title into the right margin.

- `drop` wraps the text around the title, requires care to avoid overlapping.

- `wrap` works like drop but adjusts the space for the title to match the longest text line.

- `frame` works like `display` and additionally frames the title.

- `format` may contain commands that will be applied to the label and text of the title.

- `label` prints the label, that is, the number.

- `sep` is a length that specifies the separation between the label and title text. With the `display` option, it's the vertical separation. With the `frame` option, it means the distance between the text and the frame. Otherwise, it's the horizontal separation between the label and title.

- `before` can contain code that comes before the title body. The last command is allowed to take an argument, which should then be the title text.

- `after` can contain code that comes after the title body.

That's a lot of options. Have a look at the `titlesec` documentation to learn even more by running `texdoc titlesec` or visiting `https://texdoc.org/pkg/titlesec`.

We used the `titlesec` command `\chaptertitlename`, which is `\chaptername` by default. So, it defaults to **Chapter**. In an appendix, it changes to `\appendixname`.

With the following command, we customized the spacing of all chapter headings:

```
\titlespacing*{cmd}{left}{beforesep}{aftersep}[right]
```

The arguments have the following meanings:

- `left` works differently depending on the chosen `shape`: with `drop`, `leftmargin`, and `rightmargin`, it's the title width. With `wrap`, it's the maximum width. With `runin`, it sets the indentation before the title. Otherwise, it increases the left margin. If negative, it decreases, which means overhanging into the margin.

- `beforesep` sets the vertical space before the title.

- `aftersep` sets the separation between the title and text. With a `hang`, `block`, and `display` shape, it has a vertical meaning. With a `runin`, `drop`, `wrap`, `leftmargin`, and `rightmargin` shape, it's a horizontal width. Again, it may be a negative value.

- `right` increases the right margin when a `hang`, `block`, or `display` shape is used.

If you use an *asterisk*, `titlesec` removes the indentation of the following paragraph. That's similar to standard sections – the text that follows a section heading doesn't have paragraph indentation. With `drop`, `wrap`, and `runin`, the starred version has no meaning.

In our example, we avoided the indentation of the paragraph that follows a chapter heading, and we specified a space of `30pt` before the heading and `20pt` after it. That's less compared to standard classes, which use `50pt` above chapter headings.

It's highly recommended to read the `titlesec` documentation to get the most out of it. In its appendix, it shows how the headings in standard classes would be defined with `\titleformat` and `\titlesec`. That's a great way to start by copying these definitions and beginning to modify them.

Using sans serif headings is very common today. They don't have such a heavy and ancient appearance like bold serif headings. However, serif text offers the best readability for body text. Now it's up to you to choose – you've got the tools.

In the next section, we will learn how to add color to our documents.

Coloring our documents

We could enhance our text further with colors. We haven't dealt with it yet, because most people use LaTeX to write serious books and articles or business letters where too much color may harm the appearance. But why not try something fancy? For instance, diagrams and tables in presentations are often colorful.

We just need to load the `xcolor` package:

```
\usepackage{xcolor}
```

From now on, we have to use a command to set the text color:

```
\color{name}
```

This command is a declaration that switches to the color that is named. Just try `\color{blue}`.

The corresponding command form to color a piece of text is as follows:

```
\textcolor{name}{text}
```

`\textcolor` adds grouping implicitly; it works like this:

```
{\color{name} text}
```

For coloring text snippets, `\textcolor` is the better choice, while `\color` would be a good choice for longer pieces of text enclosed by an environment or braces.

The `xcolor` package offers a lot of ready-mixed colors; you just need to call a color by its name. There are large tables of color names and samples in the documentation that you can open by running `texdoc xcolor` or on `https://texdoc.org/pkg/xcolor`.

`xcolor` provides an easy syntax of mixing colors, as follows:

```
name1!percent1!name2!percent2!name3!percent3…
```

This mixes the `name1` color with the `percent1` percentage together with the `name2` color with the `percent2` percentage and the `name3` color with `percent3`, and so on. The percentages add up to 100%, but you can omit the last percentage, and then the remaining percent of 100 is taken.

That's easier to understand with examples:

- To have a dark gray that is 60% black, we can use `\color{black!60}`.
- To mix 40% red with 60% yellow, we can use `\color{red!40!yellow}`.
- To mix 40% red with 20% green and 40% blue, we can use `\color{red!40!green!20!blue}`.

`xcolor` together with the `colortbl` package can be used to create colorful tables, such as for coloring single cells, rows, or columns, or making tables with alternating row colors. For the latter, there is a recipe in *LaTeX Cookbook* in *Chapter 6, Designing Tables*.

Summary

In this chapter, we enhanced our document with a hypertext structure including colored links and bookmarks for navigation. We can now edit the PDF metadata, customize our headings' styles, and use colors.

During our work, we may encounter errors and warnings. That's common for advanced LaTeX users as well. The following chapter will prepare us for troubleshooting.

13
Troubleshooting

During typesetting, it may happen that LaTeX prints out warning messages. It's even possible that LaTeX doesn't produce the desired output and shows error messages instead. That's absolutely normal and can be caused, for example, by minor typos in command names or by unbalanced braces. Even professional LaTeX typesetters have to deal with errors—they just know how to do it efficiently.

Don't worry too much about the potential errors—let LaTeX check it for you. Then you just need to do the corrections at the places pointed out by LaTeX.

This chapter prepares us to do the following:

- Understanding and fixing errors
- Handling warnings
- Avoiding obsolete classes and packages
- General troubleshooting

Let's first tackle error handling.

Technical requirements

You can use a local LaTeX installation, or you can compile the example code online at `https://latexguide.org/chapter-13`.

The code is available on GitHub: `https://github.com/PacktPublishing/LaTeX-Beginner-s-Guide-Second-Edition/tree/main/Chapter_13_-_Troubleshooting`.

Understanding and fixing errors

If the LaTeX typesetting engine encounters a problem, it will issue an error message. This is informative and it's intended to help you. So, read the messages carefully. Besides the line number where the error occurred, LaTeX provides a diagnostic message.

Concentrate on the very first error message. If you continue typesetting, other errors might just be a consequence of the first one that confused the compiler.

Let's create a tiny test document. For sure, you've encountered those "**Hello world!**" printing programs—we shall write one in LaTeX. Though we are used to the uncommon capitalization used in the words TeX and LaTeX, we will now try and see if the `\Latex` command works as well:

1. Create a new document containing these lines:

    ```
    \documentclass{article}
    \begin{document}
    \Latex\ says: Hello world!
    \end{document}
    ```

2. Click on **Typeset** to compile the document. LaTeX will stop and print out the following message:

    ! Undefined control sequence.

    l.3 \Latex

    \ says: Hello world!

3. Click on the cancel icon in the upper-left corner of TeXworks to stop compiling.

4. In our code from *step 1*, go to line 3, and replace `\Latex` with `\LaTeX`. Then compile again. Now, LaTeX produces output without an error:

$$\text{\LaTeX says: Hello world!}$$

Figure 13.1 – The output of the corrected document

LaTeX commands are case-sensitive. Because we did not respect that, LaTeX had to deal with a macro called \Latex, which is just unknown. As a command is also called a **control sequence**, we got an error reading **Undefined control sequence**.

If TeX encounters an error, it stops typesetting and asks for user input. You could press the *Enter* key to continue typesetting, though you may get a PDF with incorrect output. It's better to cancel and correct the error immediately.

Let's analyze the three parts of the error output:

- An error message begins with an exclamation mark, followed by a short description of the problem.
- Then LaTeX prints out the number of the input line where the error was raised and the part of the line where the problem occurred.
- After a line break, LaTeX prints the remaining part of the input line.

So, you are not on your own without a clue. LaTeX tells you exactly what you need to know:

- The kind of error
- The exact location of the error

Most editors show you the line number or allow jumping to the line number you enter. As you can now easily find the problematic place in the code, you only need to know why LaTeX is complaining—that's the topic of the following sections.

If you are using Overleaf, there's a small caveat: Overleaf hides the error messages, continues compiling, and presents output even if there was an error. The following screenshot shows our document with the error in Overleaf:

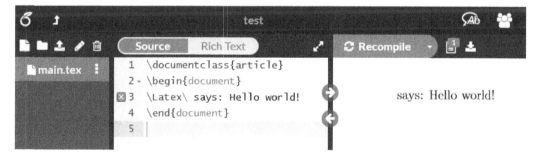

Figure 13.2 – A code error seen in Overleaf

At first glance, we do get our document. But if we look closer, we see the following:

- At the beginning, the word LaTeX is missing.

- There's a small red number above the output.

That small red number indicates that there's an error, and we should take that information seriously. Otherwise, as we saw here, we may have a document with missing or incorrect output, and in a large document that might be hard to notice.

Click on the red number, and a window with the error message opens:

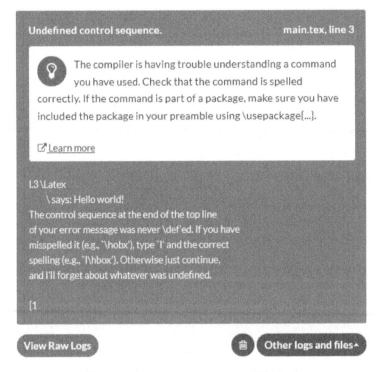

Figure 13.3 – An error message in Overleaf

Now we can see the entire error message, the explanation, and the location, **line 3**. In *Figure 13.2*, you can see that the erroneous line 3 is marked with a red cross. You can see the full log file with information, errors, and warnings by clicking on **View Raw Logs** at the bottom left.

We shall now have a closer look at frequently encountered TeX and LaTeX error messages. Let's do this in the following sections by going through each topic. We will start with the preamble.

Handling the preamble and document body

The preamble is for document-wide settings. Here, we specify the document class, load packages, set options, and define commands. The `\begin{document}` command ends the preamble and begins the document body where we can type our text. If we make a mistake in this structure, one of the following errors will occur:

- **Missing \begin{document}**: Most likely, you might have forgotten the `\begin{document}` command. But the error may occur even if you did not forget it. In that case, there may be a problem in the preamble. Specifically, if a character or a command within the preamble produces output, LaTeX would raise this error. Just remember that output is not allowed before `\begin{document}`.

- **Can be used only in preamble**: This error message refers to a command that is only allowed to be used in the preamble, not after `\begin{document}`. For example, `\usepackage` can only be used in the preamble. Move that command upward into your preamble, or remove it.

- **Option clash for package**: An option clash happens if LaTeX loads a package twice but with different options. That can happen if you have two `\usepackage{...}` lines for the same package in your document preamble. If you did that, it's usually better to reduce it to one `\usepackage` call with the desired options. But the cause might be hidden: Imagine that a class or a package implicitly loads a certain package together with some options. If you want to load the package too but with different options, there's a problem.

You could try to fix an option clash by omitting to reload the package while specifying the desired options to the document class. Remember, packages inherit class options. Some packages and classes even offer commands to set options after loading. For example, the `hyperref` package provides `\hypersetup{options}`, and similarly, the `caption` package offers `\captionsetup`.

In the following sections, we will look at common issues in the document body.

Using commands and environments

Command names might easily be misspelled or just misused. Let's check out LaTeX's common complaints:

- **Undefined control sequence**: As in our example in the previous section, LaTeX stumbled across an unknown command name. There are two possible reasons:

  a. The command name might be misspelled. In that case, you just need to correct it and restart the typesetting.

  b. The command name is correct, but it's defined by a package you didn't load. Add a \usepackage command to your preamble, which loads the required package.

- **Environment undefined**: This is similar to **Undefined control sequence**, but this time we began an unknown environment. Again, this may be caused by a misspelling or by a missing package—you know how to correct it.

- **Command already defined**: This happens when you create a command with a name that's already used, for example, with \newcommand or \newenvironment. Just choose a different name. If you would really like to override that command, use \renewcommand or \renewenvironment instead.

- **Missing control sequence inserted**: A control sequence has been expected but didn't appear. A common cause is using \newcommand, \renewcommand, or \providecommand, but not specifying a command name as its first argument.

- **\verb illegal in command argument**: The \verb command for producing verbatim text is a delicate one; it cannot be used within arguments of commands or environments. The examplep package offers commands for using verbatim text in such places.

Of this list, the very first error is probably the one that happens most often, since typing errors happen as easily as forgetting to load a package.

Writing math formulas

When LaTeX encounters an error during typesetting math expressions, one of the following error messages can occur:

- **Missing $ inserted**: There are a lot of commands that may only be used in math mode. Just think of symbols; most of them require math mode. If LaTeX is not in math mode, but encounters such a symbol, it stops and prints out that error. Usually, we can resolve such errors by inserting that missing $. Forgetting to start or end math mode is one of the most frequent mistakes. Also, remember that you cannot use paragraph breaks inside a math expression. This means that blank lines within a math expression are illegal; we have to end math mode before the blank line.

- **Command invalid in math mode**: Some commands are not applicable within math formulas. In that case, use the command outside math mode.

- **Double subscript, double superscript**: Two subsequent subscripts or superscripts cannot be compiled. For example, in a_n_1, LaTeX cannot decide if a_n should have a subscript 1, or if a should have a subscript n_1. To correct that, group them by braces, such as in a_{n_1}.

- **Bad math environment delimiter**: This can be a consequence of illegally nesting math mode. You must not start math mode if you are already inside math mode. For example, don't use \ [within an equation environment. Similarly, you must not end the math mode before you start it. Ensure that your math mode delimiters match and that braces are balanced.

In *Chapter 9, Writing Math Formulas*, we learned how to avoid such errors.

Working with files

If LaTeX cannot open a file for you, it can raise one of the following errors:

- **File not found**: LaTeX tried to open a file that doesn't exist. Possibly, you did one of the following:

  a. Used \include or \input to include a .tex file but a file with the specified name doesn't exist.

  b. Tried to use a nonexistent package or misspelled the package's name. Packages are recognized by the .sty file extension.

  c. Used a document class that doesn't exist or just has a different name. Class files have the extension .cls.

Just correct the filename in your input document or rename the file.

- **\include cannot be nested**: We learned in *Chapter 11, Developing Large Documents*, that we cannot use \include within files that are being included themselves. Instead, we use \input within such files.

> **Regarding filenames**
>
> It's good to avoid special characters and spaces in filenames. Both LaTeX and the operating system may have an issue with unusual characters in filenames, so it's good to stick to the common letters, digits, dashes, and underscores.

Creating tables and arrays

Admittedly, tabular and array environments don't have the simplest syntax. Those & and \\ might easily be misplaced, which causes LaTeX to complain. Further, we have to be careful with the formatting arguments. These are the possible errors you might see regarding arguments to the environment:

- **Illegal character in array arg**: In the argument to a tabular or an array environment, you can specify the column formatting. You line up characters such as l, c, r, p, @, and width arguments such as {1cm}. If you use any character that doesn't have such a meaning, LaTeX will tell you. The same applies to the formatting argument of \multicolumn.

- **Missing p-arg in array arg**: A bit more specific than the previous message, this tells us that the width argument to the p option is missing. Supplement p with a width such as {1cm} or change p to another option, such as l, c, or r.

- **Missing @-exp in array arg**: The expression after the @ option is missing. You just need to add it, in curly braces, or remove the @ option.

Now we shall take a look at the potential error messages concerning the table body:

- **Misplaced alignment tab character &**: As you know, the ampersand character has the special meaning of separating columns in a row of a tabular or array environment. If you accidentally use it in regular text, this error will appear. Type \& if you desire an ampersand symbol in the output.

- **Extra alignment tab has been changed to \cr**: This happens if you use too many alignment tab characters &, which are for dividing columns. For example, with two columns, we cannot have four & characters as column dividers. Such an error can happen if we forget to add \\, which ends a row.

In *Chapter 6, Creating Tables*, we discussed the proper syntax to avoid such errors.

Working with lists

Lists follow a specific structure and cannot be endlessly nested. At some point, LaTeX may complain, such as in the following error messages:

- **Too deeply nested**: We can nest up to four levels of a list. If we mix list types, we can go up to six levels. But if we go further than what LaTeX accepts, we will get this error message. Think over if you really need deep nesting. If this is the case, you could consider using sectioning commands such as `\paragraph` or `\subsubsection` for outer levels.

- **Something's wrong--perhaps a missing \item**: An `\item` command is missing. We may have simple text in an `itemize` or `enumerate` list. Then we need to insert an `\item` command before that text.

In *Chapter 4*, *Creating Lists*, we learned the proper list syntax.

Working with floating figures and tables

In *Chapter 5*, *Including Images*, and *Chapter 6*, *Creating Tables*, we learned about inserting figures and tables and how to adjust their placement. If you use a lot of floating objects, that is, figures or tables, you might encounter this error: **Too many unprocessed floats**.

If you use a floating object and LaTeX doesn't find an appropriate place as there might be no space, LaTeX saves the object for later placement. If that happens a lot, LaTeX's room for floating objects may get full, so this error appears. It may be solved as follows:

- By adding placement options, such as `[htbp!]` to the `figure` and `table` environments, thus lowering their placement requirements

- By inserting a `\clearpage` to flush out the floats at a suitable place, or perhaps even cleverer: `\afterpage{\clearpage}` with the `afterpage` package

In the final section, we take a look at other possible error situations.

General syntax errors

Just as with any markup or programming language, LaTeX's documents have to follow a syntax. For example, braces and delimiters have to match. If there's a mistake, LaTeX will point to it:

- **Missing { inserted, missing } inserted**: Though it reads like it might be caused by unbalanced braces, it may be because of a confusion of TeX. Most likely, the error occurred before the place where the error is pointed out by LaTeX. So, check the syntax used thoroughly.

- **Extra }, or forgotten $**: This time, there's a problem with unbalanced braces, or math mode delimiters don't match correctly. You need to correct the matching.

- **There's no line here to end**: Using \\ or \newline between paragraphs in vertical mode is not meaningful and causes this error. Don't try to get more vertical space by writing \\. Use \vspace instead, or other skip commands such as \bigskip, \medskip, or \smallskip. For instance, we can produce a blank line with \vspace{\baselineskip}.

The frequently asked questions list for TeX and LaTeX, called **TeX FAQ**, lists error messages together with explanations and suggestions. It's available at https://texfaq.org/#errors.

Once we fix all errors that may have occurred, there may still be some flaws in the document. LaTeX prints out warnings if it sees a potential issue. In the next section, we will see how to deal with them.

Handling warnings

Warning messages are for your information. They don't always point to a severe problem, but often it's a good idea to read these tips carefully and act accordingly. This may improve your document.

We will test this now. Let's say we want to emphasize text that is in a sans-serif font. We expect italic sans-serif text as a result.

Let's try this:

1. Take our "Hello world!" example and modify it this way:

```
\documentclass{article}
\renewcommand{\familydefault}{\sfdefault}
\begin{document}
\emph{Hello world!}
\end{document}
```

2. Compile. LaTeX will print out a warning in the log file:

```
LaTeX Font Warning: Font shape `OT1/cmss/m/it' in size
<10> not available
(Font) Font shape `OT1/cmss/m/sl' tried instead on input
line 4.
```

3. Check the output:

Hello world!

Figure 13.4 – Slanted shape instead of italic shape

The \familydefault macro stands for the default font family used in the LaTeX document. For this macro, we specified the \sfdefault value, which means the default sans-serif font. This simply means that sans-serif is now the default, no matter which font has been chosen. As you can imagine, other possible values are \rmdefault and \ttdefault. By changing \familydefault, we don't have to write \sffamily again and again.

But then we emphasized our text and got a warning. The message simply means that there's no **Computer Modern Sans Serif (cmss)** font in the default OT1 font encoding, in medium weight (m) and italic shape (it) in 10pt size. Furthermore, LaTeX told us how it tried to repair the problem – instead of italics, it chose a slanted shape. That's not too bad – at least it looks similar, and the output is produced.

This is basically what happens when warnings occur: LaTeX informs us about a potential problem or disadvantage, but it tries to choose the best alternative and continues typesetting. It's not uncommon that a longer document produces dozens of warnings, most often dealing with horizontal or vertical justification.

Often, it doesn't hurt if you ignore warnings that don't seem very serious, though following them up is a good habit. Anyone who desires to have a perfect document fixes all warnings. This way we cannot overlook a potential problem.

In the following sections, we will deal with frequently occurring situations with warnings.

Justifying text

By default, LaTeX aligns the text both at the left margin and at the right margin. LaTeX does this by adjusting the space between words and letters. That is called **full justification.**

If LaTeX cannot achieve that, we may get one of the following warnings:

Overfull \hbox: A line is too long and doesn't fit the text width. This may result in text extending past the margin. This may be caused by hyphenation problems, which we can fix by using \hyphenation or by inserting \-, as you learned in *Chapter 2, Formatting Text and Creating Macros*. You could break the line manually or polish your words otherwise.

- **Underfull \hbox**: The opposite of the previous warning; a line is not wide enough to fit to the text width, so LaTeX could not achieve full justification. This could be caused by \linebreak, if there's not enough text on the line. Also, \\ or \newline may cause it, such as \\\\, since the text justification has been interrupted.

- **Overfull \vbox**: The page is too long because TeX could not break it accordingly. The text might hang out past the bottom margin.

- **Underfull \vbox**: There's not enough text on the page. TeX had to break the page too early.

In *Chapter 2, Formatting Text and Creating Macros*, we learned how to improve the justification, reducing such warnings. Remember, already loading the microtype package may help a bit.

The \sloppy declaration switches to pretty relaxed typesetting, thus avoiding many such warnings. Its counterpart is \fussy, switching back to the default behavior. Suppose you ever want to use \sloppy because a relaxed typesetting with possibly more stretched spacing is okay for you, then it's better to keep it local by grouping or by using the respective environment—\begin{sloppypar} ... \end{sloppypar}.

Additionally, check out recommendations and alternatives regarding \sloppy in l2tabu, mentioned in *Chapter 11, Developing Large Documents*.

Referencing

Many warnings deal with referencing. Common mistakes are missing label or cite keys or keys that have been used twice, or you just need another typeset run.

The following warnings can occur:

- **Label multiply defined**: \label or \bibitem has been used with a label name that's already been used. Make label names unique.

- **There were multiply-defined labels**: Like the previous warning, but after processing the complete document; two \label commands have defined the same label.

- **Labels may have changed. Rerun to get cross-references right**: Just typeset again to let LaTeX correct the referencing.

- **Reference ... on page ... undefined**: `\ref` or `\pageref` has been used without a corresponding `\label` definition. Insert a `\label` command at a suitable place.

- **Citation ... on page ... undefined**: A `\cite` command did not have a corresponding `\bibitem` command, or no BibTeX key in the `.bib` file.

- **There were undefined references or citations**: Summarizing after processing—any `\ref` or `\cite` command did not have a corresponding `\label` or `\bibitem` command.

Whenever you get warnings regarding referencing, it's a good idea to simply rerun typesetting. Often, such warnings then disappear because LaTeX couldn't resolve all references in the first run itself.

Choosing fonts

When LaTeX cannot use a font as needed, it may print one of the following warnings:

- **Font shape ... in size <...> not available**: You chose a font that's not available. This may be a result of combining font commands that results in a nonexistent font. Also, it could just be of an unavailable size. LaTeX will choose a different font or size and inform you about that choice in detail.

- **Some font shapes were not available, defaults substituted**: LaTeX prints this after processing the entire document if any of the chosen fonts were unavailable.

Check where such a warning occurs to see if the font size and shape are okay for you. Otherwise, you may consider using another font, such as we did in *Chapter 10*, *Using Fonts*.

Placing figures and tables

Even if there is no error, LaTeX may not be able to place a figure or a table properly. In such a case, LaTeX may show one of the following warnings:

- **Float too large for page**: A figure or table is too large to fit the page. It would be printed, but the page would become too large.

- **h float specifier changed to ht**: If you specified an h option to a floating figure or table that doesn't fit there, it would be placed at the top of the next page, and that warning would be issued. The same can occur for !h and !ht.

Using all available placement options such as in \begin{figure}[!htbp] or \begin{table}[!htbp], as mentioned in *Chapter 5, Including Images*, can avoid many placement issues.

Customizing the document class

LaTeX may issue a warning reading **Unused global option(s)** if you use an illegal class option. This means you specified an option to \documentclass, which is unknown to the class and any loaded package. This could be, for example, a base font size that is not supported. Just check the option that LaTeX complains about.

Also, packages themselves may print out warnings if they foresee any problem. All these warnings are intended to help you design your document, so it's good to look at each one.

Even if you got a document without any errors and warnings, it may not be perfect if you use packages or a class that is not updated anymore. We will look at some well-known obsolete packages in the next section.

Avoiding obsolete classes and packages

At the end of *Chapter 11, Developing Large Documents*, we talked about the dangers of outdated information. LaTeX exists for decades, and so do tutorials, examples, packages, and templates. Many are totally outdated and some even refer to the old LaTeX standard 2.09, where even document classes didn't exist. We pointed to the definitive guide, l2tabu, that comes to the rescue.

Many problems just occur because of the use of obsolete packages. For example, some that aren't maintained anymore may conflict with newer packages. Often, you just need to find the recommended successor of an obsolete package and use that.

To help you in that matter, here's a short list showing obsolete packages and their respective recommended successors:

Obsolete packages	Recommended successors
a4, a4wide, anysize	geometry, typearea
backrefx	backref
bitfield	bytefield
caption2	caption
dinat	natdin
doublespace	setspace
dropping	lettrine
eps, epsfig	graphicx
euler	eulervm
eurotex	inputenx
fancyheadings	fancyhdr
floatfig	floatflt
glossary	glossaries
here	float
isolatin, isolatin1	inputenc
mathpple	mathpazo
mathptm	mathptmx
nthm	ntheorem
palatino	mathpazo
picinpar	floatflt, picins, wrapfig
prosper, HA-prosper	powerdot, beamer
ps4pdf	pst-pdf
raggedr	ragged2e
scrlettr	scrlttr2
scrpage, scrpage2	scrpage-scrlayer
seminar	powerdot, beamer
subfigure	subfig, subcaption
t1enc	fontenc
times	mathptmx
utopia	fourier
vmargin	geometry, typearea

Figure 13.5 – Obsolete packages and recommended successors

That's not set in stone. Of course, you may still use the so-called obsolete packages. They may work well even today. But check out their description on their CTAN package home page. Usually, there are comments regarding if the packages are still relevant or obsolete, and it also lists the recommended alternative packages. You can visit the package home page at the URL starting with `https://ctan.org/pkg/` followed by the package name, such as `https://ctan.org/pkg/geometry` for the `geometry` package.

You can find an updated version of that list on `https://latexguide.org/obsolete`.

Further, we will continue with some general advice in the next section.

General troubleshooting

There may be situations where we cannot solve a problem simply by reading and acting on warnings or error messages. Imagine a mysterious error, an untraceable error location, irresolvable references, or just unclear messages from classes or packages.

Locating the cause by the line number printed out by LaTeX, or by knowing what we've done since the previous typesetting run, usually helps. Once we've found a problematic line or chunk, we can remove or fix it. Otherwise, it might become difficult.

Here are the first general steps we can work through:

- Compile several times. This may be necessary for correct referencing, positioning of floating figures, creating a table of contents, bibliographies, and lists of tables and figures.

- Check the order in which you load the packages. Some packages, such as `hyperref`, don't work well if loaded before or after specific packages. You may just swap some lines to correct or test that.

- Remove auxiliary files. If anything strange happens, it's sometimes a good idea to remove all files created by LaTeX during typesetting. These files have the same name as the main document but have extensions such as `.aux`, `.toc`, `.lot`, `.lof`, `.bbl`, `.idx`, or `.nav`, just to name some examples.

If the problem persists, we could try to isolate the cause as follows:

1. Create a copy of your document. If necessary, copy the complete folder. From now on, work on the copy.

2. Remove parts of the document that are probably not involved in the problem.

3. Typeset to ensure that the problem persists. If this is the case, go back to *step 2* and remove another part of the document. If the problem is gone, you isolated the problem within the part you just removed. In this latter case, restore the deleted part since it contains the issue. If that part of the document is still too big to precisely locate the error, you can still go back to *step 2* and try again by removing smaller parts from within it.

4. After some repetitions of this process, you will have located the problem. If you didn't find it, reduce the number of loaded packages, and repeat *step 2* and *step 3*.

5. You will end up with a small but complete example document that reproduces the error. We call this a **minimal working example (MWE)**.

Removing or rewriting that identified part of your document could help. What if you really want to use that part and would like to fix that error? Now that you can show the problem with a short code example, you could post that problem to an online LaTeX forum and ask for help.

You are not dependent on just the errors and warnings that your editor shows you. LaTeX keeps track of all information, each warning and every error. These will be collected in a file with the same name as your document but carrying the extension .log. This is an ordinary text file and we can open it in any editor, including your LaTeX editor.

For instance, the log file for our `Hello world` example at the beginning of this chapter starts with information about the TeX and LaTeX format versions and looks like the following:

```
This is pdfTeX, Version 3.141592653-2.6-1.40.22 (TeX Live
2021) (preloaded format=pdflatex 2021.6.25)   12 JUL 2021
00:47
entering extended mode
 restricted \write18 enabled.
 %&-line parsing enabled.
**document
(./document.tex
LaTeX2e <2021-06-01> patch level 1
L3 programming layer <2021-06-18>
```

It continues with information about the document class, its version, and the used class options `.clo` file:

```
(/usr/local/texlive/2021/texmf-dist/tex/latex/base
/article.cls
Document Class: article 2021/02/12 v1.4n Standard LaTeX
document class
(/usr/local/texlive/2021/texmf-dist/tex/latex/base
/size10.clo
File: size10.clo 2021/02/12 v1.4n Standard LaTeX file (size
option)
)
```

It then shows the loaded packages and definitions – not much, in our case:

```
(/usr/local/texlive/2021/texmf-dist/tex/latex/l3backend
/l3backend-pdftex.def
File: l3backend-pdftex.def 2021-05-07 L3 backend support:
PDF output (pdfTeX)
\l__color_backend_stack_int=\count190
\l__pdf_internal_box=\box50
)
```

It tells us when it uses or opens a file:

```
No file document.aux.
\openout1 = `document.aux'.
```

It provides us with font information:

```
LaTeX Font Info:    Checking defaults for OML/cmm/m/it on input
line 2.
LaTeX Font Info:    ... okay on input line 2.
```

It contains all errors and warnings:

```
! Undefined control sequence.
l.3 \Latex
          \ says: Hello world!
?
! Emergency stop.
```

Once we correct the error in *step 4* of the *Understanding and fixing errors* section, LaTeX adds information about LaTeX performance and memory to the log file:

```
Here is how much of TeX's memory you used:
 385 strings out of 478510
 6981 string characters out of 5849585
 301299 words of memory out of 5000000
 18443 multiletter control sequences out of 15000+600000
 403430 words of font info for 27 fonts, out of 8000000
 for 9000
 1141 hyphenation exceptions out of 8191
 34i,5n,41p,139b,107s stack positions out of
 5000i,500n,10000p,200000b,80000s
</usr/local/texlive/2021/texmf-dist/fonts/type1/public/
amsfonts/cm/cmr10.pfb></usr/local/texlive/2021
/texmf-dist/fonts/type1/public/amsfonts/cm/cmr7.pfb>
```

The log file finishes by stating the output size as well as some statistics:

```
Output written on document.pdf (1 page, 22454 bytes).
PDF statistics:
 18 PDF objects out of 1000 (max. 8388607)
 10 compressed objects within 1 object stream
 0 named destinations out of 1000 (max. 500000)
 1 words of extra memory for PDF output out of 10000
 (max. 10000000)
```

Check out the log files of some of the documents you've produced up to now. The information therein looks very technical, but this might help you a lot in troubleshooting.

Summary

This chapter prepared us to solve problems that might occur in our LaTeX document.

Specifically, we learned about locating and fixing errors, understanding warning messages, and analyzing LaTeX's typesetting log file.

Correcting errors is absolutely necessary. Dealing with warnings is a valuable bonus. If you encounter any problem that you cannot solve on your own, don't hesitate to ask for help on a LaTeX Internet forum such as `https://latex.org`. In that forum, we have a section dedicated to this book, *LaTeX Beginner's Guide*, where I would be happy to answer your questions.

For LaTeX friends who are online, it's often an easy task to use this information to solve your problem, and definitely, a lot of LaTeX enthusiasts have fun helping other LaTeX users. The next chapter will discuss LaTeX internet forums and many other online resources.

14
Using Online Resources

There's a vast amount of LaTeX information and material on the internet, which has grown over many years. Today, thanks to the virtues of free and open-source software, a vast TeX and LaTeX community exists, sharing knowledge and expertise.

This chapter will guide you through the following resources on the internet:

- Web forums, Q&A sites, and discussion boards
- Lists of frequently asked questions
- Mailing lists
- TeX user groups sites
- Websites for LaTeX software and editors
- Graphics galleries
- LaTeX blogs
- Twitter messages

Many of the websites listed here are maintained by me and run on servers that are financially supported by DANTE e.V., the German-language TeX user group. A complete list of my websites is at `https://latex.net/about`.

As you know how to navigate the World Wide Web, this chapter does not contain practical examples. Instead, let's take a walk through the internet, beginning with interactive discussion sites.

Web forums, Q&A sites, and discussion boards

Let's go straight to where online life happens. We will start with forums.

Internet forums, or web forums, offer easy and user-friendly access to discussion and support groups. Initially, LaTeX was a topic in subforums of more general computer forums, among other software. After LaTeX became more and more popular, specific LaTeX websites were founded, some of which we will be discussing in the following sections.

LaTeX.org

Launched in January 2007, the web forum `https://latex.org/` was the first web forum dedicated to LaTeX. It's split into various subforums, each dealing with a particular LaTeX topic, such as *Math and Science* or *Fonts and Character Sets*, with a certain LaTeX distribution or a specific LaTeX editor.

Participating is as easy as in any other web forum. You don't need to register for reading, as it's freely available. Just for writing, you need to register once, choosing a login name and a password. Then you may ask questions or support other users who went there looking for help.

Questions are very welcome! They are the foundation of the site. You may increase the chance of receiving helpful answers by doing the following:

- Choosing a meaningful header to get users interested in reading your question

- Describing your problem clearly

- Quoting the error or warning messages you've got

- Including a code example, which allows others to reproduce the problem

The latter is an excellent approach; there's even a website explaining why and how at `https://texfaq.org/FAQ-minxampl`. Once a problem can be reproduced, it's close to being solved, even if it seems to be difficult at first sight. Experienced users familiar with the source code of the LaTeX kernel and packages can explain how something works and can create solutions for nearly any problem. You provide problem code; you get solution code.

There is a subforum dedicated to this book, the *LaTeX Beginner's Guide*: `https://latex.org/forum/viewforum.php?f=66`. There, you can post questions or remarks on this book, and I can answer them.

TeX and LaTeX on Stack Exchange

The website `https://tex.stackexchange.com` is a question and answer site that is different from classical web forums. While in web forums, people talk and discuss, this Q&A site has a more straightforward structure. There's a question, followed by answers. There's no discussion except in the comments.

When you post a question, follow the same advice regarding posting as with `LaTeX.org`. In addition, specify some keywords, so-called tags, which we can use to filter the site's contents.

Stack Exchange is a commercial network of Q&A sites. Since 2021, it is owned by Prosus, a technology investor. The TeX and LaTeX site, often called TeX.SE for short, was founded in 2010 specifically for users of TeX and LaTeX.

This TeX Q&A site has developed into an easily accessible knowledge base for the following reasons:

- Questions are tagged. For each question, one or more tags should be chosen, describing the subject. For example, if your question is about a problem with `\label` and `\ref` for equations, choose the tags `cross-referencing` and `equations`. This makes it easy to find answers to specific subjects. Specialized experts watch their favorite tags.

- We can vote on answers. Users vote helpful and meaningful answers up while they vote down misinformation. This way, the best answer floats to the top. So, you don't have to read through an entire multi-page thread to find the best solution, as is necessary for classical web forums.

Both tagging and voting enhance information access. We can use it for sorting and refining search results.

There's another concept called *reputation*. You don't need to worry about that, but perhaps you would like to know what it means. Users who post good questions and valuable answers earn reputation points depending on the votes on their questions and answers.

A certain number of reputation points allows you to go beyond simply asking and answering:

- You can create new tags or retag questions.

- Advertising is reduced.

- You can edit other users' posts.

- You can get access to certain moderation tools.

Reputation is a rough measurement of the user's status in the community. A high reputation means higher trust and moderation access. In that way, the site is community-moderated and shows aspects of a collaborative wiki.

For new users, there is a starter guide: `https://tex.meta.stackexchange.com/questions/1436/welcome-to-tex-sx`

You can also find further information in the help center at: `https://tex.stackexchange.com/help`.

Since TeX.SE is very strict, and questions related to already existing content may quickly be closed without answers, LaTeX.org may be a better choice for beginners with any question.

Forums in other languages

The following sites are very similar to TeX StackExchange:

- `https://texnique.fr`: A French Q&A site on LaTeX

- `https://texwelt.de`: A German Q&A site on LaTeX

And similar to LaTeX.org, `https://golatex.de` is a German web forum on LaTeX that also provides a reference wiki at `https://golatex.de/wiki`.

Usenet groups

Around 1980, a long time before the World Wide Web was born, the **Usenet** emerged. This is a discussion network that consists of many thousands of groups, so-called **newsgroups**, each dedicated to a specific subject. Unsurprisingly, there are TeX newsgroups.

The most famous one is `comp.text.tex`. The easiest way to access it is to visit `https://groups.google.com/g/comp.text.tex`, hosted by Google. Just browse it using its web interface.

Alternatively, you could install a Usenet reader program and connect to a Usenet web server. At this point, you should familiarize yourself with Usenet. A great starting point is its Wikipedia entry at `https://en.wikipedia.org/wiki/Usenet`. There you will find an introduction, links to necessary software, and further reading.

`comp.text.tex` is the classic TeX discussion board. Then and now, there are distinguished experts reading and posting messages. You can search and browse an archive reaching back over more than 20 years.

There are newsgroups in other languages as well. You could check out the German or French Usenet TeX groups if you understand those languages:

- `de.comp.text.tex`: `https://groups.google.com/g/de.comp.text.tex`

- `fr.comp.text.tex`: `https://groups.google.com/g/fr.comp.text.tex`

However, over time, Usenet newsgroups became pretty quiet. Nowadays, users tend to visit web forums and Q&A sites.

Lists of frequently asked questions

Now you know where to ask for help. However, during the long existence of online LaTeX communities, the probability that another user encountered the same problem as you is very high. There's a bunch of questions that appear again and again. If you post such a question, the community member might point you to a **Frequently Asked Questions (FAQs)** page. This refers to a list of answers to these FAQs. The following websites host famous collections:

- **TeX FAQ**: `https://texfaq.org` is an FAQ site maintained by the UK TeX Users' Group. It contains several hundred frequently asked questions and well-thought-out answers. They are sorted by topic, and that list is still growing and being continuously being improved.

- **Visual LaTeX FAQ**: `https://ctan.org/pkg/visualfaq` is a very different approach. The Visual FAQ is a PDF document containing hundreds of textual and graphic elements such as tables, figures, lists, footnotes, and math formulas. It is thirty pages, which are full of demonstration samples. Besides all document objects, key positions are marked and hyperlinked. Just clicking on any marked object leads you to the corresponding TeX FAQ entry. Take a look; it's a fancy interface.

- **MacTeX FAQ**: `https://tug.org/mactex/faq/` is made for you if you are a Mac user. It covers the installation and use of the MacTeX LaTeX distribution and the popular Mac LaTeX editor TeXShop.

- **AMS-Math FAQ**: `https://www.ams.org/faq` lists questions and answers relating to `amsmath`, the most recommended LaTeX math package.

- **LaTeX Picture FAQ**: `https://ctan.org/pkg/l2picfaq` was developed for answering a lot of questions about including pictures. It deals, for example, with the various image file formats, conversion tools, picture manipulation, and placement of floating figures. The document contains a lot of small code examples and is a handy resource for a LaTeX beginner.

  As it originated in a German LaTeX forum, it's written in German. It has been translated into English, but the translation is not yet published in 2021.

- **German TeX FAQ**: `https://texfragen.de` is a German-language list of answers to frequently asked LaTeX questions arranged by topics.

It's usually a good idea to look on an FAQ list before asking in a forum or on a mailing list, the latter being our next topic.

Mailing lists

Now we come again to a traditional media: electronic mailing lists. They are used for both announcements and discussions. If you subscribe to such a list, you will receive announcements and discussion contributions from other subscribers. You could silently receive and read all the messages, and you could send e-mails to the list address, which would then be sent to all other subscribers. Before sending a general query to the list of subscribers, you should check an FAQ list.

Today, many people prefer easily accessible media, such as web forums. However, mailing lists still exist and will be in use as long as e-mail is popular. The following mailing lists may be handy for you:

- **texhax**: `https://tug.org/mailman/listinfo/texhax` is a list for general TeX discussion, a companion to `comp.text.tex`, established in the 1980s. It has hundreds of subscribers, and there are many experts among them.

- **tex-live**: `https://tug.org/mailman/listinfo/tex-live` deals with the TeX Live collection. If you installed this software distribution, you might be interested in subscribing to get the latest news and read and write about its issues.

- **texworks**: `https://tug.org/mailman/listinfo/texworks` supports the user of the LaTeX editor TeXworks, which we used in *Chapter 1, Getting Started with LaTeX*. You may subscribe if you decide to use that editor later on and are interested in the latest builds, tricks, scripts, and news.

There are a lot more mailing lists that you can find at `https://tug.org/mailman/listinfo`. There are more than 60 mailing lists for TeX and LaTeX-specific subjects such as bibliographies, hyphenation, PostScript, pdfTeX, and development.

TeX user groups and developers of LaTeX editors, and other software, often provide mailing lists, especially for announcements. You can read about that on their home pages, but we shall now look at some of their websites now.

TeX user group sites

TeX user groups are organizations for people interested in TeX and LaTeX. They provide support for their members but also for TeX and LaTeX users in general. Let's visit a few.

The TeX Users Group

The **TeX Users Group** (**TUG**) is a not-for-profit organization with a very long history. Their website is at `https://tug.org`. Founded in 1980, the TUG always had a significant influence on the development and popularity of TeX. The TUG home page is a portal to the TeX world with links to support, documentation, and software. It hosts an extensive collection of TeX-related internet resources at `https://tug.org/interest.html`. An index and a substantial number of links show you the way to helpful material on the internet.

It publishes a journal that appears three times a year, and it holds yearly international conferences. It also hosts the LaTeX Font Catalogue at `https://tug.org/FontCatalogue`, which lists nearly all fonts available for use with LaTeX. About a dozen categories, such as sans-serif, typewriter, and calligraphy fonts, assist in finding the correct font. The fonts are displayed both briefly in overviews but also extensively with several styles and math examples. The cherries on the cake are specific code examples.

DANTE

Deutschsprachige Anwendervereinigung TeX e. V. (DANTE) is a large German-language TeX users group that funds projects and provides services for the whole TeX world. The home page, `https://www.dante.de`, is a good starting point for German language users.

DANTE provides financial support for running servers with LaTeX software, web forums, Q&A sites, FAQs, tools, and more, as mentioned in the introduction of this chapter.

The LaTeX project

The LaTeX3 project team maintains the LaTeX 2e standard and develops the next version of LaTeX. The website, `https://www.latex-project.org`, informs users about their work and LaTeX in general and publishes news regularly.

UK TUG – TeX in the United Kingdom

This user group supports and promotes TeX in the UK, holds conferences and training, and is available at `https://uk.tug.org`.

Other local user groups

There are many local TeX user groups from various countries in the world listed here:

- `https://tug.org/usergroups.html`
- `https://ntg.nl/lug`
- `https://dante.de/dante-e-v/stammtische`

Their websites often contain material in national languages and further information on the TeX world.

In the following section, we will see where we can get software, tools, and packages.

Websites for LaTeX software and editors

Like most software manufacturers and distributors, free and open-source software projects offer information on their home pages.

LaTeX distributions

Today, there are two big LaTeX distributions, both very modern and comprehensive, plus some descendants:

- **TeX Live**: `https://tug.org/texlive` is a cross-platform LaTeX software collection. It runs on Windows, Mac OS X, Linux, and other Unix systems.

- **MiKTeX**: `https://miktex.org` is a very user-friendly and popular LaTeX distribution specifically for the Windows operating system. It now supports Linux and other Unix systems as well.

- **proTeXt**: `https://tug.org/protext` is a MiKTeX-based distribution for Windows that primarily focuses on easy installation.

- **MacTeX**: `https://tug.org/mactex` is derived from TeX Live and has been explicitly customized for Mac OS X.

Most Linux versions provide a customized version of TeX Live in their repositories.

LaTeX editors

There are many LaTeX editors available, from easy-to-use to complex and professional. Most of them offer syntax highlighting, support for various (La)TeX compilers, and other tools such as BibTeX, biber, makeindex, and PDF previewers. A list to explore follows.

Cross-platform

These editors support many systems, including Windows, Mac OS X, Linux, and Unix:

- **TeXworks**: `https://tug.org/texworks` is lightweight and comfortable.

- **Texmaker**: `https://xm1math.net/texmaker` offers a lot of features.

- **TeXstudio**: `https://texstudio.org` is derived from Texmaker and nowadays provides many other capabilities in its own way.

- **Emacs**: `https://gnu.org/software/emacs` is extensible and very customizable, though not easy to use for everybody. However, it's great together with **AUCTeX**: `https://gnu.org/software/auctex`.

- **vim**: `https://www.vim.org` is based on commands given in a text interface. It's enhanced by the vim LaTeX-suite: `http://vim-latex.sourceforge.net`.

Of course, the Overleaf online compiler and editor are cross-platform as well.

Windows

In addition to the cross-platform editors, there's the powerful and popular shareware LaTeX editor called **WinEdt**. You can download it at `https://www.winedt.com`. DANTE provides licenses with a discount for its members. Also, see the WinEdt community site at `http://www.winedt.org`.

Linux

Besides all the cross-platform editors, there are the following:

- **Kile**: `https://kile.sourceforge.io` is very powerful and designed for the KDE window system. It also runs on other window managers, such as GNOME, if KDE libraries are installed.

- **gedit**: `https://wiki.gnome.org/Apps/Gedit` is the lightweight GNOME standard editor, and there's a LaTeX plugin: `https://wiki.gnome.org/Apps/Gedit/LaTeXPlugin`.

- **GNOME-LaTeX**: `https://wiki.gnome.org/Apps/GNOME-LaTeX` is another GNOME-based LaTeX editor, formerly called **LaTeXila**.

On Linux, we usually choose an editor that fits the selected window manager, KDE or GNOME, or a universal cross-platform editor.

Mac OS X

TeXshop is a very popular Mac LaTeX editor: `https://pages.uoregon.edu/koch/texshop/`.

That editor is believed to have led many new users to LaTeX because of its outstanding usability. The TeXworks editor is modeled on TeXshop.

The visual editor LyX

`https://www.lyx.org` is the home page of the cross-platform editor **LyX**, which looks and feels like a word processor software but is built on LaTeX. It combines an easy-to-use graphical user interface with the power and structure of LaTeX. You can develop documents mainly using LyX's toolbars and menus, but you may insert LaTeX code at any point.

The LyX wiki offers extensive documentation at `https://wiki.lyx.org`.

On the LyX home page, you will find links for download, news, and support. As LyX is very popular, there is a LyX dedicated support forum at `https://latex.org`.

CTAN – the Comprehensive TeX Archive Network

The network based on `https://ctan.org` consists of many servers worldwide, which store the most extensive collection of TeX-related material. CTAN serves as a repository for installing and updating LaTeX distributions such as TeX Live.

On the CTAN home page, you will find search features, or you may just start browsing the archive directories. We can find nearly every serious LaTeX package in this archive.

In the following section, we will visit websites dedicated to showing examples, images, and code.

Graphics galleries

There are showcase sites on the internet, especially for creating graphics with TeX:

- `https://texample.net` is a TikZ example gallery with hundreds of examples and complete source code, browsable by topic.

- `https://tikz.net` is another TiKZ picture gallery with source code.

- `https://pgfplots.net` focuses on plots in 2D and 3D using the `pgfplots` package.

- `https://latex-cookbook.net` is the website for the *LaTeX Cookbook* with a gallery of code examples and output.

- `https://latexguide.org` is the website for this book, the *LaTeX Beginner's Guide*, with a gallery of examples and further information.

- `https://tex.world` is a gallery of LaTeX-related websites.

These websites allow visual browsing through LaTeX graphics documents sorted by topic and with complete source code and explanations.

Now let's get personal; we will now turn to user blogs.

LaTeX blogs

Are you interested in LaTeX news and expert opinions? Then LaTeX blogs may supply you with current LaTeX information:

- `https://texblog.net` is my personal blog. Here, I write LaTeX-related news, offer tips and tricks, and provide a structured link collection sorted by subject.

- `https://www.texdev.net` is written by Joseph Wright, a member of the LaTeX project and author of various LaTeX tools.

- `https://tex-talk.net/` is a LaTeX blog with an interesting section full of interviews with LaTeX power users and developers.

- `https://latex.net` is mainly an article database with know-how accumulated over many years, but it also provides news posts like a blog.
- `http://texample.net/community` is a blog aggregator that summarizes about 30 TeX and LaTeX-related blogs and will keep you updated.
- `https://planet.dante.de` is a DANTE-hosted blog aggregator that focuses on German LaTeX related blogs but includes international blogs.

But even faster news is on Twitter, so let's look at that next.

Twitter messages

Recommended Twitter accounts to subscribe to are as follows:

- `@TeXUsersGroup`: `https://twitter.com/TeXUsersGroup` is the TUG account with news and CTAN updates.
- `@dante_ev`: `https://twitter.com/dante_ev` is the account of DANTE for TeX news, especially in the German-speaking world.
- `@overleaf`: `https://twitter.com/overleaf` is the account of the Overleaf company with its online compiler and editor.
- `@tex_tips`: `https://twitter.com/tex_tips` sends daily LaTeX tips to its subscribers.
- `@TeXgallery`: `https://twitter.com/TeXgallery` is my account that also talks for the LaTeX.org forum.

Follow the hashtag `#TeXLaTeX` to get the latest news about TeX and LaTeX: `https://twitter.com/search?q=%23TeXLaTeX`.

Summary

While you have learned about the LaTeX fundamentals in this book, this chapter gave an overview about further reading online.

Now you know about finding and downloading LaTeX software, accessing the worldwide LaTeX community knowledge, getting the latest news from blogs, and asking questions online if you encounter any problem that you cannot solve by yourself.

TeX friends will welcome you on any community website. As you have learned much in this book, you may soon become an experienced LaTeX user who supports LaTeX novices.

Hi!

I'm Stefan, author of LaTeX Beginner's Guide. I hope you enjoyed reading this book and found it helpful in using LaTeX. We had the first edition in 2011, and now we have the second edition in 2021, rewritten with a view on the newest developments. LaTeX forever! I look forward to a 2031 edition – just joking, that can be earlier. Stay tuned with upcoming developments at https://latexguide.org.

It would really help me (and other potential readers) if you could leave a review on Amazon sharing your thoughts on LaTeX Beginner's Guide Second Edition here.

Go to the link below or scan the QR code to leave your review:

```
https://packt.link/r/1801078653/qr
```

I'm reading every review. Your review will help me understand what you think worked well in this book and what I can improve for future editions, so it's really appreciated.

Best Wishes,

Stefan Kottwitz

Packt.com

Subscribe to our online digital library for full access to over 7,000 books and videos, as well as industry leading tools to help you plan your personal development and advance your career. For more information, please visit our website.

Why subscribe?

- Spend less time learning and more time coding with practical eBooks and Videos from over 4,000 industry professionals

- Improve your learning with Skill Plans built especially for you

- Get a free eBook or video every month

- Fully searchable for easy access to vital information

- Copy and paste, print, and bookmark content

Did you know that Packt offers eBook versions of every book published, with PDF and ePub files available? You can upgrade to the eBook version at packt.com and as a print book customer, you are entitled to a discount on the eBook copy. Get in touch with us at customercare@packtpub.com for more details.

At www.packt.com, you can also read a collection of free technical articles, sign up for a range of free newsletters, and receive exclusive discounts and offers on Packt books and eBooks.

Other Books You May Enjoy

If you enjoyed this book, you may be interested in these other books by Packt:

LaTex Cookbook

Stefan Kottwitz

ISBN: 978-1-78439-514-8

- Choose the right document class for your project to customize its features.
- Utilize fonts globally and locally.
- Frame, shape, arrange and annotate images.
- Create colorful graphics including diagrams, flow charts, bar charts, trees, plots in 2d and 3d, time lines, and mindmaps.
- Optimize PDF output and enrich it with meta data, annotations, popups, animations, and fill-in-fields.

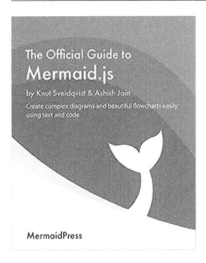

The Official Guide to Mermaid.js

Knut Sveidqvist & Ashish Jain

ISBN: 978-1-80107-802-3

- Understand good and bad documentation, and the art of effective documentation.
- Become well-versed with maintaining complex diagrams with ease.
- Discover how to draw different types of Mermaid diagrams such as flowcharts.
- Implement Mermaid diagrams in your workflows
- Understand how to set up themes for a Mermaid diagram or an entire site.

Packt is searching for authors like you

If you're interested in becoming an author for Packt, please visit `authors.packtpub.com` and apply today. We have worked with thousands of developers and tech professionals, just like you, to help them share their insight with the global tech community. You can make a general application, apply for a specific hot topic that we are recruiting an author for, or submit your own idea.

Index

Symbols

@dante_ev
  reference link 316
@overleaf
  reference link 316
@TeXgallery
  reference link 316
@tex_tips
  reference link 316
@TeXUsersGroup
  reference link 316

A

accents
  setting 222
admin mode 6
advanced referencing
  using 161
all caps 78
AMS-Math FAQ
  reference link 310
amsmath matrix environments 220
amsmath multi-line environments 211

arbitrary fonts
  main font, selecting 242, 243
  multiple font families, selecting 243-245
  using 242
arev 237
arguments
  about 32
  used, for creating macro 44, 45
  using 44
arrays
  creating 219
arrows 214
automatic naming
  intelligent references,
    combining with 167
automatic reference names
  using 164-166

B

back matter
  creating 254-256
backtick 60
basic formulas
  writing 198-200
Bera Mono 240

bibliography
  BibTeX entry types 191, 192
  creating 185, 186
  databases, using with BibTeX 187-189
  looking, at BibTeX entry fields 189, 190
  references, listing without citing 194
  referring, to Internet resources 190
  standard environment, using 186, 187
  style, selecting 192, 193
BibTeX
  about 187
  bibliography databases,
    using with 187-189
  entry fields 189, 190
  entry types 191, 192
binary operation symbols 213
binary relation symbols 213
binomial coefficients
  writing 220
book
  creating, with chapters 66-68
bookman 235, 236
bookmarks
  creating, manually 277
  math formulas, using 277-279
  special symbols, using 277-279
  using 270
boxes
  using, to limit paragraph width 46
bulleted lists
  creating 100-103
  corresponding environments 109
bullets format
  selecting 110-112

C

Calligra 240
calligraphic fonts
  about 240
  Calligra 240
  Miama Nueva 241
caption package 126
capt-of package 126
Charter 234
class
  about 31
  options, using 72-75
classes 4
columns
  writing, with tab stops 132-135
commands
  about 31
  creating 42
  macro, using for simple text 42, 43
  manual spacing 43, 44
Comprehensive TeX Archive
    Network (CTAN)
  about 314
  URL 314
Computer Modern 228
Computer Modern Bright 237
Computer Modern Roman 233
Computer Modern Sans Serif (cmss) 295
Concrete Roman 235
container formats 120
control sequence 287
Cork encoding 230
Courier 239
cross-platform editors 313
cross-references 158

D

declaration 32
decorative lines
  using, in headers and footers 80
definitions
  list, producing 105, 106
  writing 223
description lists
  about 105
  corresponding environments 109
Detexify 217
Deutschsprachige Anwendervereinigung
    TeX e. V. (DANTE)
  about 311
  URL 311
Device Independent File
    Format (DVI) 119
discussion boards 306
displayed formulas
  customizing 209
displayed quoting 61
document body
  handling 289
document class
  customizing 298
  options 72
documents
  coloring 283, 284

E

ellipsis
  producing 207
Encapsulated PostScript (EPS) 119, 120
enumerated list
  building 103, 104
epstopdf 121

equations
  numbering 202
errors
  about 286-288
  arrays, creating 292
  commands, using 290
  document body, handling 289
  environments, using 290
  fixing 286-288
  math formulas, writing 291
  message 288
  output, parts analyzing 287
  preamble, handling 289
  syntax 293, 294
  tables, creating 292
  working, with files 291
  working, with floating figures 293
  working, with floating tables 293
  working, with lists 293
eso-pic package 122
extensible accents 222

F

FAQ, list
  mailing 310, 311
figures
  output, forcing 125
  placement options 125
  placing, warnings 297
filenames 292
floating
  avoiding 126, 127
  images, managing 122-124
  limiting 126
floats 122

font bundles
  Kp-Fonts 231, 232
  Latin Modern 231
  using 228-231
font encoding 230
font families
  about 37
  calligraphic fonts 240
  sans-serif fonts 236
  serif fonts 233
  typewriter fonts 239
  using 232
fonts
  selecting, warnings 297
footnote line
  modifying 82, 83
footnotes
  styles, expanding with packages 83, 84
  using 81, 82
formulas
  displaying 201
  text, inserting into 212
fractions
  writing 205
Frequently Asked Question (FAQs)
  lists 309, 310
front matter
  creating 254-256
Frutiger font 237
full justification
  about 295
  center text 57
  environments, using 58, 59
  ragged-left text, creating 57
  ragged-right text, creating 56
  turning off 56

G

Garamond font 234
geometry package
  about 69
  reference link 72, 300
German TeX FAQ
  URL 310
Graphical User Interface (GUI) 8
graphics with TeX
  galleries 315
graphicx package 118
Greek letters
  writing 205, 206

H

handwritten symbol recognition 216
harpoons 215
headers and footers
  customizing 79, 80
  decorative lines, using in 80
  designing 75-78
headings
  designing 279-283
  modifying 194, 195
Helvetica 238
hyperlinks
  adding 270- 272
  creating, manually 276
  customizing 272-275
  references, turning into 168
  using 270
hyperref package
  reference link 169

I

images
  arranging 127
  including, in document 118-120
  placing, behind text 122
  scaling 121
Inconsolata 240
index
  fine-tuning page numbers 183
  generating 179-181
  layout, designing 184, 185
  page ranges, specifying 182
  referring, to other index entries 183
  symbols and macros, using in 182
index entries
  defining 181
inequality relation symbols 214
inline quoting 61
inner margins, versus outer margins 69
input command
  code, including 251
  document, compiling 252, 253
  document, including 251
  splitting 248-250
input encoding 231
intelligent page references
  producing 161, 162
intelligent references
  combining, with automatic naming 167
Internet resources
  referring 190
itemize 101

K

Kerkis font 236
Kile
  reference link 16
KOMA-Script
  about 75
  reference link 75
  classes 126, 236
Kp-Fonts 231, 232
Kurier 238

L

label
  assigning 159, 160
  referring to 160
labels
  referring, in documents 167, 168
  setting 156-158
landscape orientation
  using 153
LaTeX
  about 2
  approaches, to working with 5
  benefits 3
  blogs 315
  distributions 312
  documentation, accessing 25
  document, creating 14, 15
  form and content, separation 4
  header marks, modifying 80
  installing 5-7
  on Stack Exchange 307, 308

open source, virtues 3
portability 4
URL 84, 156
using 5, 7
working with 5
work, protection 4
writing modes 198
LaTeX commands 32
LaTeX editors
about 313
checking, out advanced 15, 16
cross-platform 313
features 15
Linux 314
Mac OS X 314
visual editor LyX 314
windows 313
LaTeX environments
about 33
input reading 33, 34
symbols, printing out 34, 35
LaTeX Font Catalogue
reference link 241
LaTeX online
working with, using Overleaf 16
LaTeX.org 306
LaTeX Picture FAQ
reference link 310
LaTeX project
about 312
URL 312
LaTeX software and editors
websites 312
LaTeX Templates
URL 259
Latin Modern 228, 231
leading 93
left-to-right mode 198

line breaking
about 51
hyphenation, improving 51
hyphenation, preventing 52
manual, implementation 53, 54
options, exploring 55
pdfTeX, improving 53
prevention 55
line spacing
modifying 91, 93
Linux editors 314
lipsum 68
list of figures (LOF)
about 273
creating 177, 178
customizing 177, 178
list of tables (LOT)
about 273
creating 178
lists
building 100
bullets and numbering format,
selecting 110-112
compact lists, obtaining 107-109
continuing 113-115
customizing 106
suspending 113-115
logical formatting
about 28
document, creating with heading 29, 30
document, creating with title 29, 30
document structure, exploring 31
LaTeX commands 31, 32
LaTeX environments 32, 33
working with 28
longer text
quoting 61-63

Lorem ipsum filler text 68
LyX wiki
   URL 314

M

Mac OS X editors 314
macro
   about 31, 32, 42
   creating, with arguments 44, 45
   creating, with optional arguments 45, 46
MacTeX 4, 5
MacTeX FAQ
   reference link 310
margins
   defining 69, 70
   inner versus outer margins 69
   paper size, selecting 70
   setting 71, 72
   text area, specifying 70
mathematical text
   example 200
math expressions
   embedding, within text 200
math formulas
   writing 291
math mode 198
math structures
   building 219
math symbols
   exploring 212
mathtools package 225
matrices
   typesetting 219
Miama Nueva 241
MiKTeX
   URL 6
minimal working example (MWE) 301

miscellaneous symbols 215
monospaced 37, 239
multi-line formulas
   rows, numbering 212
   typesetting 209-211
multi-page tables
   generating 152

N

nested lists 102
net installer wizard
   used, for installing TeX Live 8-11
ntheorem package 224
numbered lists
   corresponding environments 109
numbering format
   selecting 110-112

O

obsolete classes
   avoiding 298-300
obsolete packages
   avoiding 298-300
obsolete packages and
         recommended successors
   about 298
   reference link 300
open source 3
operating systems
   TeX Live, installing on 12
operators
   using 203
optimal file type
   selecting 120, 121
optional arguments
   used, for creating macro 45, 46

Overleaf
  benefits 17
  caveats, of working online 18
  commenting 24
  document online, creating 18-20
  exploring 20-22
  requires and delivers 16, 17
  reviewing 24
  URL 265
  used, for working with LaTeX online 16
overlining 221

P

packages
  about 4
  options 52
  styles 83, 84
  used, for expanding footnote styles,
      for customizations 151
page
  breaking 84-87
  enlarging 88-91
  referring to 160, 161
page ranges
  fine-tuning 163
  referring to 164
page style 78, 79
Palatino text font 233
pangram 228
paragraph boxes
  features, exploring 49
  mini pages, using 49, 50
  narrow text box, creating 47
  producing 48, 49
paragraph breaking 51
paragraph mode 198

paragraph width
  limiting, with boxes 46
pdfLaTeX 53
pdfpages package
  reference link 122
pdfTeX 53
physical formatting 28
placeins package 126
Portable Document Format
      (PDF) 119, 120
PostScript (PS) 119
preamble
  handling 289
preamble document 31

Q

Q&A sites 306
quotes
  displaying 60

R

references
  setting 156-158
  turning, into hyperlinks 168
referencing
  warnings 296
Roman font 37
roots
  taking 204
rotating package 121
rows
  numbering, in multi-line formulas 212
running titles 175

S

sans-serif fonts
  about 37, 236
  Arev 237
  Computer Modern Bright 237
  Helvetica 238
  Kurier 238
scope 40
script letters
  writing 206, 207
script typefaces 240
search feature 217
serif 233
serif fonts
  about 37, 233
  Bookman 235, 236
  Charter 234
  Concrete Roman 235
  New Century Schoolbook 234, 235
  Palatino 233
  Times Roman 233
single-user mode 6
Stack Exchange
  LaTeX on 307, 308
  TeX on 307, 308
style file 7
subcaption package 127
subentries
  defining 181
subfig package 127
subfigure package 127
subscripts
  adding 202
subset symbol 214
superscripts
  adding 203

superset symbol 214
symbol
  placing, above or below another one 222
symbols
  derived from letter 215
  reference link 216

T

table of contents (TOC)
  about 273
  creating 93-96
  customizing 172-174
  depth, adjusting of 174, 175
  entries, adding manually 176
  entries, shortening 175
  list of tables, creating 178
  lists of figures, creating 177, 178
  lists of figures, customizing 177, 178
  packages, using to customizing 178
tables
  beautifying 141, 142
  captions, adding to 147-150
  captions, customizing 151
  captions, placing above 150
  code, inserting column-wise 145, 146
  coloring 153
  columns, aligning at decimal point 153
  customizations, with packages 151
  entries, spanning over multiple
    columns 144, 145
  entries, spanning over multiple
    rows 146, 147
  formatting arguments 138-140
  landscape orientation, using 153
  lengths, adjusting 143
  lines, drawing 138

narrow columns, handling 154
  placing, warnings 297
  row height, increasing 140, 141
  typesetting 136, 137
table width
  auto-fitting columns to 151, 152
tab stops
  using, to write columns 132-135
templates
  working with 258-266
TeX
  on Stack Exchange 307, 308
TeX distributions 4
TeX FAQ
  about 294
  reference link 294
  URL 309
TeX Gyre Bonum 236
texhax 310
tex-live 310
TeX Live
  about 5
  installing, on other operating systems 12
  installing, with net installer wizard 8-11
  new packages, installing 12-14
  offline installation 11, 12
  updating 12-14
TeX Live Manager 12
TeX Live Shell 12
Texmaker
  reference link 15
TeXshop
  reference link 314
TeXstudio
  reference link 15, 16
text
  flowing, around images 128, 129
  inserting, into formulas 212

justifying 295, 296
  math expressions, embedding
    within 200
text font
  commands, implementing 40
  font family, selecting 37-39
  font shape, displaying 36, 37
  modifying 35, 207
  sizes, exploring 41
textpos package
  reference link 122
text size
  modifying 208
text style
  modifying 208
TeX Users Group (TUG)
  about 42, 311
  local user groups 312
  sites 311
  URL 311
texworks 311
TeXworks 4
TeXworks template
  selection 260
theorems
  writing 223
Times Roman 233
title page
  designing 256-258
troubleshooting 300-303
Twitter
  messages 316
typeface 37
typewriter fonts
  about 37, 239
  Bera Mono 240
  Courier 239
  Inconsolata 240

U

UK TUG
about 312
URL 312
underlining 221
units
writing 217
universal commands
creating 44
Usenet
groups 308, 309
UTF8-Unicode 231
Utopia font 234

V

variable sized delimiters 218
variable sized operators 217, 218
varioref package 161-163
Vera Sans font 237
verso pages 71
visual editor LyX 314
Visual LaTeX FAQ
reference link 309

W

warnings
figures, placing 297
fonts, selecting 297
handling 294, 295
referencing 296
tables, placing 297
text, justifying 295, 296
web forums
about 306
languages 308
whole pages
including 121
wide accents 222
windows editors 313
WinEdt 313
wrapfigure environment
reference link 129
Writefull Overleaf
grammar and language feedback with 23
writing modes, LaTeX
left-to-right mode 198
math mode 198
paragraph mode 198